Abhidhamma in Daily Life

Nina van Gorkom
Zolag 2014
4th Edition

4th edition published in 2014 by
Zolag
32 Woodnook Road
Streatham
London
SW16 6TZ
www.zolag.co.uk

ISBN 978-1897633-27-4

British Library Cataloguing in Publication Data
A CIP record for this book is available from the British Library
Printed in the UK and USA by Lightningsource.
$Id: abh.texi,v 1.26 2014/01/04 12.32 alan$

Table of Contents

Preface

The Buddha's teachings, contained in the "Tipiṭaka" (Three Baskets) are: the Vinaya (Book of Discipline for the monks), the Suttanta (Discourses) and the Abhidhamma. All three parts of the Tipiṭaka can be an inexhaustible source of inspiration and encouragement to the practice, the development of right understanding of realities. The development of right understanding will eventually lead to the eradication of wrong view and the other defilements. In all three parts of the Tipiṭaka we are taught about *dhamma*, about everything which is real. Seeing is a dhamma, it is real. Colour is a dhamma, it is real. Feeling is a dhamma, it is real. Our defilements are dhammas, they are realities.

When the Buddha attained enlightenment he clearly knew all dhammas as they really are. He taught the "Dhamma", the teaching on realities, to us in order that we also may know dhammas as they are. Without the Buddha's teaching we would be ignorant of reality. We are inclined to take for permanent what is impermanent, for pleasant what is sorrowful and unsatisfactory (dukkha), and for "self" what is nonself. The aim of all three parts of the Tipiṭaka is to teach people the development of the way leading to the end of defilements.

The Vinaya contains the rules for the monks and these rules help them to live to perfection the "brahman life" and to reach "...that unsurpassed goal of the brahman life, realizing it by personal knowledge even in this life; for the sake of which clansmen rightly go forth from the home into the homeless life..." (Gradual Sayings, Book of the Fives, chapter VI, paragraph 6, The Preceptor). The goal of the "brahman life" is the eradication of defilements.

Not only monks, but also laymen should study the Vinaya. We read about the instances that monks deviated from their purity of life; when there was such a case, a rule was laid down in order to help them to be watchful. When we read the Vinaya we are reminded of our own attachment (lobha), aversion (dosa) and ignorance (moha); they are realities. So long as they have not been eradicated they can arise at any time. We are reminded how deeply rooted defilements are and what they can lead to. When we consider this, we are motivated to develop the eightfold Path which leads to the eradication of wrong view, jealousy, stinginess, conceit and all other defilements.

In the Suttanta, the "Discourses", the Dhamma is explained to different people at different places on various occasions. The Buddha taught about all realities appearing through the "six doors" of eyes, ears, nose, tongue, body-sense and mind. He taught about cause and effect and about the practice leading to the end of all sorrow.

As regards the *Abhidhamma*, this is an exposition of all realities in detail. The prefix "abhi" is used in the sense of "preponderance" or "distinction". "Abhidhamma" means "higher dhamma" or "dhamma in detail". The form of this part of the Tipiṭaka is different, but the aim is the same: the eradication of wrong view and eventually of all defilements. Thus, when we study the many enumerations of realities, we should not forget the real purpose of our study. The theory (pariyatti) should encourage us to the practice (paṭipatti) which is necessary for the realization of the truth (paṭivedha). While we are studying the different mental phenomena (nāmas) and physical phenomena (rūpas) and while we are pondering over them, we can be reminded to be aware of the nāma and rūpa which appear at that moment. In this way we will discover more and more that the Abhidhamma explains everything which is real, that is, the "worlds" appearing through the six doors of the senses and the mind.

This book is meant as an introduction to the study of the Abhidhamma. In order to understand this book, some basic knowledge of Buddhism is necessary. My book The Buddha's Path could be helpful to make the reader acquainted with the basic principles and tenets of Buddhism before he starts to read this book on the Abhidhamma.

I am using terms in Pāli which is the original language of the scriptures of the old Theravāda tradition. The English equivalents of the Pāli terms are often unsatisfactory since they stem from Western philosophy and psychology and therefore give an association of meaning which is different from the meaning intended by the Buddhist teachings. I hope that the reader, instead of being discouraged by the Pāli terms and by the many enumerations which are used in this book, will develop a growing interest in the realities to be experienced in and around himself.

Ms. Sujin Boriharnwanaket has been of immense assistance and inspiration to me in my study of the Abhidhamma. She encouraged me to discover for myself that the Abhidhamma deals with realities to be experienced through the senses and the mind. Thus I learnt that the study of the Abhidhamma is a process which continues throughout life. I hope that the reader will have a similar experience and that he will be full of enthusiasm and gladness every time he studies realities which can be experienced!

I have quoted many times from the suttas in order to show that the teaching contained in the Abhidhamma is not different from the teaching in the other parts of the Tipiṭaka. I have mostly used the English translation of the "Pāli Text Society" (Translation Series). For the quotations from the Visuddhimagga (Path of Purification) I have used the translation by Bhikkhu Ñāṇamoli (Colombo, Sri Lanka, 1964). The Visuddhimagga is an Encyclopedia on Buddhism written by the commentator Buddhaghosa in the fifth century A.D. He also edited the commentaries to most parts of the Tipiṭaka, thereby basing his works on older commentarial traditions.

The Abhidhamma consists of the following seven books[1]:

- Dhammasangaṇi (Buddhist Psychological Ethics)
- Vibhaṅga (Book of Analysis)
- Dhātukathā (Discussion on the Elements)
- Puggalapaññatti (A Designation of Human Types)
- Kathāvatthu (Points of Controversy)
- Yamaka (the Book of Pairs)
- Paṭṭhāna (Conditional Relations)

[1] For a synopsis of their contents see: Guide through the Abhidhamma Pitaka by Ven. Nyanatiloka.

When I first started to write this book my sources were the Visuddhimagga and the Atthasālinī (Expositor), the commentary to the Dhammasangaṇi, written by Buddhaghosa. I also used the Abhidhammattha Sangaha, an Encyclopedia of the Abhidhamma, written by Anuruddha[2]. These works helped me greatly with the study of the Abhidhamma itself, of the Dhammasangaṇi and some of the other books of the abhidhamma I gradually acquired later on.

The commentaries give a detailed explanation and nomenclature of the different cittas, moments of consciousness, which each perform their own function, and they deal with the different processes of cittas experiencing an object through a sense-door or through the mind-door. Although not all the details concerning the processes of cittas can be found in the scriptures themselves, the commentaries are firmly based on the scriptures. The essence of the subjects explained by the commentaries can be found in the scriptures. The Dhammasangaṇi, which is an analytical exposition of realities, enumerates different cittas arising in processes. The Vibhaṅga, under "Analysis of the Elements", refers to cittas performing their functions in processes and also the Paṭṭhāna refers to processes of cittas under the heading of some of the conditions it deals with. Moreover, the Paṭisambhidāmagga (Khuddaka Nikāya) mentions (I, Treatise on Knowledge, in chapter XVII, under "behaviour of citta", viññāṇa cariya) different functions of citta in a process. I hope that these few references show that the commentator did not give his own personal views, but was faithful to the tradition of the original scriptures.

In the last four chapters of this book I explain about the cittas which attain jhāna, absorption, and the cittas which attain enlightenment. Some readers may wonder why they should know details about these subjects. It is useful to study details about jhāna and enlightenment because people may have wrong notions about them. The study of the Abhidhamma will help one not to be deluded about realities. Moreover, it will help one to understand the suttas where there is often reference to jhāna and to the attainment of enlightenment.

I have added some questions after the chapters which may help the reader to ponder over what he has read.

The late Bhikkhu Dhammadharo (Alan Driver) and also Mr. Jonothan Abbott gave me most helpful corrections and suggestions for the text of the first edition of this book. I also want to acknowledge my gratitude to the "Dhamma Study and Propagation Foundation" and to the publisher Alan Weller who have made possible the third edition of this book.

Nina van Gorkom

---

[2] This work was composed some time between the 8th and the 12th century A.D. It has been translated into English and published by the P.T.S. under the title of "Compendium of Philosophy", and by Ven. Nārada, Colombo, under the title of "A Manual of Abhidhamma". It has also been translated by the Venerable Bikkhu Bodhi as "A Comprehensive Manual of Abhidhamma". Moreover, it has been translated together with its commentary as "Summary of the Topics of Abhidhamma" and "Exposition of the Topics of Abhidhamma", by R.P. Wijeratne and Rupert Gethin.

1 The Four Paramattha Dhammas

There are two kinds of reality: mental phenomena or **nāma** and physical phenomena or **rūpa**. Nāma experiences something; rūpa does not experience anything. What we take for "self" are only nāma and rūpa which arise and fall away. The Visuddhimagga (Path of Purification chapter XVIII, 25) explains:

For this has been said:

```
''As with the assembly of parts
The word 'chariot' is countenanced,
So, when the khandhas are present,
'A being' is said in common usage''.
     (Kindred Sayings I, 135)
```

> ...So in many hundred suttas there is only mentality-materiality which is illustrated, not a being, not a person. Therefore, just as when the component parts (of a chariot) such as axles, wheels, frame, poles... are arranged in a certain way, there comes to be the mere conventional term 'chariot', yet in the ultimate sense, when each part is examined, there is no chariot... so too, when there are the five khandhas of clinging there comes to be the mere conventional term 'a being', 'a person', yet in the ultimate sense, when each component is examined, there is no being as a basis for the assumption 'I am' or 'I'; in the ultimate sense there is only mentality-materiality. The vision of one who sees in this way is called correct vision.

All phenomena in and around ourselves are only nāma and rūpa which arise and fall away; they are impermanent. Nāma and rūpa are absolute realities, in Pāli: *paramattha dhammas*. We can experience their characteristics when they appear, no matter how we name them; we do not necessarily have to call them nāma and rūpa. Those who have developed "insight" can experience them as they really are: impermanent and not self. Seeing, hearing, smelling, tasting, experiencing tangible object through the bodysense and thinking, all these nāmas are impermanent. We are used to thinking that there is a self who performs different functions such as seeing, hearing or thinking; but where is the self? Is it one of those nāmas? The more we know different nāmas and rūpas by experiencing their characteristics, the more will we see that "self" is only a concept; it is not a paramattha dhamma (absolute or ultimate reality).

Nāmas are mental phenomena, rūpas are physical phenomena. Nāma and rūpa are different types of realities. If we do not distinguish them from each other and learn the characteristic of each we will continue to take them for self. For example, hearing is nāma; it has no form or shape, it has no ears. Hearing is different from earsense, but it has earsense as a necessary condition. The nāma which hears experiences sound. Earsense and sound are rūpas, they do not experience anything; they are entirely different from the nāma which hears. If we do not learn that hearing, earsense and sound are realities which are altogether different from each other, we will continue to think that it is self who hears.

The Visuddhimagga (XVIII, 34) explains:

> Furthermore, nāma has no efficient power, it cannot occur by its own efficient power. . . It does not eat, it does not drink, it does not speak, it does not adopt postures. And rūpa is without efficient power; it cannot occur by its own efficient power. For it has no desire to eat, it has no desire to drink, it has no desire to speak, it has no desire to adopt postures. But it is when supported by rūpa that nāma occurs; and it is when supported by nāma that rūpa occurs. When nāma has the desire to eat, the desire to drink, the desire to speak, the desire to adopt a posture, it is rūpa that eats, drinks, speaks and adopts a posture. . .

Furthermore (XVIII, 36) we read:

```
And just as men depend upon
A boat for traversing the sea,
So does the mental body need
The matter-body for occurrence.

And as the boat depends upon
The men for traversing the sea,
So does the matter-body need
The mental body for occurrence.

Depending each upon the other
The boat and men go on the sea.
And so do mind and matter both
Depend the one upon the other.
```

There are two kinds of conditioned nāma : *citta* (consciousness) and *cetasika* (mental factors arising together with consciousness). They are nāmas which arise because of conditions and fall away again.

As regards citta, citta knows or experiences an object. Each citta has its object, in Pāli: ārammaṇa. Knowing or experiencing an object does not necessarily mean thinking about it. The citta which sees has what is visible as object; it is different from the cittas which arise afterwards, such as the cittas which know what it is that was perceived and which think about it. The citta which hears (hearing-consciousness) has sound as its object. Even when we are sound asleep and not dreaming, citta experiences an object. There isn't any citta without an object. There are many different types of citta which can be classified in different ways.

Some cittas are *kusala* (wholesome), some are *akusala* (unwholesome). Kusala cittas and akusala cittas are cittas which are cause; they can motivate wholesome or unwholesome deeds through body, speech or mind which are able to bring about their appropriate results. Some cittas are the result of wholesome or unwholesome deeds; they are vipākacittas. Some cittas are neither cause nor result; they are *kiriyacittas* (sometimes translated as "inoperative")[1].

Cittas can be classified by way of jāti (jāti literally means "birth" or "nature"). There are four jātis:

- *kusala*
- *akusala*
- *vipāka*
- *kiriya*

Both kusala vipāka (the result of a wholesome deed) and akusala vipāka (the result of an unwholesome deed) are one jāti, the jāti of vipāka.

It is important to know which jāti a citta is. We cannot develop wholesomeness in our life if we take akusala for kusala or if we take akusala for vipāka. For instance, when someone speaks unpleasant words to us, the moment of experiencing the sound (hearing-consciousness) is akusala vipāka, the result of an unwholesome deed we performed ourselves. But the aversion which may arise very shortly afterwards is not vipāka, but it arises with akusala citta. We can learn to distinguish these moments from each other by realizing their different characteristics.

Another way of classifying citta is by plane of consciousness, in Pāli: *bhūmi*. There are different planes of consciousness. The sensuous plane of consciousness (kāmāvacara cittas) is the plane of sense-impressions, which are: seeing, hearing, smelling, tasting and the experiencing of tangible object through the bodysense. On account of pleasant and unpleasant objects experienced through the senses, kusala cittas (wholesome cittas) and akusala cittas (unwholesome cittas) arise. There are other planes of citta which do not experience sense-impressions. Those who cultivate samatha (tranquil meditation) and attain absorption (jhāna), have jhānacittas. The jhānacitta is another plane of citta; it does not experience sense-impressions. The lokuttara citta ("supramundane consciousness") is the highest plane of consciousness because it is the citta which directly experiences nibbāna.

There are still other ways of classifying citta and if we consider the different intensities of citta there are many more distinctions to be made. For instance, *akusala* cittas, which are rooted in attachment (*lobha*), aversion (*dosa*) and ignorance (*moha*), can be of many different intensities. Sometimes they may motivate deeds, sometimes they may not, depending on the degree of akusala. Kusala cittas too are of many different intensities. It is useful to know different ways of classification because in this way we learn about different aspects of citta. There are altogether eighty-nine (or, in another classification, hundred-and-twenty-one) types of citta[2]. If we develop our knowledge of cittas and if we are aware of them when they appear, we will be less inclined to take them for "self".

---

[1] In chapter 3 and the following ones I will explain more about akusala, kusala, vipāka and kiriya.

[2] Cittas are classified as 121 when one takes into account the lokuttara cittas of those who have cultivated both samatha and vipassanā and attain enlightenment with lokuttara jhānacittas, lokuttara cittas accompanied by jhāna-factors of different stages of jhāna, absorption. This will be explained in chapter 23.

Cetasika is the second paramattha dhamma which is nāma. As we have seen, citta experiences an object: seeing has what is visible as its object, hearing has sound as its object, the citta which thinks experiences the object it is thinking of. However, there is not only citta, there are also mental factors, cetasikas, which accompany citta. One can think of something with aversion, with pleasant feeling or with wisdom. Aversion, feeling and wisdom are mental phenomena which are not citta; they are cetasikas which accompany different cittas. There is only one citta at a time, but there are several cetasikas arising together with the citta and falling away together with the citta; citta never arises alone. For example, feeling, in Pāli: *vedanā*, is a cetasika which arises with every citta. Citta only knows or experiences its object; it does not feel. Feeling, vedanā, however, has the function of feeling. Feeling is sometimes pleasant, sometimes unpleasant. When we do not have a pleasant or an unpleasant feeling, there is still feeling: at that moment the feeling is neutral or indifferent. There is always feeling; there isn't any moment of citta without feeling. When, for example, seeing-consciousness arises, feeling arises together with the citta. The citta which sees perceives only visible object; there is not yet like or dislike. The feeling which accompanies this type of citta is indifferent feeling. After seeing-consciousness has fallen away, other cittas arise and there may be cittas which dislike the object. The feeling which accompanies this type of citta is unpleasant feeling. The function of citta is to cognize an object; citta is the "chief in knowing". Cetasikas share the same object with the citta, but they each have their own specific quality and function. Some cetasikas arise with every citta whereas others do not[3].

As we have seen, feeling, *vedanā* is a cetasika which arises with every citta. Contact, in Pāli: *phassa*, is another cetasika which arises with every citta; it "contacts" the object so that citta can experience it. Perception or remembrance, in Pāli: *saññā*, is also a cetasika which arises with every citta. In the Visuddhimagga (XIV, 130) we read that saññā has the function of perceiving:

> . . . Its function is to make a sign as a condition for perceiving again that "this is the same", as carpenters, etc., do in the case of timber. . .

Citta only experiences or cognizes an object; it does not "mark" the object. Saññā marks the object so that it can be recognized later. Whenever we remember something it is saññā, not self, which remembers. It is saññā which, for example, remembers that this colour is red, that this is a house, or that this is the sound of a bird.

There are also types of cetasika which do not arise with every citta. Akusala (unwholesome) cetasikas arise only with akusala cittas. Sobhana (beautiful) cetasikas[4] arise with sobhana cittas. Lobha (attachment), dosa (aversion) and moha (ignorance) are akusala cetasikas which arise only with akusala cittas. For example, when we see something beautiful, cittas with attachment to what we have seen may arise. The cetasika which is lobha arises with the citta at that moment. Lobha has the function of attachment or clinging. There are several other akusala cetasikas

---

[3] There are seven types of cetasika which have to arise with every citta.

[4] See chapter 19 for the meaning of sobhana. Sobhana cittas include not only kusala cittas, but also vipakacittas and kiriyacittas which are accompanied by sobhana cetasikas.

which arise with akusala cittas, such as conceit (*māna*), wrong view (*diṭṭhi*) and envy (*issā*). Sobhana cetasikas accompanying wholesome cittas are for example *alobha* (generosity), *adosa* (loving kindness), *amoha* (or *paññā*, wisdom). When we are generous alobha and adosa arise with the kusala citta. Paññā, wisdom, may arise too with the kusala citta, and moreover, there are other kinds of sobhana cetasikas arising with the kusala citta as well. Defilements and wholesome qualities are cetasikas, they are non-self. Altogether there are fifty-two different cetasikas.

Although citta and cetasika are both nāma, they each have different characteristics. One may wonder how cetasikas can be experienced. When we notice a change in citta, a characteristic of cetasika can be experienced. For instance, when akusala cittas with stinginess arise after kusala cittas with generosity have fallen away, we can notice a change. Stinginess and generosity are cetasikas which can be experienced; they have different characteristics. We may notice as well the change from attachment to aversion, from pleasant feeling to unpleasant feeling. Feeling is a cetasika we can experience, because feeling is sometimes predominant and there are different kinds of feeling. We can experience that unpleasant feeling is different from pleasant feeling and from indifferent feeling. These different cetasikas arise with different cittas and they fall away immediately, together with the citta they accompany. If we know more about the variety of citta and cetasika, it will help us to see the truth.

Since citta and cetasika arise together it is difficult to experience the difference in their characteristics. The Buddha was able to directly experience the different characteristics of all cittas and cetasikas because his wisdom was of the highest degree. We read in the Questions of King Milinda (Book III, "The Removal of Difficulties", chapter 7, 87[5]) that the arahat Nāgasena said to King Milinda:

> "A hard thing there is, O King, which the Blessed One has done." "And what is that?" "The fixing of all those mental conditions which depend on one organ of sense, telling us that such is contact, such is feeling, such is saññā (perception), such is volition and such is citta." "Give me an illustration." "Suppose, O King, a man were to wade down into the sea, and taking some water in the palm of his hand, were to taste it with his tongue. Would he distinguish whether it were water from the Ganges, or from the Jamunā, or from the Aciravatī, or from the Sarabhū, or from the Mahī?" "Impossible, Sir." "More difficult than that, great King, is it to have distinguished between the mental conditions which follow on the exercise of any one of the organs of sense!"

Citta and cetasika are *paramattha* dhammas (absolute realities) which each have their own unchangeable characteristic. These characteristics can be experienced, regardless how one names them. Paramattha dhammas are not words or concepts, they are realities. Pleasant feeling and unpleasant feeling are real; their characteristics can be experienced without having to call them "pleasant feeling" or "unpleasant feeling". Aversion is real; it can be experienced when it presents itself.

---

5 I am using the translation by T.W. Rhys Davids, Part I, Dover Publications, New York.

There are not only mental phenomena, there are also physical phenomena. Physical phenomena or rūpa are the third paramattha dhamma. There are several kinds of rūpas which each have their own characteristic[6]. There are four principle rūpas which are called the Great Elements (in Pāli: mahā-bhūta-rūpa). They are:

- Element of Earth or solidity (to be experienced as hardness or softness)
- Element of Water or cohesion
- Element of Fire or temperature (to be experienced as heat or cold)
- Element of Wind or motion (to be experienced as oscillation or pressure)

These "Great Elements" are the principle rūpas which arise together with all the other kinds of rūpa, which are the derived rūpas (in Pāli: upādā-rūpa). Rūpas never arise alone; they arise in "groups" or "units". There have to be at least eight kinds of rūpa arising together. For example, whenever the rūpa which is temperature arises, solidity, cohesion, motion and other rūpas have to arise as well. "Derived rūpas" are, for example, the physical sense-organs of eyesense, earsense, smellingsense, tastingsense and bodysense, and the sense-objects of visible object, sound, odour and flavour.

Different characteristics of rūpa can be experienced through eyes, ears, nose, tongue, bodysense and mind. These characteristics are real since they can be experienced. We use conventional terms such as "body" and "table"; both have the characteristic of hardness which can be experienced through touch. In this way we can prove that the characteristic of hardness is the same, no matter whether it is in the body or in the table. Hardness is a paramattha dhamma; "body" and "table" are not paramattha dhammas but only concepts. We take it for granted that the body stays and we take it for "self", but what we call "body" are only different rūpas arising and falling away. The conventional term "body" may delude us about reality. We will know the truth if we learn to experience different characteristics of rūpa when they appear.

Citta, cetasika and rūpa only arise when there are the right conditions, they are conditioned dhammas (in Pāli: saṅkhāra dhammas[7]). Seeing cannot arise when there is no eyesense and when there is no visible object; these are necessary conditions for its arising. Sound can only arise when there are the right conditions for its arising. When it has arisen it falls away again. Everything which arises because of conditions has to fall away again when the conditions have ceased. One may think that sound stays, but what we take for a long, lasting moment of sound are actually many different rūpas succeeding one another.

The fourth paramattha dhamma is *nibbāna*. Nibbāna is a paramattha dhamma because it is real. Nibbāna can be experienced through the mind-door if one follows the right Path leading towards it: the development of the wisdom which sees things as they are. Nibbāna is nāma. However, it is not citta or cetasika, paramattha

---

[6] There are twenty-eight classes of rūpa in all.

[7] Saṅkhāra dhammas are conditioned dhammas that arise together depending on each other. The Pāli term "saṅkhata" is also used. Saṅkhata means what has been put together, composed by a combination of factors. Saṅkhata dhamma is what has arisen because of conditions.

dhammas which arise because of conditions and fall way. Nibbāna is the nāma which is an unconditioned reality[8]; therefore it does not arise and it does not fall away. Citta and cetasika are nāmas which experience an object; nibbāna is the nāma which does not experience an object, but nibbāna itself can be the object of citta and cetasika which experience it. Nibbāna is not a person, it is non-self, anattā.

Summarising the four paramattha dhammas, they are:

- citta
- cetasika
- rūpa
- nibbāna

When we study Dhamma it is essential to know which paramattha dhamma such or such reality is. If we do not know this we may be misled by conventional terms. We should, for example, know that what we call "body" are actually different rūpa-paramattha dhammas, not citta or cetasika. We should know that nibbāna is not citta or cetasika, but the fourth paramattha dhamma. Nibbāna is the end of all conditioned realities which arise and fall away: for the arahat, the perfected one, who passes away, there is no more rebirth, no more nāmas and rūpas which arise and fall away.

- All conditioned dhammas, citta, cetasika and rūpa, are impermanent, "anicca".
- All conditioned dhammas are "dukkha"; they are "suffering" or unsatisfactory, since they are impermanent.
- All dhammas are non-self, "anattā" (in Pāli: sabbe dhammā anattā, Dhammapada, vs. 279).

Thus, the conditioned dhammas, not nibbāna, are impermanent and dukkha. But all dhammas, that is, the four paramattha dhammas, nibbāna included, have the characteristic of anattā, non-self.

Questions

1. What is the difference between nāma and rūpa?
2. What is the difference between citta and cetasika?
3. Do cetasikas experience an object?
4. Is there more than one cetasika arising together with the citta?
5. Can nibbāna experience an object?
6. Is nibbāna a "self"?

[8] In Pāli: asaṅkhata: not conditioned, the opposite of saṅkhata. In the Dhammasangaṇi nibbāna is referred to as asaṅkhatā dhatu, the unconditioned element. Sometimes the term visaṅkhāra dhamma, the dhamma which is not saṅkhāra (vi is negation), is used.

2 The Five Khandhas

The Buddha discovered the truth of all phenomena. He knew the characteristic of each phenomenon by his own experience. Out of compassion he taught other people to see reality in many different ways, so that they would have a deeper understanding of the phenomena in and around themselves. When realities are classified by way of paramattha dhammas (absolute realities), they are classified as:

- citta
- cetasika
- rūpa
- nibbāna

Citta, cetasika and rūpa are conditioned realities (saṅkhāra dhammas). They arise because of conditions and fall away again; they are impermanent. One paramattha dhamma, nibbāna, is an unconditioned reality (asaṅkhata dhamma); it does not arise and fall away. All four paramattha dhammas are anattā, non-self.

Citta, cetasika and rūpa, the conditioned realities, can be classified by way of the five khandhas. *Khandha* means "group" or "aggregate". What is classified as khandha arises because of conditions and falls away again. The five khandhas are not different from the three paramattha dhammas which are citta, cetasika and rūpa. Realities can be classified in many different ways and thus different names are given to them. The five khandhas are:

- *Rūpakkhandha*, which are all physical phenomena
- *Vedanākkhandha*, which is feeling (vedanā)
- *Saññākkhandha*, which is remembrance or "perception" (saññā)
- *Saṅkhārakkhandha*, comprising fifty cetasikas (mental factors arising with the citta)
- *Viññāṇakkhandha*, comprising all cittas (89 or 121)[1]

As regards the fifty-two kinds of cetasika which may arise with citta, they are classified as three khandhas: the cetasika which is feeling (vedanā) is classified as one khandha, the vedanākkhandha; the cetasika which is remembrance or "perception" (saññā) is classified as one khandha, the saññākkhandha; as regards the other fifty cetasikas, they are classified altogether as one khandha, the saṅkhārakkhandha. For example, in saṅkhārakkhandha are included the following cetasikas: volition or intention (cetanā), attachment (lobha), aversion (dosa), ignorance (moha), loving kindness (mettā), generosity (alobha) and wisdom (paññā). All defilements and all good qualities are included in saṅkhārakkhandha, they are impermanent not "self". Saṅkhārakkhandha is sometimes translated as "activities" or "mental formations"[2]

As regards citta, all cittas are one khandha: viññāṇakkhandha. The Pāli terms viññāṇa, mano and citta are three terms for the same reality: that which has the

---

[1] See chapter 1.

[2] Saṅkhāra has different meanings in different contexts. Saṅkhāra dhamma comprises all conditioned realities. Saṅkhārakkhandha comprises fifty cetasikas.

characteristic of knowing or experiencing something. When citta is classified as khandha the word viññāṇa is used. Thus, one khandha is rūpakkhandha and the other four khandhas are nāmakkhandhas. Three nāmakkhandhas are cetasika and one nāmakkhandha is citta.

Anything which is khandha does not last; as soon as it has arisen it falls away again. Although khandhas arise and fall away, they are real; we can experience them when they present themselves. Nibbāna, the unconditioned dhamma which does not arise and fall away, is not a khandha.

The Visuddhimagga (XX, 96) explains about the arising and falling away of nāma and rūpa:

> There is no heap or store of unarisen nāma-rūpa (existing) prior to its arising. When it arises it does not come from any heap or store; and when it ceases, it does not go in any direction. There is nowhere any depository in the way of heap or store or hoard of what has ceased. But just as there is no store, prior to its arising, of the sound that arises when a lute is played, nor does it come from any store when it arises, nor does it go in any direction when it ceases, nor does it persist as a store when it has ceased ("Kindred Sayings" IV, 197), but on the contrary, not having been, it is brought into being owing to the lute, the lute's neck, and the man's appropriate effort, and having been, it vanishes – so too all material and immaterial states (rūpa and nāma), not having been, are brought into being, having been, they vanish.

The khandhas are realities which can be experienced. We experience rūpakkhandha when, for example, we feel hardness. This phenomenon does not stay; it arises and falls away. Rūpakkhandha is impermanent. Not only rūpas of the body, but the other physical phenomena are included in rūpakkhandha as well. For example, sound is rūpakkhandha; it arises and falls away, it is impermanent.

Vedanākkhandha (feeling) is real; we can experience feelings. Vedanākkhandha comprises all kinds of feelings. Feeling can be classified in different ways. Sometimes feelings are classified as threefold:

- pleasant feeling
- unpleasant feeling
- indifferent feeling

Sometimes they are classified as fivefold. In addition to pleasant feeling, unpleasant feeling and indifferent feeling there are:

- pleasant bodily feeling
- painful bodily feeling

Bodily feeling is feeling which has bodysense, the rūpa which has the capacity to receive bodily impressions, as condition; the feeling itself is nāma, but it has rūpa (bodysense) as condition. When an object contacts the bodysense, the feeling is either painful or pleasant; there is no indifferent bodily feeling. When the bodily feeling is painful it is akusala vipāka (the result of an unwholesome deed), and when the bodily feeling is pleasant it is kusala vipāka (the result of a wholesome deed).

Since there are many different moments of feeling arising and falling away it is difficult to distinguish them from each other. For instance, we are inclined to confuse pleasant bodily feeling which is vipāka and the pleasant feeling which may arise shortly afterwards together with attachment to that pleasant bodily feeling. Or we may confuse painful bodily feeling and unpleasant feeling which may arise afterwards together with aversion. When there is bodily pain, the painful feeling is vipāka, it accompanies the vipākacitta which experiences the unpleasant object impinging on the bodysense[3]. Unpleasant (mental) feeling may arise afterwards; it is not vipāka, but it accompanies the akusala citta with aversion, and thus it is akusala. The akusala citta with aversion arises because of our accumulated aversion (dosa). Though bodily feeling and mental feeling are both nāma, they are entirely different kinds of feelings, arising because of different conditions. When there are no more conditions for dosa there can still be painful bodily feeling, but there is no longer unpleasant (mental) feeling. The arahat, the perfected one who has eradicated all defilements, may still have akusala vipāka so long as his life has not terminated yet, but he has no aversion.

We read in the Kindred Sayings (I, Sagāthā-vagga, the Māra-suttas, chapter II, paragraph 3, The Splinter):

> Thus have I heard: The Exalted One was once staying at Rājagaha, in the Maddakucchi, at the Deer-preserve. Now at that time his foot was injured by a splinter. Sorely indeed did the Exalted One feel it, grievous the pains he suffered in the body, keen and sharp, acute, distressing and unwelcome. He truly bore them, mindful and deliberate, nor was he cast down. . .

Feelings are sixfold when they are classified by way of the contacts occurring through the six doors: there is feeling which arises because of what is experienced through the eyes, the ears, the nose, the tongue, the bodysense and the mind. All these feelings are different; they arise because of different conditions. Feeling arises and falls away together with the citta it accompanies and thus at each moment feeling is different.

We read in the Kindred Sayings (IV, Saḷāyatana-vagga, Part II, Kindred Sayings about Feeling, paragraph 8, Sickness II) that the Buddha said to the monks:

> . . . Monks, a monk should meet his end collected and composed. This is our instruction to you.
>
> . . . Now, monks, as that monk dwells collected, composed, earnest, ardent, strenuous, there arises in him feeling that is pleasant, and he thus understands: "There is arisen in me this pleasant feeling. Now that is owing to something, not without cause. It is owing to this contact. Now this contact is impermanent, compounded, arisen owing to something. Owing to this impermanent contact which has so arisen, this pleasant feeling has

[3] The experiences through the senses which are seeing, hearing, smelling, tasting and body-consciousness are vipākacittas, the results of kamma. When these cittas experience a pleasant object they are kusala vipāka, the result of kusala kamma, and when they experience an unpleasant object they are akusala vipāka, the result of akusala kamma.

> arisen: How can that be permanent?" Thus he dwells contemplating the impermanence in contact and pleasant feeling, contemplating their transience, their waning, their ceasing, the giving of them up. Thus as he dwells contemplating their impermanence...the lurking tendency to lust for contact and pleasant feeling is abandoned in him.
>
> So also as regards contact and painful feeling...contact and neutral feeling...

There are still many more ways of classifying feelings. If we know about different ways of classifying feelings it will help us to realize that feeling is only a mental phenomenon which arises because of conditions. We are inclined to cling to feeling which has fallen away, instead of being aware of the reality of the present moment as it appears through eyes, ears, nose, tongue, bodysense or mind. In the passage of the Visuddhimagga which was quoted above (XX, 96) nāma and rūpa are compared to the sound of a lute which does not come from any "store" when it arises, nor goes in any direction when it ceases, nor persists as a "store" when it has ceased. However, we cling so much to feelings that we do not realize that the feeling which has fallen away does not exist any more, that it has ceased completely. Vedanākkhandha (feeling) is impermanent.

Saññākkhandha (perception) is real; it can be experienced whenever we remember something. Saññā accompanies every moment of citta. Each citta which arises experiences an object and saññā which arises with the citta remembers and "marks" that object so that it can be recognized. Even when there is a moment that one does not recognize something citta still experiences an object and saññā which arises with the citta "marks" that object. Saññā arises and falls away with the citta; saññā is impermanent. So long as we do not see saññā as it really is: only a mental phenomenon which falls away as soon as it has arisen, we will take saññā for self.

Saṅkhārakkhandha (all the cetasikas other than vedanā and saññā) is real; it can be experienced. When beautiful mental factors (sobhana cetasikas) arise, such as generosity and compassion, or when unwholesome mental factors arise, such as anger and stinginess, we can experience saṅkhārakkhandha. All these phenomena arise and fall away; saṅkhārakkhandha is impermanent.

Viññāṇakkhandha (citta) is real; we can experience it when there is seeing, hearing, smelling, tasting, experiencing tangible object through the bodysense or thinking. Viññāṇakkhandha arises and falls away; it is impermanent. All saṅkhāra dhammas (conditioned phenomena), that is, the five khandhas, are impermanent.

Sometimes the khandhas are called the "khandhas of clinging" (in Pāli: upādānakkhandha). Those who are not arahats still cling to the khandhas. We take the body for self; thus we cling to rūpakkhandha. We take mentality for self; thus we cling to vedanākkhandha, to saññākkhandha, to saṅkhārakkhandha and to viññāṇakkhandha. If we cling to the khandhas and do not see them as they are, we will have sorrow. So long as the khandhas are still objects of clinging for us, we are like people afflicted by sickness.

We read in the Kindred Sayings (III, Khandha-vagga, the First Fifty, paragraph 1, Nakulapitar) that the housefather Nakulapitar, who was an old, sick man, came to see the Buddha at Crocodile Haunt in the Deerpark. The Buddha said to him that he should train himself thus:

> "Though my body is sick, my mind shall not be sick."

Later on Sāriputta gave him a further explanation of the Buddha's words:

> Herein, housefather, the untaught many-folk. . . who are unskilled in the worthy doctrine, untrained in the worthy doctrine – these regard body as the self, they regard the self as having body, body as being in the self, the self as being in the body. "I am the body", they say, "body is mine", and are possessed by this idea; and so, possessed by this idea, when body alters and changes, owing to the unstable and changeable nature of the body, then sorrow and grief, woe, lamentation and despair arise in them. They regard feeling (vedanā) as the self. . . They regard perception (saññā) as the self. . . They regard the activities (saṅkhārakkhandha) as the self. . . They regard consciousness (viññāṇa) as the self. . . That, housefather, is how body is sick and mind is sick too.
>
> And how is body sick, but mind is not sick?
>
> Herein, housefather, the well-taught ariyan disciple. . . regards not body as the self, regards not the self as having body, nor body as being in the self, nor self as being in the body. He says not "I am body", he says not "body is mine", nor is possessed by this idea. As he is not so possessed, when body alters and changes owing to the unstable and changeable nature of body, then sorrow and grief, woe, lamentation and despair do not arise in him. He regards not feeling (vedanā) as the self. . . He regards not perception (saññā) as the self. . . He regards not the activities (saṅkhārakkhandha) as the self. . . He regards not consciousness (viññāṇa) as the self. . . Thus, housefather, body is sick, but mind is not sick.

So long as we are still clinging to the khandhas we are like sick people, but we can be cured of our sickness if we see the khandhas as they are. The khandhas are impermanent and thus they are dukkha (unsatisfactory). We read in the Kindred Sayings (III, Khandha-vagga, Last Fifty, paragraph 104, Suffering) that the Buddha taught to the monks the four noble Truths: the Truth of dukkha, the Truth of the arising of dukkha, the Truth of the ceasing of dukkha, the Truth of the way leading to the ceasing of dukkha. He said:

> Monks, I will teach you dukkha[4], the arising of dukkha, the ceasing of dukkha, the way leading to the ceasing of dukkha. Do you listen to it.
>
> And what, monks, is dukkha? It is to be called the five khandhas of grasping. What five? The rūpakkhandha of grasping, the vedanākkhandha of grasping, the saññākkhandha of grasping, the saṅkhārakkhandha of grasping, the viññāṇakkhandha of grasping. This, monks, is called dukkha.

[4] In the English translation "dukkha" is sometimes translated as "suffering", sometimes as "ill". Here the English text uses the word "suffering".

> And what, monks, is the arising of dukkha? It is that craving. . . that leads downward to rebirth. . . the craving for feeling, for rebirth, for no rebirth. . . This, monks, is called the arising of dukkha.
> And what, monks, is the ceasing of dukkha? It is the utter passionless ceasing, the giving up, the abandonment of, the release from, the freedom from attachment to that craving. . .
> This, monks, is called the ceasing of dukkha.
> And what, monks, is the way going to the ceasing of dukkha?
> It is the ariyan eightfold Path. . . This, monks, is the way going to the ceasing of dukkha.

So long as we still cling to the khandhas they will arise at rebirth, and this means sorrow. If we develop the eightfold Path, the development of right understanding of realities, we will learn to see what the khandhas really are. Then we are on the way leading to the ceasing of dukkha, which means: no more birth, old age, sickness and death. Those who have attained the last stage of enlightenment, the stage of the arahat, will be, after their life-span is over, free from the khandhas.

Questions

1. Which paramattha dhammas are nāma?
2. Which paramattha dhammas are saṅkhāra dhamma (conditioned realities)?
3. Which paramattha dhamma is the unconditioned reality?
4. Which saṅkhāra dhammas are nāma?
5. Are all cetasikas saṅkhārakkhandha?
6. Is vedanā cetasika (feeling) a khandha?
7. Is saññā cetasika (remembrance or perception) a khandha?
8. Is painful bodily feeling vipāka?
9. Is unhappy mental feeling vipāka?
10. Which khandhas are nāma?
11. Is seeing-consciousness a khandha?
12. Is the concept "human being" a khandha?
13. Is sound a khandha?
14. Which paramattha dhammas are khandha?

3 Different Aspects of Citta

The Buddha spoke about everything which is real. What he taught can be proved by our own experience. However, we do not really know the most common realities of daily life: the mental phenomena and physical phenomena which appear through eyes, ears, nose, tongue, bodysense and mind. It seems that we are mostly interested in the past or the future. However, we will find out what life really is if we know more about the realities of the present moment, and if we learn to be aware of them when they appear.

The Buddha explained that citta (consciousness) is a reality. We may doubt whether cittas are real. How can we prove that there are cittas? Could it be that there are only physical phenomena and not mental phenomena? There are many things in our life we take for granted such as our homes, meals, clothes, or the tools we use every day. These things do not appear by themselves. They are brought about by a thinking mind, by citta.*Citta* is a mental phenomenon; it knows or experiences something. Citta is not like a physical phenomenon which does not experience anything. We listen to music which was written by a composer. It was citta which had the idea for the music; it was citta which made the composer's hand move in order to write down the notes. His hand could not have moved without citta.

Citta can achieve many different effects. We read in the Atthasālinī (the commentary to the Dhammasaṅgaṇi, the first book of the Abhidhamma) Book I, Part II, Analysis of Terms, 64:

> How is consciousness (i.e. mind) capable of producing a variety or diversity of effects in action? There is no art in the world more variegated than the art of painting. In painting, the painter's masterpiece is more artistic than the rest of his pictures. An artistic design occurs to the painters of masterpieces that such and such pictures should be drawn in such and such a way. Through this artistic design there arise operations of the mind (or artistic operations) accomplishing such things as sketching the outline, putting on the paint, touching up, and embellishing... Thus all classes of arts in the world, specific or generic, are achieved by the mind. And owing to its capacity thus to produce a variety or diversity of effects in action, the mind, which achieves all these arts, is in itself artistic like the arts themselves. Nay, it is even more artistic than the art itself, because the latter cannot execute every design perfectly. For that reason the Blessed One has said, "Monks, have you seen a masterpiece of painting?" "Yes, Lord." "Monks, that masterpiece of art is designed by the mind. Indeed, monks, the mind is even more artistic than that masterpiece." (Kindred Sayings, III, 151)

We then read about the many different things which are accomplished by citta: good deeds, such as deeds of generosity, and bad deeds, such as deeds of cruelty and deceit, are accomplished by citta and these deeds produce different results. There is not just one type of citta, but there are many different types of cittas.

Different people react differently to what they experience, thus, different types of citta arise. What one person likes, another dislikes. We can also notice how different people are when they make or produce something. Even when two people plan to make the same thing the result is quite different. For example, when two people make a painting of the same tree, the paintings are not at all the same. People have different talents and capacities; some people have no difficulty with their studies, whereas others are incapable of study. Cittas are beyond control; they each have their own conditions for their arising.

Why are people so different from one another? The reason is that they accumulate different inclinations. When a child has been taught from his youth to be generous he accumulates generosity. People who are angry very often accumulate a great deal of anger. We all have accumulated different inclinations, tastes and skills.

Each citta which arises falls away completely and is succeeded by the next citta. How then can there be accumulation of good and bad inclinations? The reason is that each citta which falls away is succeeded by the next citta. Our life is an uninterrupted series of cittas and each citta conditions the next citta and this again the next, and thus the past can condition the present. It is a fact that our good cittas and bad cittas in the past condition our inclinations today. Thus, good and bad inclinations are accumulated.

We all have accumulated many impure inclinations and defilements (in Pāli: kilesa). Defilements are for example greed or attachment (lobha), anger (dosa) and ignorance (moha). There are different degrees of defilements: there are subtle defilements or latent tendencies, medium defilements and gross defilements. Subtle defilements do not appear with the citta, but they are latent tendencies which are accumulated and lie dormant in the citta. At the time we are asleep and not dreaming, there are no akusala cittas but there are unwholesome latent tendencies. When we wake up akusala cittas arise again. How could they appear if there were not in each citta accumulated unwholesome latent tendencies? Even when the citta is not akusala there are unwholesome latent tendencies so long as they have not been eradicated by wisdom. Medium defilement is different from subtle defilement since it arises together with the citta. Medium defilement arises with akusala cittas rooted in attachment, lobha, aversion, dosa, and ignorance, moha. Medium defilement is, for example, attachment to what one sees, hears or experiences through the bodysense, or aversion towards the objects one experiences. Medium defilement does not motivate ill deeds. Gross defilement motivates unwholesome actions, akusala kamma, through body, speech and mind, such as killing, slandering or the intention to take away other people's possessions. *Kamma* is actually volition or intention; it can motivate good deeds or bad deeds. Kamma is a mental phenomenon and thus it can be accumulated. People accumulate different defilements and different kammas.

Different accumulations of kamma are the condition for different results in life. This is the law of kamma and vipāka, of cause and result. We see that people are born into different circumstances. Some people live in agreeable surroundings and they have many pleasant experiences in their lives. Other people may often have disagreeable experiences; they are poor or they suffer from ill health. When we hear about children who suffer from malnutrition, we wonder why they have to suffer whereas other children receive everything they need. The Buddha taught that everyone receives the results of his own deeds. A deed or kamma of the past can bring about its result later on, because akusala kamma and kusala kamma are accumulated. When there are the right conditions the result can be brought about in the form of *vipāka*. When the word "result" is used, people may think of the consequences of their deeds for other people, but "result" in the sense of vipāka has a different meaning. Vipākacitta is a citta which experiences an unpleasant object or a pleasant object and this citta is the result of a deed we did ourselves. We are used to thinking of a self who experiences unpleasant and pleasant things. However, there is no self; there are only cittas which experience different objects. Some cittas are cause; they can motivate good deeds or bad deeds which are capable of bringing about their appropriate results. Some cittas are result or vipāka. When we see something unpleasant, it is not self who sees; it is a citta, seeing-consciousness, which is the result of an unwholesome deed (akusala kamma) we performed either in this life or in a past life. This kind of citta is akusala vipāka. When we see something pleasant, it is a citta which is kusala vipāka, the result of a wholesome deed we performed. Every time we experience an unpleasant object through one of the five senses, there is akusala vipāka. Every time we experience a pleasant object through one of the five senses there is kusala vipāka.

If one is being hit by someone else, the pain one feels is not the vipāka (result) of the deed performed by the other person. The person who is being hit receives the result of a bad deed he performed himself; for him there is akusala vipāka through the bodysense. The other person's action is the proximate cause of his pain. As regards the other person who performs the bad deed, it is his akusala citta which motivates that deed. Sooner or later he will receive the result of his own bad deed. When we have more understanding of kamma and vipāka we will see many events of our life more clearly.

The Atthasālinī (Book I, Analysis of Terms, Part II, 65) explains that kamma of different people causes different results at birth and throughout life. Even bodily features are the result of kamma. We read:

> ...In dependence on the difference in kamma appears the difference in the destiny of beings without legs, with two legs, four legs, many legs, vegetative, spiritual, with perception, without perception, with neither perception nor without perception. Depending on the difference in kamma appears the difference in the births of beings, high and low, base and exalted, happy and miserable. Depending on the difference in kamma appears the difference in the individual features of beings as beautiful or ugly, high-born or low-born, well-built or deformed. Depending on the difference in kamma appears the difference in the worldly conditions of beings as gain and loss, fame and disgrace, blame and praise, happiness and misery.

Further on we read: ("Sutta Nipāta", 654)

```
By kamma the world moves, by kamma men
Live, and by kamma are all beings bound
As by its pin the rolling chariot wheel.
```

The Buddha taught that everything arises because of conditions; it is not by chance that people are so different in bodily features and character, and that they live in such different circumstances. Even the difference in bodily features of animals is due to different kamma. Animals have citta too; they may behave badly or they may behave well. Thus they accumulate different kammas which produce different results. If we understand that each kamma brings about its own result, we will know that there is no reason to be proud if we are born into a rich family or if we receive praise, honour or other pleasant things. When we have to suffer we will understand that suffering is due to our own deeds. Thus we will be less inclined to blame other people for our unhappiness or to be jealous when others receive pleasant things. When we understand reality we know that it is not self who receives something pleasant or who has to suffer; it is only vipāka, a citta which arises because of conditions and which falls away immediately.

We see that people who are born into the same circumstances still behave differently. For example, among people who are born into rich families, some are stingy, others are not. The fact that one is born into a rich family is the result of kamma. Stinginess is conditioned by one's accumulated defilements. There are many different types of conditions which play their part in the life of each person. Kamma causes one to be born into certain circumstances and one's accumulated tendencies condition one's character.

One may have doubts about past lives and future lives, since one only experiences the present life. However, in the present life we notice that different people experience different results. These results must have their causes in the past. The past conditions the present and the deeds we perform now will bring about their results in the future. In understanding the present we will be able to know more about the past and the future.

Past, present and future lives are an uninterrupted series of cittas. Each citta which arises falls away immediately to be succeeded by the next citta. Cittas do not last, but there isn't any moment without citta. If there were moments without citta the body would be a dead body. Even when we are sound asleep there is citta. Just as each citta that falls away is succeeded by the next citta, even so the last citta of this life is succeeded by the first citta of the next life, the rebirth-consciousness. Therefore, accumulations can continue on from one citta to the next citta, from life to life. Thus we see that life goes on and on. We are moving in a cycle, the cycle of birth and death.

The next citta cannot arise until the previous citta has passed away. There can be only one citta at a time, but cittas arise and fall away so rapidly that one has the impression that there can be more than one citta at a time. We may think that we can see and hear at the same time, but in reality each of these cittas arises at a different moment. We can verify through our own experience that seeing is a type of citta which is different from hearing; these cittas arise because of different conditions and experience different objects.

A citta is that which experiences something; it experiences an object. Each citta must experience an object, there cannot be any citta without an object. Cittas experience different objects through the six doors of eyes, ears, nose, tongue, bodysense and mind. Seeing is a citta experiencing that which appears through the eyes. We can use the word "visible object" for the object which is seen but it is not necessary to name it "visible object". When visible object contacts the eyesense there are conditions for seeing. Seeing is different from thinking about what we see; the latter is a type of citta which experiences something through the mind-door. Hearing is a citta which is different from seeing; it has different conditions and it experiences a different object. When sound contacts the earsense, there are conditions for a citta which experiences sound. There have to be the right conditions for the arising of each citta. We cannot smell through the ears and taste with the eyes. A citta which smells experiences odour through the nose. A citta which tastes experiences flavour through the tongue. A citta which experiences tangible object experiences this through the bodysense. Through the mind-door cittas are able to experience all kinds of objects. There can be only one citta at a time and citta can experience only one object at a time.

We may understand in theory that a citta which sees has a characteristic which is different from a citta which hears, and that citta is different from a physical phenomenon which does not experience anything. Knowing this may seem quite simple to us, but theoretical knowledge is different from knowing the truth by one's own experience. Theoretical knowledge is not very deep; it cannot eradicate the concept of self. Only in being aware of phenomena as they appear through the six doors, will we know the truth by our own experience. This kind of understanding can eradicate the concept of self.

The objects which we experience are the world in which we live. At the moment we see, the world is visible object. The world of visible object does not last, it falls away immediately. When we hear, the world is sound, but it falls away again. We are absorbed in and infatuated with the objects we experience through eyes, ears, nose, tongue, bodysense and mind-door, but not one of these objects lasts. What is impermanent should not be taken for self.

In the Gradual Sayings (Book of the Fours, chapter V, paragraph 5, Rohitassa) we read that Rohitassa, a deva, asked the Buddha about reaching the world's end. He said to the Buddha:

> "Pray, lord, is it possible for us, by going, to know, to see, to reach world's end, where there is no more being born or growing old, no more dying, no more falling (from one existence) and rising up (in another)?"
>
> "Your reverence, where there is no more being born or growing old, no more dying, no more falling from one existence and rising up in another, I declare that end of the world is not by going to be known, seen or reached."
>
> "It is wonderful, lord! It is marvellous, lord, how well it is said by the Exalted One: 'Where there is no more being born... that end of the world is not by going to be known, seen or reached!'
>
> Formerly, lord, I was the hermit called Rohitassa, Bhoja's son, one of psychic power, a skywalker... The extent of my stride was as the distance between the eastern and the western ocean. To me, lord, possessed of such

speed and of such a stride, there came a longing thus: I will reach the world's end by going.

But, lord, not to speak of (the time spent over) food and drink, eating, tasting and calls of nature, not to speak of struggles to banish sleep and weariness, though my life-span was a hundred years, though I travelled a hundred years, yet I reached not world's end but died ere that. Wonderful indeed, lord! Marvellous it is, lord, how well it has been said by the Exalted One: 'Your reverence, where there is no more being born. . . that end of the world is not by going to be known, seen or reached."'

"But your reverence, I declare not that there is any making an end of ill (dukkha) without reaching the world's end. Nay, your reverence, in this very fathom-long body, along with its perceptions and thoughts, I proclaim the world to be, likewise the origin of the world and the making of the world to end, likewise the practice going to the ending of the world.

```
Not to be reached by going is world's end.
Yet there is no release for man from ill
Unless he reach the world's end. Then let a man
Become world-knower, wise, world-ender,
Let him be one who lives the holy life[1].
Knowing the world's end by becoming calmed
He longs not for this world or another.''
```

The Buddha taught people about the "world" and the way to reach the end of the world, that is, the end of suffering, dukkha. The way to realize this is knowing the world, that is, knowing "this very fathom-long body, along with its perceptions and thoughts", knowing oneself.

Questions

1. People are born into different circumstances: some are born rich, others are born poor. What is the cause of this?
2. People behave differently: some are stingy, others are generous. By what is this conditioned?
3. Each citta which arises falls away completely. How is it possible that defilements can be accumulated?

[1] In Pāli:
brahmacariya.

4 The Characteristic of Lobha

Cittas are of different types. They can be classified as kusala cittas (wholesome cittas), akusala cittas (unwholesome cittas), vipākacittas (cittas which are result) and kiriyacittas (cittas which are neither cause nor result). All these kinds of cittas arise in a day, yet we know so little about them. Most of the time we do not know whether the citta is kusala, akusala, vipāka or kiriya. If we learn to classify our mind we will have more understanding of ourselves and of others. We will have more compassion and loving kindness towards others, even when they behave in a disagreeable way. We do not like the akusala cittas of others; we find it unpleasant when they are stingy or speak harsh words. However, do we realize at which moments we ourselves have akusala cittas? When we dislike other people's harsh words, we ourselves have akusala cittas with aversion at that moment. Instead of paying attention to the akusala cittas of others we should be aware of our own akusala cittas. If one has not studied the Abhidhamma which explains realities in detail, one may not know what is akusala. People may take what is unwholesome for wholesome and thus accumulate unwholesomeness without knowing it. If we know more about different types of citta we can see for ourselves which types arise more often, kusala cittas or akusala cittas, and thus we will understand ourselves better.

We should know the difference between kusala and akusala. The Atthasālinī (Book I, Part I, chapter I, 38) speaks about the meaning of the word "*kusala*". The word "kusala" has many meanings; it can mean "of good health", "faultless", "skillful", "productive of happy results".

When we perform dāna (generosity), sīla (good moral conduct) and bhāvanā (mental development), the citta is kusala. All different kinds of wholesomeness such as the appreciation of other people's good deeds, helping others, politeness, paying respect, observing the precepts, studying and teaching Dhamma, samatha (tranquil meditation) and vipassanā (development of "insight", right understanding of realities), are included in dāna, sīla or bhāvanā. Kusala is "productive of happy results"; each good deed will bring a pleasant result. The Atthasālinī (Book I, Part I, chapter I, 39) states about akusala:

> "A-kusala means "not kusala". Just as the opposite to friendship is enmity, or the opposite to greed, etc. is disinterestedness, etc., so "akusala" is opposed to "kusala"...

Unwholesome deeds will bring unhappy results. Nobody wishes to experience an unhappy result, but many people are ignorant about the cause which brings an unhappy result, about akusala. They do not realize when the citta is unwholesome, and they do not always know it when they perform unwholesome deeds.

When we study the Abhidhamma we learn that there are three groups of akusala cittas. They are:

- *Lobha-mūla-cittas*, or cittas rooted in attachment (lobha)
- *Dosa-mūla-cittas*, or cittas rooted in aversion (dosa)
- *Moha-mūla-cittas*, or cittas rooted in ignorance (moha)

Moha (ignorance) arises with every akusala citta. Akusala cittas rooted in lobha (attachment) actually have two roots: moha and lobha[1]. They are named "lobha-mūla-cittas", because there is not only moha, which arises with every akusala citta, but lobha as well. Lobha-mūla-cittas are thus named after the root which is lobha. Akusala cittas rooted in dosa (aversion) have two roots as well: moha and dosa. They are named "dosa-mūla-cittas" after the root which is dosa. Akusala cittas rooted in moha (ignorance), have only one root which is moha. Each of these three classes of akusala cittas includes again different types of akusala citta and thus we see that there is a great variety of cittas.

Now I shall deal first with lobha-mūla-citta. Lobha is the paramattha dhamma (absolute reality) which is cetasika (mental factor arising with the citta); it is a reality and thus it can be experienced.

Lobha is "clinging" or "attachment". The Visuddhimagga (XIV, 162) states:

> . . . lobha has the characteristic of grasping an object, like birdlime (lit. "monkey lime"). Its function is sticking, like meat put in a hot pan. It is manifested as not giving up, like the dye of lampblack. Its proximate cause is seeing enjoyment in things that lead to bondage. Swelling with the current of craving, it should be regarded as taking (beings) with it to states of loss, as a swift-flowing river does to the great ocean.

Lobha is sometimes translated as "greed" or "craving"; it can be translated by different words, since there are many degrees of lobha. Lobha can be coarse, medium or subtle. Most people can recognize lobha when it is very obvious, but not when it is of a lesser degree. For example, we can recognize lobha when we are inclined to eat too much of a delicious meal, or when we are attached to alcoholic drinks and cigarettes. We are attached to people and we suffer when we lose those who are dear to us through death. Then we can see that attachment brings sorrow. Sometimes attachment is very obvious, but there are many degrees of lobha and often we may not know that we have lobha. Cittas arise and fall away very rapidly and we may not realize it when lobha arises on account of what we experience in daily life through the six doors, especially if the degree of lobha is not as intense as greed or lust. Every time there is a pleasant sight, sound, odour, taste or tangible object, lobha is likely to arise. It arises many times a day.

Lobha arises when there are conditions for its arising; it is beyond control. In many suttas the Buddha speaks about lobha, points out the dangers of it and the way to overcome it. The pleasant objects which can be experienced through the five senses are in several suttas called the "five strands of sense-pleasures". We read in the Mahā-dukkhakkhandha-sutta ("Greater Discourse on the Stems of Anguish", Middle Length Sayings I, no. 13) that the Buddha, when he was staying near Sāvatthī, in the Jeta Grove, said to the monks:

> And what, monks, is the satisfaction in pleasures of the senses? These five, monks, are the strands of sense-pleasures. What five? Visible objects cognizable by the eye, agreeable, pleasant, liked, enticing, connected with sensual pleasures, alluring. Sounds, cognizable by the ear. . . Smells, cog-

---

[1] Mūla or hetu are the Pāli terms for root. There are three akusala hetus: lobha, dosa and moha. Akusala cittas are classified by way of the accompanying roots.

> nizable by the nose. . . Tastes cognizable by the tongue. . . Touches, cognizable by the body, agreeable, pleasant, liked, enticing, connected with sensual pleasures, alluring. These, monks, are the five strands of sense-pleasures. Whatever pleasure, whatever happiness arises in consequence of these five strands of sense-pleasures, this is the satisfaction in sense-pleasures.

The satisfaction in sense-pleasures is not true happiness. Those who do not know the Buddha's teachings may think that attachment is wholesome, especially when it arises with pleasant feeling. They may not know the difference between attachment and loving kindness (mettā), phenomena which may both arise with pleasant feeling. However, a citta accompanied by pleasant feeling is not necessarily kusala citta. When we learn more about akusala cittas and kusala cittas and when we are mindful of their characteristics, we will notice that the pleasant feeling which may arise with lobha-mūla-citta (citta rooted in attachment) is different from the pleasant feeling which may arise with kusala citta. Feeling (vedanā) is a cetasika which arises with every citta. When the citta is akusala, the feeling is also akusala, and when the citta is kusala, the feeling is also kusala. We may be able to know the difference between the characteristic of the pleasant feeling arising when we are attached to an agreeable sight or sound, and the characteristic of the pleasant feeling arising when we are generous.

The Buddha pointed out that lobha brings sorrow. When we lose people who are dear to us or when we lose the things we enjoy, we have sorrow. If we are attached to a comfortable life we may have aversion when we have to endure hardship or when things do not turn out the way we want them to be. We read in the Greater Discourse on the Stems of Anguish, which was quoted above, that the Buddha spoke to the monks about the dangers in the pleasures of the senses:

> And what, monks, is the peril in sense-pleasures? In this case, monks, a young man of family earns his living by some craft . . . He is afflicted by the cold, he is afflicted by the heat, suffering from the touch of gadflies, mosquitos, wind, sun, creeping things, dying of hunger and thirst. This, monks, is a peril in pleasures of the senses that is present, a stem of ill. . .
>
> If, monks, this young man of family rouses himself, exerts himself, strives thus, but if these possessions do not come to his hand, he grieves, mourns, laments, beating his breast and wailing, he falls into disillusionment, and thinks: "Indeed my exertion is in vain, indeed my striving is fruitless." This too, monks, is a peril in the pleasures of the senses that is present. . .
>
> And again, monks, when sense-pleasures are the cause. . . kings dispute with kings, nobles dispute with nobles, brahmans dispute with brahmans, householders dispute with householders, a mother disputes with her son, a son disputes with his mother, a father disputes with his son, a son disputes with his father, a brother disputes with a brother, a brother disputes with a sister, a sister disputes with a brother, a friend disputes with a friend. Those who enter into quarrel, contention, dispute and attack one another with their hands and with stones and with sticks and with weapons, these

suffer dying then and pain like unto dying. This too, monks, is a peril in the pleasures of the senses that is present. . .

We then read about many more perils in pleasures of the senses, and about the bad results they will cause in the future. The Buddha also explained about the satisfaction and peril in "material shapes". We read:

"And what, monks, is the satisfaction in material shapes? Monks, it is like a girl in a noble's family or a brahman's family or a householder's family who at the age of fifteen or sixteen is not too tall, not too short, not too thin, not too fat, not too dark, not too fair – is she, monks, at the height of her beauty and loveliness at that time?"

"Yes, Lord."

"Monks, whatever happiness and pleasure arise because of beauty and loveliness, this is satisfaction in material shapes.

And what, monks, is peril in material shapes? As to this, monks, one might see that same lady after a time, eighty or ninety or a hundred years old, aged, crooked as a rafter, bent, leaning on a stick, going along palsied, miserable, youth gone, teeth broken, hair thinned, skin wrinkled, stumbling along, the limbs discoloured. . .

. . . And again, monks, one might see that same lady, her body thrown aside in a cemetery, dead for one, two or three days, swollen, discoloured, decomposing. What would you think, monks? That which was former beauty and loveliness has vanished, a peril has appeared?"

"Yes, Lord."

"This too, monks, is a peril in material shapes. . ."

What the Buddha told the monks may sound crude to us, but it is reality. We find it difficult to accept life as it really is: birth, old age, sickness and death. We cannot bear to think of our own body or the body of someone who is dear to us as being a corpse. We accept being born, but we find it difficult to accept the consequences of birth, which are old age, sickness and death. We wish to ignore the impermanence of all conditioned things. When we look into the mirror and when we take care of our body we are inclined to take it for something which stays and which belongs to us. However, the body is only rūpa, elements which fall away as soon as they have arisen. There is no particle of the body which lasts.

One may cling to the body with wrong view, in Pāli: diṭṭhi. Diṭṭhi is a cetasika which can arise with lobha-mūla-citta (citta rooted in attachment). Sometimes there is lobha without wrong view, diṭṭhi, and sometimes with wrong view.

There are different kinds of diṭṭhi. The belief in a "self" is one kind of diṭṭhi. We may cling to mental phenomena as well as to physical phenomena with the wrong view of self. Some people believe that there is a self who exists in this life and who will continue to exist after this life-span is over. This is the "eternity-belief". Others believe in a self who, existing only in this life, will be annihilated after this life-span is over. This is the "annihilation-belief". Another form of diṭṭhi is the belief that there is no kamma which produces vipāka, that deeds do not bring their results. There have always been people in different countries who think that they can be purified of their imperfections merely by ablution in water or by prayers.

They believe that the results of ill deeds they committed can thus be warded off. They do not know that each deed can bring about its own result. We can only purify ourselves of imperfections if the wisdom is cultivated which can eradicate them. If one thinks that deeds do not bring about their appropriate results one may easily be inclined to believe that the cultivation of wholesomeness is useless. This kind of belief may lead to ill deeds and to the corruption of society.

There are eight types of lobha-mūla-citta and of these, four types arise with wrong view, diṭṭhi (in Pāli: diṭṭhigata-sampayutta; sampayutta means: associated with). Four types of lobha-mūla-citta arise without wrong view (in Pāli: diṭṭhigata-vippayutta; vippayutta means: dissociated from).

As regards the feeling which accompanies the lobha-mūla-citta, lobha-mūla-cittas can arise either with pleasant feeling or indifferent feeling, never with unpleasant feeling. Of the four types of lobha-mūla-citta which are accompanied by diṭṭhi, two types arise with pleasant feeling, somanassa (in Pāli: somanassa-sahagata; sahagata means: accompanied by); two types arise with indifferent feeling, upekkhā (in Pāli: upekkhā-sahagata). For example, when one clings to the view that there is a self who will continue to exist, the citta can be accompanied by pleasant feeling or by indifferent feeling. Of the four lobha-mūla-cittas arising without diṭṭhi, two types are accompanied by pleasant feeling and two types are accompanied by indifferent feeling. Thus, of the eight types of lobha-mūla-citta, four types arise with pleasant feeling and four types arise with indifferent feeling.

In classifying lobha-mūla-cittas there is yet another distinction to be made. Lobha-mūla-cittas can be "unprompted", asaṅkhārika, or "prompted", sasaṅkhārika. "Asaṅkhārika" can be translated a "unprompted", "not induced", or "spontaneous"; sasaṅkhārika can be translated as "prompted" or "induced". The Visuddhimagga(XIV, 91) states about lobha-mūla-citta that it is "sasaṅkhārika" "when it is with consciousness which is sluggish and urged on."

The lobha-mūla-cittas which are sasaṅkhārika can be prompted by the advice or request of someone else, or they arise induced by oneself. When the cittas are sasaṅkhārika, they are "sluggish and urged on"; they are not keen, they are weaker than when they are asaṅkhārika.

Of the four lobha-mūla-cittas arising with diṭṭhi, two types are unprompted, asaṅkhārika, and two types are prompted, sasaṅkhārika. As regards the lobha-mūla-cittas arising without diṭṭhi, two types are unprompted, asaṅkhārika, and two types are prompted, sasaṅkhārika. Thus, of the eight types of lobha-mūla-cittas, four types are unprompted and four types are prompted.

It is useful to learn the Pāli terms and their meaning, because the English translation does not render the meaning of realities very clearly.

The eight types of lobha-mūla-citta are:

- Accompanied by pleasant feeling, with wrong view, unprompted. (Somanassa-sahagataṃ, diṭṭhigata-sampayuttaṃ, asaṅkhārikam ekaṃ[2]).
- Accompanied by pleasant feeling, with wrong view, prompted. (Somanassa-sahagataṃ, diṭṭhigata-sampayuttaṃ, sasaṅkhārikam ekaṃ).

---

[2] ekaṃ means "one". The ṃ at the end of a word is pronounced as "ng".

- Accompanied by pleasant feeling, without wrong view, unprompted. (Somanassa-sahagataṃ, diṭṭhigata-vippayuttaṃ, asaṅkhārikam ekaṃ).
- Accompanied by pleasant feeling, without wrong view, prompted. (Somanassa-sahagataṃ, diṭṭhigata-vippayuttaṃ, sasaṅkhārikam ekaṃ).
- Accompanied by indifferent feeling, with wrong view, unprompted. (Upekkhā-sahagataṃ, diṭṭhigata-sampayuttaṃ, asaṅkhārikam ekaṃ).
- Accompanied by indifferent feeling, with wrong view, prompted. (Upekkhā-sahagataṃ, diṭṭhigata-sampayuttaṃ, sasaṅkhārikam ekaṃ).
- Accompanied by indifferent feeling, without wrong view, unprompted. (Upekkhā-sahagataṃ, diṭṭhigata-vippayuttaṃ, asaṅkhārikam ekaṃ).
- Accompanied by indifferent feeling, without wrong view, prompted. (Upekkhā-sahagataṃ, diṭṭhigata-vippayuttaṃ, sasaṅkhārikam ekaṃ).

As we have seen, lobha-mūla-cittas can be unprompted or prompted. The Atthasālinī (Book II, Part IX, chapter III, 225) gives an example of lobha-mūla-cittas, accompanied by diṭṭhi, which are prompted. A son of a noble family marries a woman who has wrong views and therefore he associates with people who have wrong views. Gradually he accepts those wrong views and then they are pleasing to him.

Lobha-mūla-cittas without diṭṭhi which are sasaṅkhārika arise, for example, when one, though at first not attached to alcoholic drink, takes pleasure in it after someone else persuades one to drink.

As we have seen, lobha-mūla-cittas can be accompanied by pleasant feeling or by indifferent feeling. Lobha-mūla-cittas without diṭṭhi, accompanied by pleasant feeling, can arise, for example, when we enjoy ourselves while seeing a beautiful colour or hearing an agreeable sound. At such moments we can be attached without wrong view about realities. When we enjoy beautiful clothes, go to the cinema, or laugh and talk with others about pleasurable things there can be many moments of enjoyment without the idea of self, but there can also be moments with diṭṭhi, moments of clinging to a "self".

Lobha-mūla-cittas without diṭṭhi, accompanied by indifferent feeling, may arise, for example, when we like to stand up, or like to take hold of different objects. Since we generally do not have happy feeling with these actions, there may be lobha with indifferent feeling at such moments. Thus we see that lobha often motivates the most common actions of our daily life.

Questions

1. When there is lobha is there always pleasant feeling, somanassa, as well?
2. Does diṭṭhi, wrong view, arise only with lobha-mūla-citta?
3. How many types of lobha-mūla-citta are there? Why is it useful to know this?

5 Different Degrees of Lobha

Lobha, attachment, leads to sorrow. If we really understand this, we will wish to eradicate lobha. The eradication of lobha, however, cannot be done immediately. We may be able to suppress lobha for a while, but it will appear again when there are the right conditions for its arising. Even though we know that lobha brings sorrow, it is bound to arise time and again. However, there is a way to eradicate it: it can be eradicated by the wisdom which sees things as they are.

When we study cittas more in detail it will help us to know ourselves. We should know not only the gross lobha but also the degrees of lobha which are more subtle. The following sutta gives an example of lobha which is more subtle. We read in the Kindred Sayings (I, Sagāthā-vagga IX, Forest Suttas paragraph 14):

> A certain monk was once staying among the Kosalese in a certain forest-tract. Now while there was that monk, after he had returned from his alms-round and had broken his fast, plunged into the lotus-pool and sniffed up the perfume of a red lotus. Then the deva who haunted that forest tract, moved with compassion for that monk, desiring his welfare, and wishing to agitate him, drew near and addressed him in the verse:

```
''That blossom, water-born, thing not given,
You stand sniffing up the scent of it.
This is one class of things that may be stolen.
And you a smell-thief must I call, dear sir.''

(The monk:)

''Nay, nought I bear away, I nothing break.
Standing apart I smell the water's child.
Now for what reason am I smell-thief called?
One who does dig up water-lilies, one
Who feeds on lotuses, in motley tasks
Engaged: why have you no such name for him?''

(The Deva:)

''A man of ruthless, wicked character,
Foul-flecked as is a handmaid's dirty cloth:
With such the words I say have no concern.
But this it is meet that I should say (to you):
To him whose character is void of vice,
Who ever makes quest for what is pure:
What to the wicked but a hair-tip seems,
To him does great as a rain-cloud appear...''
```

We should also know the more subtle lobha which arises when we enjoy a fragrant smell or beautiful music. It seems that there are no akusala cittas when we do not harm others, but also the more subtle lobha is akusala; it is different from generosity which is kusala. We cannot force ourselves not to have lobha, but we can come to know the characteristic of lobha when it appears.

Not only the suttas, but also the Vinaya (Book of Discipline for the monks) gives examples of lobha which is more subtle. Each part of the teachings, the Vinaya, the Suttanta and the Abhidhamma can help us to know ourselves better. When we read the Vinaya we see that even monks who lead a life with contentment with little, still have accumulated conditions for lobha. Every time there was a case where monks deviated from their purity of life, a rule was laid down in order to help them to be more watchful. Thus we can understand the usefulness of the rules, which go into even the smallest details of the monk's behaviour. The rules help the monk to be watchful even when performing the most common actions of daily life such as eating, drinking, robing himself and walking. There are rules which forbid seemingly innocent actions like playing in the water or with the water (Expiation, Pācittiya 53), or teasing other monks. Such actions are not done with kusala cittas, but with akusala cittas.

We read in the Vinaya (III, Suttavibhaṅga, Expiation, Pācittiya 85) that the monks should not enter a village at the wrong time. The reason is that they would indulge more easily in worldly talk. We read:

> Now at that time the group of six monks, having entered a village at the wrong time, having sat down in a hall, talked a variety of worldly talk, that is to say: talk of kings, of thieves, of great ministers, of armies, of fears, of battles, of food, of drink, of clothes, of beds, of garlands, of scents, of relations, of vehicles, of villages, of little towns, of towns, of the country, of women, of strong drink, of streets, of wells, of those departed before, of diversity, of speculation about the world, about the sea, on becoming and not becoming thus and thus. . .

This passage is useful for laypeople as well. We cannot help talking about worldly matters, but we should know that our talking, even if it seems innocent, is often motivated by lobha-mūla-cittas or by dosa-mūla-cittas (cittas rooted in aversion). In order to know ourselves we should find out by what kind of citta our talking is motivated.

Every time a lobha-mūla-citta arises lobha is accumulated. When the conditions are there, lobha can motivate ill deeds through body, speech or mind. When we see to what kinds of deeds lobha can lead we will be more inclined to develop the wisdom which eventually will lead to its eradication.

Ill deeds are called in Pāli: akusala kamma. Kamma is the cetasika (mental factor arising with the citta) which is intention or volition, in Pāli: cetanā. However, the word "kamma" is also used in a more general sense for the deeds which are intended by cetanā. The term kamma-patha (literally "course of action") is used as well in this sense. There are akusala kamma-pathas and kusala kamma-pathas, ill deeds and good deeds, accomplished through body, speech and mind. As regards akusala kamma-patha, there are ten akusala kamma-pathas and these are conditioned by lobha, dosa and moha. Moha, ignorance, accompanies every akusala citta, it is the root of all evil. Thus, whenever there is akusala kamma-patha, there must be moha. Some akusala kamma-pathas can sometimes be performed with lobha-mūla-citta and sometimes with dosa-mūla-citta. Therefore, when we see someone else committing an ill deed we cannot always be sure which kind of citta motivates that deed.

The ten akusala kamma-pathas are the following:

1. Killing
2. Stealing
3. Sexual misbehaviour
4. Lying
5. Slandering
6. Rude speech
7. Frivolous talk
8. Covetousness
9. Ill-will
10. Wrong view (diṭṭhi)

Killing, stealing and sexual misbehaviour are three akusala kamma-pathas accomplished through the body. Lying, slandering, rude speech and frivolous talk are four akusala kamma-pathas accomplished through speech. Covetousness, ill-will and wrong view are three akusala kamma-pathas accomplished through the mind. As regards akusala kamma-patha through the body, killing is done with dosa-mūla-citta. Stealing can sometimes be performed with lobha-mūla-citta and sometimes with dosa-mūla-citta. It is done with lobha-mūla-citta if one wishes to take what belongs to someone else in order to enjoy it oneself. It is done with dosa-mūla-citta if one wishes someone else to suffer damage. Sexual misbehaviour is performed with lobha-mūla-citta.

As far as the akusala kamma-pathas through speech are concerned, lying, slandering and frivolous talk are performed with lobha-mūla-citta if one wishes to obtain something for oneself, or if one wishes to endear oneself to other people. As regards lying, we may think that there is no harm in a so-called "white lie" or a lie said for fun. However, all kinds of lies are motivated by akusala cittas. We read in the "Discourse on an Exhortation to Rāhula at Ambalaṭṭhikā" (Middle Length Sayings II, no. 61, Bhikkhu-vagga) that the Buddha spoke to his son Rāhula about lying. The Buddha said:

> Even so, Rāhula, of anyone for whom there is no shame at intentional lying, of him I say that there is no evil he cannot do. Wherefore, for you, Rāhula, "I will not speak a lie, even for fun" – this is how you must train yourself, Rāhula.

Lying can also be done with dosa-mūla-citta and this is the case when one wants to harm someone else.

As regards slandering, we all are inclined to talk about others. When there is no intention to harm the reputation of others, there is no akusala kamma-patha. However, when talking about others becomes a habit, there can easily be an occasion for akusala kamma-patha. This kind of akusala kamma-patha is performed with lobha-mūla-citta if one slanders in order to obtain something for oneself or in order to please others. It is performed with dosa-mūla-citta if one wants to harm someone else. We will be less inclined to talk about others or to judge them when we see ourselves and others as phenomena which arise because of conditions and which do not stay. At the moment we talk about other people's actions, these phenomena have fallen away already; what they said or did exists no more.

Rude speech is performed with dosa-mūla-citta. Frivolous talk is talk about idle, senseless things. This kind of talk can be performed with lobha-mūla-citta or with dosa-mūla-citta. Frivolous talk is not always akusala kamma-patha. It can be done with akusala citta which does not have the intensity of akusala kamma-patha.

As regards akusala kamma-patha through the mind, ill-will, the intention to hurt or harm someone else, is motivated by dosa-mūla-citta; covetousness and wrong view are motivated by lobha-mūla-citta[1]. There is akusala kamma-patha which is covetousness when one intends to obtain by dishonest means what belongs to someone else. As regards diṭṭhi (wrong view), there are many kinds of diṭṭhi; however, three kinds of diṭṭhi are akusala kamma-patha through the mind. One of them is ahetuka-diṭṭhi, the belief that there is no cause for the existence of beings and no cause for their purity or corruption. Another wrong view which is akusala kamma-patha through the mind is akiriyā-diṭṭhi, the belief that there are no good and bad deeds which produce their results. The third wrong view which is akusala kamma-patha through the mind is natthika-diṭṭhi or annihilation view. Natthika-diṭṭhi is the belief that there is no result of kamma and that there is no further life after death.

All degrees of lobha, be it coarse or more subtle, bring sorrow. We are like slaves so long as we are absorbed in and infatuated with the objects which present themselves through eyes, ears, nose, tongue, bodysense and mind. We are not free if our happiness depends on the situation we are in, and the way others behave towards us. One moment people may be kind to us, but the next moment they may behave in an unpleasant way towards us. If we attach too much importance to the affection of others, we shall be easily disturbed in mind, and thus become slaves of our moods and emotions.

We can become more independent and free if we realize that both we ourselves and other people are only nāma and rūpa, phenomena arising because of conditions and falling away again. When others speak in an unpleasant way to us there are conditions which cause them to speak in that way, and there are conditions which cause us to hear such speech. Other people's behaviour and our reactions to it are conditioned phenomena which do not stay. At the moment we are thinking about these phenomena, they have fallen away already. The development of insight is the way to become less dependent on the vicissitudes of life. When there is more understanding of the present moment, we will attach less importance to the way people behave towards us.

Since lobha is rooted so deeply, it can only be eradicated in different stages. Diṭṭhi has to be eradicated first. The sotāpanna, the person who has realized

[1] As we have seen (in Ch 4), wrong view accompanies lobha-mūla-cittas. Whenever there is wrong view there is clinging to such view.

the first stage of enlightenment, has eradicated diṭṭhi. He has developed the wisdom which realizes that all phenomena are nāma and rūpa, not self. Since he has eradicated diṭṭhi, the lobha-mūla-cittas with diṭṭhi do not arise anymore. As we have seen, four types of lobha-mūla-citta arise with diṭṭhi (they are diṭṭhigata-sampayutta), and four types arise without diṭṭhi (they are diṭṭhigatha-vippayutta). As for the sotāpanna, the four types of lobha-mūla-citta without diṭṭhi still arise; he has not yet eradicated all kinds of attachment. The sotāpanna still has conceit. Conceit can arise with the four types of lobha-mūla-citta which are without diṭṭhi (diṭṭhigata-vippayutta). There may be conceit when one compares oneself with others, when one, for example, thinks that one has more wisdom than others. When we consider ourselves better, equal or less in comparison with others we may find ourselves important and then there is conceit. When we think ourselves less than someone else it is not necessarily kusala; there may still be a kind of upholding of ourselves and then there is conceit. Conceit is rooted so deeply that it is eradicated only when one has become an arahat.

The person who has attained the second stage of enlightenment, the sakadāgāmī (once-returner), has less lobha than the sotāpanna. The person who has attained the third stage of enlightenment, the anāgāmī (never-returner), has no more clinging to the objects which present themselves through the five senses, but he still has conceit and he clings to rebirth. The arahat, the perfected one who has attained the fourth and last stage of enlightenment, has eradicated all forms of lobha completely.

The arahat is completely free since he has eradicated all defilements. We read in the Kindred Sayings (IV, Saḷāyatanavagga, Kindred Sayings on Sense, Third Fifty, chapter IV, paragraph 136, Not including), that the Buddha said to the monks, while he was staying among the Sakkas at Devadaha:

> Devas and mankind, monks, delight in objects, they are excited by objects. It is owing to the instability, the coming to an end, the ceasing of objects, monks, that devas and mankind live woefully. They delight in sounds, scents, savours, in touch, they delight in mindstates, and are excited by them. It is owing to the instability, the coming to an end, the ceasing of mindstates, monks, that devas and mankind live woefully.
>
> But the Tathāgata, monks, who is arahat, a Fully-enlightened One, seeing, as they really are, both the arising and the destruction, the satisfaction, the misery and the way of escape from objects, – he delights not in objects, takes not pleasure in them, is not excited by them. It is owing to the instability, the coming to an end, the ceasing of objects that the Tathāgata dwells at ease. . .

The Buddha and all those who are arahats have eradicated clinging to all objects which are experienced. They have penetrated the true nature of conditioned realities which arise and fall away, which are impermanent. The arahat will attain the end of rebirth, the cessation of the arising of conditioned realities and therefore, he is "dwelling at ease".

Questions

1. When the objective is not dāna (generosity), sīla (morality) or bhāvanā (mental development), can talking be done with kusala citta?
2. Which cetasika is kamma?
3. Which are the ten akusala kamma-pathas?
4. Are all kinds of wrong view, diṭṭhi, akusala kamma-patha?
5. Why does attachment always lead to sorrow?
6. Who has eradicated all kinds of lobha?

6 The Characteristic of Dosa

When we are angry with other people we harm ourselves by our anger. The Buddha pointed out the adverse effects of anger (dosa). We read in the Gradual Sayings (Book of the Sevens, chapter VI, paragraph 10, Anger) about the ills a rival wishes his rival to have and which are actually the ills coming upon an angry woman or man. The sutta states:

> . . . Monks, there is the case of a rival, who wishes thus of a rival: "Would that he were ugly!" And why? A rival, monks, does not like a handsome rival. Monks, this sort of person, being angry, is overwhelmed by anger; he is subverted by anger: and however well he be bathed, anointed, trimmed as to the hair and beard, clad in spotless linen; yet for all that he is ugly, being overwhelmed by anger. Monks, this is the first condition, fostered by rivals, causing rivals, which comes upon an angry woman or man.
>
> Again, there is the case of a rival, who wishes thus of a rival: "Would that he might sleep badly!" And why? A rival, monks, does not like a rival to sleep well. Monks, this sort of person, being angry, is overwhelmed by anger; he is subverted by anger: and in spite of his lying on a couch, spread with a fleecy cover, spread with a white blanket, spread with a woollen coverlet, flower embroidered, covered with rugs of antelope skins, with awnings above; or on a sofa, with crimson cushions at either end; yet for all that he lies in discomfort, being overwhelmed by anger. Monks, this is the second condition. . .

We then read about other misfortunes a rival wishes for his rival, which come upon an angry woman or man. We read that a rival wishes his rival to be without prosperity, wealth and fame. Further we read that a rival wishes a rival to be without friends and this happens to someone who is an angry person. The text states:

> Monks, this sort of person, being angry. . . whatever friends, intimates, relations and kinsmen he may have, they will avoid him and keep far away from him, because he is overwhelmed by anger. . .

A rival wishes his rival to have an unhappy rebirth and this can happen to an angry person. We read:

> . . . Monks, this sort of person, being angry. . . he misconducts himself in deed, in word and thought; so living, so speaking and so thinking, on breaking up of the body after death he is reborn in the untoward way, the ill way, the abyss, hell. . .

We would like to live in a world of harmony and unity among nations and we are disturbed when people commit acts of violence. We should consider what the real cause is of war and discord between people: it is the defilements which people have accumulated. When we have aversion we think that other people or unpleasant situations are the cause of our aversion. However, our accumulation of dosa is the real cause for aversion to arise time and again. If we want to have less dosa we should know the characteristic of dosa and we should be aware of it when it arises.

Dosa has many degrees; it can be a slight aversion or it can be more coarse, such as anger. We can recognize dosa when it is coarse, but do we realize that we have dosa when it is more subtle? Through the study of the Abhidhamma we learn more about the characteristic of dosa. Dosa is an akusala cetasika (mental factor) arising with akusala citta; it is a cetasika that is an unwholesome root, akusala hetu. A citta rooted in dosa is called in Pāli: dosa-mūla-citta. The characteristic of dosa is different from the characteristic of lobha. When there is lobha, the citta likes the object which it experiences at that moment, whereas when there is dosa, the citta has aversion towards the object it experiences. We can recognize dosa when we are angry with someone and when we speak disagreeable words to him. But when we are afraid of something there is dosa as well, because one has aversion towards the object one is afraid of. There are so many things in life we are afraid of; we are afraid of the future, of diseases, of accidents, of death. We look for many means in order to be cured of anguish, but the only way is the development of the wisdom which eradicates the latent tendency of dosa.

Dosa is conditioned by lobha: we do not want to lose what is dear to us and when this actually happens we are sad. Sadness is dosa, it is akusala. If we do not know things as they are, we believe that people and things last. However, people and things are only phenomena which arise and then fall away immediately. The next moment they have changed already. If we can see things as they are we will be less overwhelmed by sadness. It makes no sense to be sad about what has happened already.

In the Psalms of the Sisters (Therīgāthā, 33) we read that the King's wife Ubbirī mourned the loss of her daughter Jīvā. Every day she went to the cemetery. She met the Buddha who told her that in that cemetery about eighty-four thousand of her daughters (in past lives) had been burnt. The Buddha said to her:

O, Ubbirī, who wails in the wood
Crying, ''O Jīvā! O my daughter dear!''
Come to yourself! See, in this burying-ground
Are burnt full many a thousand daughters dear,
And all of them were named like her.
Now which of all those Jīvās do you mourn?

After Ubbirī pondered over the Dhamma thus taught by the Buddha she developed insight and saw things as they really are; she even attained arahatship.

There are other akusala cetasikas which can arise with cittas rooted in dosa. Regret or worry, in Pāli: *kukkucca*, is an akusala cetasika which arises with dosa-mūla-citta at the moment we regret something bad we did or something good we omitted to do. When there is regret we are thinking of the past instead of knowing the present moment. When we have done something wrong it is of no use to have aversion.

Envy (*issā*) is another cetasika which can arise with dosa-mūla-citta. There is envy when we do not like someone else to enjoy pleasant things. At that moment the citta does not like the object it experiences. We should find out how often envy arises, even when it is more subtle. This is a way to know whether we really care for someone else or whether we only think of ourselves when we associate with others.

Stinginess (*macchariya*) is another akusala cetasika which may arise with dosa-mūla-citta. When we are stingy there is dosa as well. At that moment we do not like someone else to share in our good fortune.

Dosa always arises with an unpleasant feeling (domanassa vedanā). Most people do not like to have dosa because they do not like to have an unpleasant feeling. As we develop more understanding of realities we want to eradicate dosa not so much because we dislike unpleasant feeling, but rather because we realize the adverse effects of akusala.

Dosa can arise on account of the objects experienced through the five sense-doors and the mind-door. It can arise when we see ugly sights, hear harsh sounds, smell unpleasant odours, taste unappetizing food, experience unpleasant tangible objects through the bodysense and think of disagreeable things. Whenever there is a feeling of uneasiness, no matter how slight, it is evident that there is dosa. Dosa may often arise when there is the experience of unpleasant objects through the senses, for example, when the temperature is too hot or too cold. Whenever there is a slightly unpleasant bodily sensation dosa may arise, be it only of a lesser degree.

Dosa arises when there are conditions for it. It arises so long as there is still attachment to the objects which can be experienced through the five senses. Everybody would like to experience only pleasant things and when one does not have them any more, dosa may arise.

Another condition for dosa is ignorance of the Dhamma. If we are ignorant of kamma and vipāka, cause and result, dosa may arise very easily on account of an unpleasant experience through one of the senses and thus dosa is accumulated time and again. An unpleasant experience through one of the senses is akusala vipāka caused by an unwholesome deed we performed. When, for example, someone speaks unpleasant words to us, we may be angry with that person. Those who have studied the Dhamma know that hearing an unpleasant sound is akusala vipāka which is not caused by someone else but by an unwholesome deed performed by oneself. A moment of vipāka falls away immediately, it does not stay. Are we not inclined to keep on thinking about an unpleasant experience? If there is more awareness of the present moment one will be less inclined to think with aversion about one's akusala vipāka.

When we study the Abhidhamma we learn that there are two types of dosa-mūla-citta: one of these is unprompted (*asaṅkhārika*) and one is prompted (*sasaṅkhārika*). Dosa is prompted (sasaṅkhārika) when, for example, one becomes angry after having been reminded of the disagreeable actions of someone else. Dosa-mūla-cittas are always accompanied by domanassa (unpleasant feeling). There are two types of dosa-mūla-citta which are the following:

1. Accompanied by unpleasant feeling, arising with anger, unprompted (Domanassa-sahagataṃ, paṭigha-sampayuttaṃ[1], asaṅkhārikam ekaṃ).

[1] Paṭigha is another word for dosa.

2. Accompanied by unpleasant feeling, arising with anger, prompted (Domanassa-sahagataṃ, paṭigha-sampayuttaṃ, sasaṅkhārikam ekaṃ).

As we have seen, there are many degrees of dosa; it may be coarse or more subtle. When dosa is coarse, it causes akusala kamma-patha (unwholesome deeds) through body, speech or mind. Two kinds of akusala kamma-patha through the body can be performed with dosa-mūla-citta: killing and stealing. If we want less violence in the world we should try not to kill. When we kill we accumulate a great deal of dosa. The monk's life should be a life of non-violence; he should not hurt any living being in the world. However, not everyone is able to live like the monks. Defilements are anattā (not self); they arise because of conditions. The purpose of the Buddha's teaching is not to lay down rules which forbid people to commit ill deeds, but to help people to develop the wisdom which eradicates defilements. There are precepts for laypeople, but these are rules of training rather than commandments.

As regards stealing, this can either be performed with lobha-mūla-citta or with dosa-mūla-citta. It is done with dosa-mūla-citta when there is the intention to harm someone else. Doing damage to someone else's possessions is included in this kamma-patha.

Four kinds of akusala kamma-patha through speech can be performed with dosa-mūla-citta: lying, slandering, rude speech and frivolous talk. Lying, slandering and frivolous talk can either be performed with lobha-mūla-citta or with dosa-mūla-citta. Slandering, for example, is performed with dosa-mūla-citta when there is the intention to cause damage to someone else, such as doing harm to his good name and causing him to be looked down upon by others. Most people think that the use of weapons is to be avoided, but they forget that the tongue can be a weapon as well, a weapon which can badly wound. Evil speech does a great deal of harm in the world; it causes discord between people. When we speak evil we harm ourselves, because at such moments akusala kamma is accumulated and it is capable of producing akusala vipāka.

We read in the Sutta Nipāta (Chapter III, the Great Chapter, 10, Kokāliya, "Khuddaka Nikāya") that while the Buddha was staying at Sāvatthī, the bhikkhu Kokāliya visited him. Kokāliya spoke evil of Sāriputta and Moggallāna, saying that they had evil desires. Three times the Buddha told him not to speak in that way. After Kokāliya had departed boils developed all over his body which became bigger and bigger and discharged pus and blood. He died and was reborn in the Paduma hell. Later on the Buddha told the monks about Kokāliya's evil speech and his rebirth in hell. We read (vs. 657, 658) that the Buddha said:

> "Surely in the mouth of a man, when born, an axe is born, with which the fool cuts himself, saying a badly-spoken (utterance).
>
> He who praises him who is to be blamed, or blames him who is to be praised, accumulates evil by his mouth. Because of that evil he does not find happiness...

As regards akusala kamma-patha through the mind performed with dosa-mūla-citta, this is the intention to hurt or harm someone else.

People often speak about violence and the ways to cure it. Who of us can say that he is free from dosa and that he will never kill? We do not know how much dosa we have accumulated in the course of many lives. When the conditions are present we might commit an act of violence we did not realize we were capable of. When we understand how ugly dosa is and to what deeds it can lead we want to eradicate it.

In performing kind deeds we cannot eradicate the latent tendency of dosa, but at least at those moments we do not accumulate more dosa. The Buddha exhorted people to cultivate loving kindness (mettā). We read in the Karaniya Mettā-sutta (Sutta Nipāta, vs. 143-152)[2] that the Buddha spoke the following words.

```
What should be done by one skillful in good
So as to gain the State of Peace is this:

Let him be able, and upright, and straight.
Easy to speak to, gentle, and not proud,
Contented too, supported easily,
With few tasks, and living very lightly,
His faculties serene, prudent and modest,
Unswayed by the emotions of the clans;
And let him never do the slightest thing
That other wise men might hold blamable.

(And let him think) ``In safety and in bliss
May creatures all be of a blissful heart.
Whatever breathing beings there may be,
No matter whether they are frail or firm,
With none excepted, be they long or big
Or middle-sized, or be they short or small
Or thick, as well as those seen or unseen,
Or whether they are dwelling far or near,
Existing or yet seeking to exist,
May creatures all be of a blissful heart.
Let no one work another one's undoing
Or even slight him at all anywhere;
And never let them wish each other ill
Through provocation or resentful
thought.''

And just as might a mother with her life
Protect the son that was her only child,
So let him then for every living thing
Maintain unbounded consciousness in being,
And let him too with love for all the world
Maintain unbounded consciousness in being
```

[2] I am using the translation by the venerable Bhikkhu Ñanamoli, Buddhist Publication Society, Wheel 7, Kandy, Sri Lanka.

```
Above, below, and all around in between,
Untroubled, with no enemy or foe.
And while he stands, or walks or while he sits
Or while he lies down, free from drowsiness,
Let him resolve upon mindfulness:
This is Divine Abiding here, they say.

But when he has no trafficking with views[3],
Is virtuous, and has perfected seeing,
And purges greed for sensual desires,
He surely comes no more to any womb.
```

The Buddha taught us not to be angry with those who are unpleasant to us. We read in the Vinaya (Mahāvagga X, 349) that the Buddha said to the monks:

```
They who (in thought) belabour this: That man
has me abused, has hurt, has worsted me,
has me despoiled: in these wrath is not allayed.

They who do not belabour this: That man
has me abused, has hurt, has worsted me,
has me despoiled: in them wrath is allayed.

Nay, not by wrath are wrathful moods allayed
    here (and) at any time,
but by not-wrath are they allayed:
    this is an (ageless) endless rule.
```

At times it seems impossible for us to have mettā instead of dosa. For example, when people treat us badly we may feel very unhappy and we keep on pondering over our misery. So long as dosa has not been eradicated there are still conditions for its arising. By being mindful of all realities which appear the wisdom is developed which can eventually eradicate dosa.

Dosa can only be eradicated stage by stage. The sotāpanna (the streamwinner, who has attained the first stage of enlightenment) has not yet eradicated dosa and also at the subsequent stage of enlightenment, the stage of the sakadāgāmī (once-returner), dosa is not yet eradicated completely. The anāgāmī (the non-returner, who has attained the third stage of enlightenment) has eradicated dosa completely; he has no more latent tendency of dosa.

We have not eradicated dosa, but when dosa appears, we can be mindful of its characteristic in order to know it as a type of nāma, arising because of conditions. When there is no mindfulness of dosa when it appears, dosa seems to last and we take it for self. Through mindfulness of nāmas and rūpas which present themselves one at a time, we will learn that there are different characteristics of nāma and

[3] Wrong view.

rūpa, none of which lasts and we will also know the characteristic of dosa as only a type of nāma, not self.

When a clearer understanding of realities is developed we will be less inclined to ponder for a long time over an unpleasant experience, since it is only a type of nāma which does not last. We will attend more to the present moment instead of thinking about the past or the future. We will also be less inclined to tell other people about unpleasant things which have happened to us, since that may be a condition for both ourselves and others to accumulate more dosa. When someone is angry with us we will have more understanding of his situation; he may be tired or not feeling well. Those who treat us badly deserve compassion because they actually make themselves unhappy.

Right understanding of realities will help us most of all to have more loving kindness and compassion towards others instead of dosa.

Questions

1. Why is lobha a condition for dosa?
2. Lying, slandering and frivolous talk are akusala kamma-patha through speech which can be performed either with lobha-mūla-citta or with dosa-mūla-citta. When are they performed with dosa-mūla-citta?
3. Is there akusala kamma-patha through the mind performed with dosa-mūla-citta?

7 Ignorance

We may know when we have akusala cittas rooted in lobha (attachment) or akusala cittas rooted in dosa (aversion), but do we know when we have akusala cittas rooted in *moha* (ignorance)? What is the characteristic of moha? We may think someone ignorant who does not have much education, who does not speak foreign languages, who does not know anything about history or politics. We call someone ignorant who does not know what is happening in the world. Is that the kind of ignorance which should be eradicated? If that were true it would mean that there is more wholesomeness in one's life if one speaks foreign languages or if one knows about history and politics. We can find out that this is not true.

In order to understand the characteristic of moha we should know what we are ignorant of when there is moha. There is the world of concepts which in our daily, ordinary language are denoted by conventional terms and there is the world of paramattha dhammas or ultimate realities. When we think of the concept which in conventional language is denoted by "world", we may think of people, animals and things and we call them by their appropriate names. But do we know the phenomena in ourselves and around ourselves as they really are: only nāma and rūpa which do not last?

The world of paramattha dhammas is real. Nāma and rūpa are paramattha dhammas. The nāmas and rūpas which appear in our daily life can be directly experienced through the five sense-doors and the mind-door, no matter how we name them. This is the world which is real. When we see, there is the world of visible object. When we hear, there is the world of sound. When we experience an object through touch there is the world of tangible object. Visible object and seeing are real. Their characteristics cannot be altered and they can be directly experienced; it does not matter whether we call them "visible object" and "seeing", or whether we give them another name. But when we cling to concepts which are denoted by conventional terms such as "tree" or "chair", we do not experience any characteristic of reality. What is real when we look at a tree? What can be directly experienced? Visible object is a paramattha dhamma, a reality; it is a kind of rūpa which can be directly experienced through the eyes. Through touch hardness can be experienced; this is a kind of rūpa which can be directly experienced through the bodysense, it is real. "Tree" is a concept or idea of which we can think, but it is not a paramattha dhamma, not a reality which has its own unchangeable characteristic. Visible object and hardness are paramattha dhammas, they have their own characteristics which can be directly experienced, no matter how one names them.

The world experienced through the six doors is real, but it does not last; it is impermanent. When we see, there is the world of the visible, but it falls away immediately. When we hear, there is the world of sound, but it does not last either. It is the same with the world of smell, the world of flavour, the world of tangible object and the world of objects experienced through the mind-door. However, we usually know only the world of concepts, because ignorance and wrong view have been accumulated for so long. Ignorance of paramattha dhammas is the kind of ignorance which should be eradicated; it brings sorrow. Ignorance conditions the wrong view of self and all other defilements. So long as there is ignorance we are deluding ourselves, we do not know what our life really is: conditioned phenomena which arise and fall away.

The world in the sense of paramattha dhammas is in the teachings called "the world in the ariyan sense". The ariyan has developed the wisdom which sees things as they are; he truly knows "the world". We read in the Kindred Sayings (IV, Saḷāyatana-vagga, Kindred Sayings on Sense, Second Fifty, chapter IV, paragraph 84, Transitory) that Ānanda said to the Buddha:

> " 'The world! The world!' is the saying lord. Pray, how far, lord, does this saying go?"
>
> "What is transitory by nature, Ānanda, is called 'the world' in the ariyan sense. And what, Ānanda, is transitory by nature? The eye, Ānanda, is transitory by nature. . . objects. . . tongue. . . mind[1] is transitory by nature, mind-states, mind-consciousness, mind-contact, whatsoever pleasant feeling, unpleasant feeling or indifferent feeling which arises owing to mind-contact, that also is transitory by nature. What is thus transitory, Ānanda, is called 'the world' in the ariyan sense."

Someone may think that he can truly know himself without knowing the world as it appears through the six doors. He may think that he knows his anger and attachment, but, in fact, he has not experienced them as they are: only different types of nāma and not self. So long as he has wrong view of realities he does not really know himself and he cannot eradicate defilements. He clings to an idea, to the concept of self; he has not directly experienced any characteristic of reality. It is difficult to know when there are lobha, dosa and moha, and it is difficult to be aware also of the more subtle degrees of akusala. When we start to develop "insight", right understanding of realities, we realize how little we know ourselves.

When there is moha we live in darkness. It was the Buddha's great compassion which moved him to teach people Dhamma. Dhamma is the light which can dispel darkness. If we do not know Dhamma we are ignorant of the world, of ourselves; we are ignorant of good and ill deeds and their results; we are ignorant of the way to eradicate defilements.

The study of the Abhidhamma will help us to have more understanding of the characteristic of moha. The Atthasālinī (Book II, Part IX, chapter I, 249) states about moha:

> "Delusion" (moha) has the characteristic of blindness or opposition to knowledge; the essence of non-penetration, or the function of covering the intrinsic nature of the object; the manifestation of being opposed to right conduct or causing blindness; the proximate cause of unwise attention; and it should be regarded as the root of all akusala. . .

There are many degrees of moha. When we study Dhamma we become less ignorant of realities; we will have more understanding of paramattha dhammas, of kamma and vipāka. However, this does not mean that we can already eradicate

[1] The Pāli text is abridged, but also included are: the ear. . . the nose. . . the bodysense, all realities appearing through the six doors.

moha. Moha cannot be eradicated merely by thinking of the truth; it can only be eradicated by developing the wisdom which knows "the world in the ariyan sense": eyesense, visible object, seeing-consciousness, earsense, sound, hearing-consciousness, and all realities appearing through the six doors.

When we study the Abhidhamma we learn that moha arises with all akusala cittas. Lobha-mūla-cittas have moha and lobha as roots; dosa-mūla-cittas have moha and dosa as roots. There are two types of akusala citta which have moha as their only root, these are moha-mūla-cittas. One type of moha-mūla-citta is moha-mūla-citta accompanied by doubt (in Pāli: *vicikicchā*), and one type is moha-mūla-citta accompanied by restlessness (in Pāli: uddhacca). The feeling which accompanies moha-mūla-cittas is always indifferent feeling (upekkhā). When the citta is moha-mūla-citta there is no like or dislike; one does not have pleasant or unpleasant feeling. Both types of moha-mūla-citta are unprompted (asaṅkhārika).

The characteristic of moha should not be confused with the characteristic of diṭṭhi (wrong view), which only arises with lobha-mūla-cittas. When diṭṭhi arises one takes, for example, what is impermanent for permanent, or one believes that there is a self. Moha is not wrong view, it is ignorance of realities. Moha conditions diṭṭhi, but the characteristic of moha is different from the characteristic of diṭṭhi.

The two types of moha-mūla-citta are:

1. Arising with indifferent feeling, accompanied by doubt (Upekkhā-sahagataṃ, vicikicchā-sampayuttaṃ).
2. Arising with indifferent feeling, accompanied by restlessness (Upekkhā-sahagataṃ, uddhacca-sampayuttaṃ).

When we have the type of moha-mūla-citta which is accompanied by doubt, we doubt about the Buddha, the Dhamma and the Sangha[2]. We may doubt whether the Buddha really discovered the truth, whether he taught the Path leading to the end of defilements, whether there are other people who can become enlightened as well. We may doubt about past and future lives, about kamma and vipāka. There are many degrees of doubt. When we start to develop insight we may have doubt about the reality of the present moment; we may doubt whether it is nāma or rūpa. For example, when there is hearing, there is sound as well, but there can be awareness of only one reality at a time, since only one object at a time can be experienced by citta. We may doubt whether the reality which appears at the present moment is the nāma which hears or the rūpa which is sound. Nāma and rūpa arise and fall away so rapidly and when a precise understanding of their different characteristics has not been developed one does not know which reality appears at the present moment. There will be doubt about the world of paramattha dhammas until paññā (wisdom) clearly knows the characteristics of nāma and rūpa as they appear through the six doors.

The Atthasālinī (Book II, Part IX, chapter III, 259) states about doubt:

> Here doubt means exclusion from the cure (of knowledge). Or, one investigating the intrinsic nature by means of it suffers pain and fatigue

[2] The Sangha is the order of monks, but it also means the "ariyan Sangha", the noble persons who have attained enlightenment.

(kicchati)—thus it is doubt. It has shifting about as characteristic, mental wavering as function, indecision or uncertainty in grasp as manifestation, unsystematic thought (unwise attention) as proximate cause, and it should be regarded as a danger to attainment.

Doubt is different from wrong view (diṭṭhi). When there is diṭṭhi one clings, for example, to the view that phenomena are permanent or that they are self. When vicikicchā, doubt, arises, one wonders whether the mind is different from the body or not, whether phenomena are permanent or impermanent. There is no other way to eradicate doubt but the development of paññā which sees realities as they are. People who have doubts about the Buddha and his teachings may think that doubt can be cured by studying historical facts. They want to find out more details about the time the Buddha lived and about the places where he moved about; they want to know the exact time the texts were written down. They cannot be cured of their doubt by studying historical events; this does not lead to the goal of the Buddha's teachings which is the eradication of defilements.

People in the Buddha's time too were speculating about things which do not lead to the goal of the teachings. They were wondering whether the world is finite or infinite, whether the world is eternal or not eternal, whether the Tathāgata (the Buddha) exists after his final passing away or not. We read in the Lesser Discourse to Māluṅkyā (Middle Length Sayings II, no. 63) that Māluṅkyāputta was displeased that the Buddha did not give explanations with regard to speculative views. He wanted to question the Buddha on these views and if the Buddha would not give him an explanation with regard to these views he wanted to leave the order. He spoke to the Buddha about this matter and the Buddha asked him whether he had ever said to Māluṅkyāputta:

"Come you, Māluṅkyāputta, fare the Brahma-faring[3] under me and I will explain to you either that the world is eternal or that the world is not eternal. . . or that the Tathāgata is. . . is not after dying. . . both is and is not after dying. . . neither is nor is not after dying?"

We read that Māluṅkyāputta answered: "No, revered sir." The Buddha also asked him whether he (Māluṅkyāputta) had said that he would "fare the Brahma-faring" under the Lord if the Lord would give him an explanation with regard to these views and again Māluṅkyāputta answered: "No, revered sir." The Buddha then compared his situation with the case of a man who is pierced by a poisoned arrow and who will not draw out the arrow until he knows whether the man who pierced him is a noble, a brahman, a merchant or a worker; until he knows the name of the man and his clan; until he knows his outward appearance; until he knows about the bow, the bowstring, the material of the shaft, the kind of arrow. However, he will pass away before he knows all this. It is the same with the person who only wants to "fare the Brahma-faring" under the Lord if explanations with regard to speculative views are given to him. We read that the Buddha said:

[3] The Brahma-faring is the "holy life" of the monk who develops the eightfold Path in order to become an arahat. In a wider sense: all those who develop the eightfold Path leading to enlightenment, laypeople included, are "faring the Brahma-faring", in Pāli: brahma-cariya.

> The living of the Brahma-faring, Māluṅkyāputta, could not be said to depend on the view that the world is eternal. Nor could the living of the Brahma-faring, Māluṅkyāputta, be said to depend on the view that the world is not eternal. Whether there is the view that the world is eternal or whether there is the view that the world is not eternal, there is birth, there is ageing, there is dying, there are grief, sorrow, suffering, lamentation and despair, the destruction of which I lay down here and now...
>
> Wherefore, Māluṅkyāputta, understand as not explained what has not been explained by me, and understand as explained what has been explained by me. And what, Māluṅkyāputta, has not been explained by me? That the world is eternal...that the world is not eternal has not been explained by me...And why, Māluṅkyāputta, has this not been explained by me? It is because it is not connected with the goal, it is not fundamental to the Brahma-faring, and does not conduce to turning away from, nor to dispassion, stopping, calming, superknowledge, awakening, nor to nibbāna. Therefore it has not been explained by me, Māluṅkyāputta. And what has been explained by me, Māluṅkyāputta? "This is dukkha" has been explained by me, Māluṅkyāputta. "This is the arising of dukkha" has been explained by me. "This is the stopping of dukkha" has been explained by me. "This is the course leading to the stopping of dukkha" has been explained by me. And why, Māluṅkyāputta, has this been explained by me? It is because it is connected with the goal, it is fundamental to the Brahma-faring, and conduces to turning away from, to dispassion, stopping, calming, super-knowledge, awakening and nibbāna...

Doubt cannot be cured by speculating about matters which do not lead to the goal; it can only be cured by being aware of the nāma and rūpa which present themselves now. Even when there is doubt, this can be realized as only a type of nāma which arises because of conditions and which is not self. Thus the reality of the present moment will be known more clearly.

The second type of moha-mūla-citta is accompanied by indifferent feeling, arising with restlessness (upekkhā-sahagataṃ, uddhacca-sampayuttaṃ). *Uddhacca* is translated as restlessness or excitement. Uddhacca arises with all akusala cittas. When there is uddhacca there is no sati (mindfulness) with the citta. Sati arises with each wholesome citta; it is mindful, non-forgetful, of what is wholesome. There is sati not only in vipassanā, the development of right understanding of realities, but also with each kind of kusala. There is sati when one performs dāna (generosity), observes sīla (good moral conduct) or applies oneself to bhāvanā, mental development, which comprises studying or teaching the Dhamma, the development of samatha, tranquil meditation, and vipassanā. Sati in vipassanā is aware of a characteristic of nāma or rūpa.

When there is uddhacca, the citta cannot be wholesome; one cannot at that moment apply oneself to dāna, sīla or bhāvanā. Uddhacca distracts the citta from kusala. Uddhacca is restlessness with regard to kusala. Thus, uddhacca is different from what we in conventional language mean by restlessness.

Uddhacca arises also with the moha-mūla-citta which is accompanied by doubt, since it arises with each akusala citta. The second type of moha-mūla-citta, however, is called uddhacca-sampayutta; it is different from the first type of moha-mūla-citta which is called vicikicchā-sampayutta.

The second type of moha-mūla-citta, the moha-mūla-citta which is uddhacca-sampayutta, accompanied by restlessness, arises countless times a day, but it is difficult to know its characteristic. If one has not developed vipassanā one does not know this type of citta. When we are forgetful of realities and "day-dreaming", there is not necessarily this type of citta. When we are "day-dreaming"there is not only the second type of moha-mūla-citta (uddhacca-sampayutta), but also lobha-mūla-cittas (cittas rooted in attachment) and dosa-mūla-cittas (cittas rooted in aversion) may arise.

Moha-mūla-citta can arise on account of what we experience through the five sense-doors and through the mind-door. When, for example, we have heard sound, moha-mūla-citta may arise. When the second type of moha-mūla-citta which is uddhacca-sampayutta arises, there is ignorance and forgetfulness with regard to the object which is experienced at that moment. We may not see the danger of this type of citta since it is accompanied by indifferent feeling and thus less obvious. However, all kinds of akusala are dangerous.

Moha is dangerous, it is the root of all akusala. When we are ignorant of realities, we accumulate a great deal of akusala. Moha conditions lobha; when we do not know realities as they are we become absorbed in the things we experience through the senses. Moha also conditions dosa; when we are ignorant of realities we have aversion towards unpleasant experiences. Moha accompanies each akusala citta and it conditions all ten kinds of akusala kamma patha (killing, stealing, lying etc.) which are accomplished through body, speech and mind[4]. Only when there is mindfulness of the realities which appear through the six doors, the wisdom is developed which can eradicate moha.

The sotāpanna (the "streamwinner", who has attained the first stage of enlightenment) has eradicated the moha-mūla-citta which is accompanied by doubt, vicikicchā; he has no more doubts about paramattha dhammas, he knows the "world in the ariyan sense". He has no doubts about the Buddha, the Dhamma and the Sangha. He has no doubts about the Path leading to the end of defilements. The sotāpanna, the sakadāgāmī (the "once-returner, who has attained the second stage of enlightenment) and the anāgāmī (the "non-returner", who has attained the third stage of enlightenment) still have the type of moha-mūla-citta accompanied by uddhacca, restlessness. Only the arahat has eradicated all akusala.

Ignorance is not seeing the true characteristics of realities, not knowing the four noble Truths. Out of ignorance one does not see the first noble Truth, the Truth of dukkha: one does not realize the nāma and rūpa which appear as impermanent and therefore one does not see them as dukkha, unsatisfactory. One does not know the second noble Truth: the origin of dukkha which is craving. Because of clinging

[4] See chapter 5.

to nāma and rūpa there is no end to the cycle of birth and death and thus there is no end to dukkha. One does not know the noble truth of the cessation of dukkha, which is nibbāna. One does not know the noble Truth of the way leading to the cessation of dukkha, which is the eightfold Path. The eightfold Path is developed through vipassanā.

We read in the Kindred Sayings (IV, Saḷāyatana-vagga, Kindred Sayings about Jambukhādaka, paragraph 9) that Jambukhādaka asked Sāriputta:

> " 'Ignorance, ignorance!' is the saying, friend Sāriputta. Pray, what is ignorance?"
>
> "Not understanding about dukkha, friend, not understanding about the arising of dukkha, the ceasing of dukkha, the way leading to the ceasing of dukkha – this, friend, is called 'ignorance'."
>
> "But is there any way, friend, any approach to the abandoning of this ignorance?"
>
> "There is indeed a way, friend, to such abandoning."
>
> "And what, friend, is that way, that approach to the abandoning of this ignorance?"
>
> "It is this ariyan eightfold Path, friend..."

The ariyan eightfold Path leads to the eradication of moha.

Questions

1. What is ignorance? Why should it be eradicated?
2. How can it be eradicated?
3. When there is doubt (vicikicchā) about realities, is there moha as well?
4. On account of experiences through which doors can moha arise?

8 Ahetuka Cittas (Rootless Cittas)

If we want to know ourselves we should not merely know the moments of akusala cittas or kusala cittas but other moments as well. When we see something ugly, we dislike what we see. At the moment of dislike there is akusala citta rooted in dosa (aversion). Before there is dislike, however, there must be moments of merely seeing visible object. At these moments there are not yet akusala cittas, but cittas which are without "root" (in Pāli: *hetu*).

There are six cetasikas which are hetu or root. Three of these hetus are akusala; they are: lobha (attachment), dosa (aversion) and moha (ignorance). Three hetus are sobhana (beautiful); they are: alobha[1] (greedlessness or generosity), adosa (non-hate or loving kindness) and amoha (paññā or wisdom). The citta or cetasika which is accompanied by a hetu is sahetuka ("sa" means "with"). For example, dosa-mūla-citta is sahetuka; moha and dosa are the hetus which arise with dosa-mūla-citta.

Cittas without hetu are *ahetuka* cittas. There are many ahetuka cittas arising in a day. Whenever we see, hear, smell, taste or experience tangible object through the bodysense, there are ahetuka cittas before cittas with akusala hetus or with sobhana hetus arise. We are inclined to pay attention only to the moments of like and dislike, but we should know other moments as well; we should know ahetuka cittas.

There are altogether eighteen types of ahetuka citta. As I will explain, fifteen types of ahetuka cittas are vipākacittas and three types are kiriyacittas (cittas which are "inoperative", neither cause nor result). Seven of the fifteen ahetuka vipākacittas are akusala vipākacittas (results of unwholesome deeds) and eight of them are kusala vipākacittas (results of wholesome deeds). When a pleasant or an unpleasant object impinges on the eyesense, seeing-consciousness only experiences what appears through the eyes, there is no like or dislike yet of the object. Seeing-consciousness is an ahetuka vipākacitta. Cittas which like or dislike the object arise later on; these are sahetuka cittas (arising with hetus). Seeing is not the same as thinking of what is seen. The citta which pays attention to the shape and form of something and knows what it is, does not experience an object through the eye-door but through the mind-door; it has a different characteristic. When one uses the word "seeing" one usually means: paying attention to the shape and form of something and knowing what it is. However, there must also be a kind of citta which merely sees visible object, and this citta does not know anything else. What we see we can call "visible object" or "colour"; what is meant is: what appears through the eyes. When there is hearing, we can experience that hearing has a characteristic which is different from seeing; the citta which hears experiences sound through the ears. Only in being aware of the different characteristics of realities and investigating them over and over again, will we come to know them as they are. People may think that there is a self who can see and hear at the same time, but through which door can the self be experienced? The belief in a self is wrong view.

Seeing, hearing, smelling, tasting and the experience of tangible object through the bodysense do not arise without conditions; they are the results of kamma.

[1] In Pāli "a" is a negative.

Eyesense, earsense, smelling-sense, tasting-sense and bodysense are rūpas which are produced by kamma, they are the corporal result of kamma. Only the mental result of kamma is called vipāka, and thus only citta and cetasika (mental factors arising with the citta) can be vipāka. Rūpa is not vipāka.

The Buddha taught that everything which arises must have conditions for its arising. When we see something unpleasant there must be a condition for it: it is the result of akusala kamma. Akusala vipāka cannot be the result of kusala kamma. Seeing something pleasant is kusala vipāka; this can only be the result of kusala kamma. The vipākacitta which experiences an unpleasant or pleasant object through one of the five senses is ahetuka. At that moment there are no akusala hetus (unwholesome roots) or sobhana hetus (beautiful roots) arising with the citta.

Seeing-consciousness, hearing-consciousness and the other sense-cognitions which experience a pleasant object or an unpleasant object through the corresponding sense-doors are ahetuka vipākacittas. There are two kinds of ahetuka vipāka experiencing an object through each of the five sense-doors: one is akusala vipāka and one is kusala vipāka. Thus there are five pairs of ahetuka vipākacittas which arise depending on the five sense-doors. There are also other kinds of ahetuka vipākacitta which will be dealt with later on. The ten ahetuka vipākacittas which are the five pairs are called in Pāli: dvi-pañca-viññāṇa (two times five viññāṇa[2]). Summing them up they are:

1. Seeing-consciousness (cakkhu-viññāṇa, "cakkhu" means eye): akusala vipāka, accompanied by indifferent feeling (upekkhā): kusala vipāka, accompanied by indifferent feeling.
2. Hearing-consciousness (sota-viññāṇa, "sota" means ear): akusala vipāka, accompanied by indifferent feeling: kusala vipāka, accompanied by indifferent feeling.
3. Smelling-consciousness (ghāna-viññāṇa, "ghāna" means nose): akusala vipāka, accompanied by indifferent feeling: kusala vipāka, accompanied by indifferent feeling.
4. Tasting-consciousness (jivhā-viññāṇa, "jivhā" means tongue): akusala vipāka, accompanied by indifferent feeling: kusala vipāka, accompanied by indifferent feeling.
5. Body-consciousness (kāya-viññāṇa, "kāya" means body): akusala vipāka, accompanied by painful bodily feeling (dukkha-vedanā): kusala vipāka, accompanied by pleasant bodily feeling (sukha-vedanā).

The ahetuka vipākacittas which see, hear, smell and taste are invariably accompanied by indifferent feeling, upekkhā, no matter whether they are akusala vipāka or kusala vipāka. The citta which dislikes the object may arise afterwards. This citta is "sahetuka", with hetus (roots), and it is accompanied by unpleasant feeling. Or the citta which likes the object may arise; this citta which is also "sahetuka", with roots, may be accompanied by pleasant feeling or by indifferent feeling. We are inclined to think that the dvi-pañca-viññāṇas, such as seeing or hearing, can

[2] "dvi" is "two" and "pañca" is "five".

occur at the same time as like or dislike of the object, but this is not so. Different cittas arise at different moments and the feelings which accompany the cittas are different too; these realities arise each because of their own conditions and they are non-self.

The feeling arising with body-consciousness which experiences tangible object through the bodysense cannot be indifferent feeling; it arises either with painful bodily feeling or with pleasant bodily feeling. When an unpleasant tangible object is experienced the feeling which accompanies the ahetuka vipākacitta is painful bodily feeling, dukkha-vedanā. When a pleasant tangible object is experienced the feeling which accompanies the ahetuka vipākacitta is pleasant bodily feeling, sukha-vedanā. Painful bodily feeling and pleasant bodily feeling are nāma which can arise only with the vipākacitta which experiences an object through the bodysense. Bodily feeling is conditioned by impact on the bodysense. Both bodily feeling and mental feeling are nāma, but they arise because of different conditions and at different moments. For example, we may have pleasant bodily feeling when we are in comfortable surroundings, but in spite of that, we may still be worried and also have moments of "mental" unpleasant feeling which accompanies dosa-mūla-citta; these feelings arise at different moments and because of different conditions. Pleasant bodily feeling is the result of kusala kamma. The mental unpleasant feeling which arises when we are unhappy is conditioned by our accumulation of dosa (aversion); it is akusala. The whole day there are tangible objects experienced through the bodysense, which is a kind of rūpa. Tangible object can be experienced all over the body, also inside the body, and thus the door of the bodysense can be anywhere in the body. Whenever we touch hard or soft objects, when cold or heat contacts the body, and when we move, bend or stretch, there are unpleasant or pleasant objects experienced through the bodysense. One may wonder whether at each moment there is a bodily impression, pleasant bodily feeling or painful bodily feeling arises. One may notice the coarse bodily feelings, but not the subtle bodily feelings. For example, when something is a little too hard, too cold or too hot, there is painful bodily feeling, dukkha-vedanā, arising with the ahetuka vipākacitta which experiences the object through the bodysense. One may not notice the subtle bodily feelings if one has not learned to be aware of realities.

The arahat, when he experiences an unpleasant object or a pleasant object through the bodysense, has painful bodily feeling or pleasant bodily feeling arising with the ahetuka vipākacitta which is body-consciousness, but he has no akusala cittas or kusala cittas after the vipākacitta; instead he has kiriyacittas ("inoperative cittas"[3]). We read in the Kindred Sayings (IV, Saḷāyatana-vagga, Kindred Sayings about Feeling, Book I, paragraph 6) that the Buddha said to the monks:

> "The untaught manyfolk, monks, feels feeling that is pleasant, feeling that is painful and feeling that is neutral. The well-taught ariyan disciple, monks, feels the same three feelings.

[3] The arahat does not perform kusala kamma or akusala kamma, deeds which produce results. For him there is no kamma which could produce rebirth.

Now herein, monks, what is the distinction, what is the specific feature, what is the difference between the well-taught ariyan disciple and the untaught manyfolk?"

"For us, lord, things are rooted in the Exalted One..."

" The untaught manyfolk, monks, being touched by feeling that is painful, weeps and wails, cries aloud, knocks the breast, falls into utter bewilderment. For he feels a twofold feeling, bodily and mental...Touched by that painful feeling he feels repugnance for it. Feeling that repugnance for the painful feeling, the lurking tendency to repugnance fastens on him. Touched by the painful feeling, he delights in pleasant feeling. Why so? The untaught manyfolk, monks, knows of no refuge from painful feeling save sensual pleasure. Delighting in that sensual pleasure, the lurking tendency to sensual pleasure fastens on him..."

Is this not real life? Touched by painful feeling, we long for pleasant feeling; we believe that it is real happiness. We do not see life as it really is: dukkha. We wish to ignore sickness, old age and death, "lamentation and despair", and the impermanence of all conditioned realities. We expect happiness in life and when we have to suffer we think that pleasant feeling might cure us of suffering and we cling to it. In the Buddha's teaching of the "Dependent Origination"[4] it is said that feeling conditions craving. Not only pleasant feeling and indifferent feeling condition craving, but also unpleasant feeling conditions craving, since one wishes to be liberated from unpleasant feeling (Visuddhimagga, XVII, 238). Furthermore, we read in the sutta:

...If he feels feeling that is pleasant, he feels it as one in bondage. If he feels feeling that is painful, he feels it as one in bondage. If he feels feeling that is neutral, he feels it as one in bondage. This untaught manyfolk, monks, is called 'in bondage to birth, death, sorrow and grief, woe, lamentation and despair. He is in bondage to dukkha'. So I declare.

But, monks, the well-taught ariyan disciple, when touched by painful feeling, weeps not, wails not, cries not aloud, knocks not the breast, falls not into utter bewilderment. He feels but one feeling, the bodily, not the mental...[5] If he feels a feeling that is pleasant, he feels it as one freed from bondage. If he feels a feeling that is painful, he feels it as one that is freed from bondage. If he feels a neutral feeling, he feels it as one that is freed from bondage. This well-taught ariyan disciple, monks, is called 'freed from the bondage of birth, old age, from sorrow and grief, from woe, lamentation and despair, freed from the bondage of dukkha.' So I declare..."

Feelings arise because of conditions and fall away again. They are impermanent and they should not be taken for self. We read in the Kindred Sayings (Saḷāyatana-vagga, Kindred Sayings on Sense, Third Fifty, paragraph 130, Hāliddaka):

---

[4] In Pāli: Paṭiccasamuppāda. The teaching of the conditionality of all nāmas and rūpas of our life.

[5] He feels bodily pain, not mental pain.

> Once the venerable Kaccāna the Great was staying among the folk of Avanti, at Osprey's Haunt, on a sheer mountain crag. Then the housefather Hāliddakāni came to the venerable Kaccāna the Great. Seated at one side he said this:
>
> " It has been said by the Exalted One, sir, 'Owing to diversity in elements arises diversity of contact. Owing to diversity of contact arises diversity of feeling.' Pray, sir, how far is this so?"
>
> "Herein, housefather, after having seen with the eye a pleasant object, a monk comes to know as such[6] eye-consciousness that is a pleasant experience. Owing to contact that is pleasant to experience arises happy feeling.
>
> After having seen with the eye an unpleasant object, a monk comes to know as such eye-consciousness that is an unpleasant experience. Owing to contact that is unpleasant to experience arises unpleasant feeling.
>
> After having seen with the eye an object that is of indifferent effect, a monk comes to know as such eye-consciousness that experiences an object which is of indifferent effect. Owing to contact that is indifferent to experience arises feeling that is indifferent.
>
> So also, housefather, after having heard a sound with the ear, smelt a scent with the nose, tasted a savour with the tongue, experienced tangible object with the body, cognized with the mind a mental object that is pleasant. . . Owing to contact that is pleasant to experience arises happy feeling. But after having cognized a mental object which is unpleasant. . . owing to contact that is unpleasant to experience arises unhappy feeling. Again, after having cognized with the mind a mental object that is indifferent in effect, he comes to know as such mind-consciousness that experiences an object which is of indifferent effect. Owing to contact that is indifferent arises feeling that is indifferent. Thus, housefather, owing to diversity in elements arises diversity of contact. Owing to diversity of contact arises diversity of feeling."

If we are mindful of realities which appear through the different doorways we will come to know from direct experience different characteristics of nāmas and rūpas; we will know different types of citta and different kinds of feeling. We will understand that all these realities are only conditioned elements and not self. We will know from direct experience that there are not only cittas accompanied by lobha, dosa and moha, and cittas accompanied by "beautiful" roots, but also cittas which are ahetuka, cittas without roots. One may not find it useful and interesting to know more about seeing, hearing and the other realities appearing through the different doorways. However, in order to see things as they are, it is essential to know that the citta which, for example hears sound, has a characteristic which is different from the citta which likes or dislikes the sound and that these cittas arise because of different conditions. What the Buddha taught can be proved by being mindful of realities.

---

[6] The P.T.S. translation has: at the thought "This is such and such", comes to know eye-consciousness that is a pleasant experience.

Questions

1. Which are the six hetus (roots)?
2. When there is seeing it may be kusala vipāka or akusala vipāka. Are there hetus accompanying seeing-consciousness?

9 Ahetuka Cittas which are Unknown in Daily Life

There are eighteen types of ahetuka citta, cittas arising without hetu (root). Fifteen types of ahetuka cittas are vipāka. As we have seen, ten of these fifteen cittas are dvi-pañca-viññāṇas (five pairs). They are the pairs of:

- seeing-consciousness
- hearing-consciousness
- smelling-consciousness
- tasting-consciousness
- body-consciousness

Each of these is a pair of which one is akusala vipāka and one kusala vipāka.

Seeing-consciousness is the result of kamma. When it is the result of an ill deed, seeing-consciousness is akusala vipākacitta which experiences an unpleasant object; when it is the result of a good deed, it is kusala vipākacitta which experiences a pleasant object. The function of seeing-consciousness is experiencing visible object.

Kamma which produces the vipākacitta which is seeing-consciousness does not only produce that type of vipākacitta, it also produces two other types of vipākacitta which succeed seeing-consciousness. Seeing-consciousness is succeeded by another vipākacitta which receives the object. This citta, which still has the same object as seeing-consciousness, is called the receiving-consciousness, sampaṭicchana-citta. Visible object which is experienced by seeing-consciousness does not fall away when seeing-consciousness falls away, because it is rūpa; rūpa does not fall away as rapidly as nāma. When an object is experienced through one of the six doors, there is not merely one citta experiencing that object, but there is a series or process of cittas succeeding one another, which share the same object.

If the seeing-consciousness is akusala vipāka, the sampaṭicchana-citta (receiving-consciousness) is also akusala vipāka; if the seeing-consciousness is kusala vipāka, the sampaṭicchana-citta is also kusala vipāka. Thus, there are two types of sampaṭicchana-citta: one is akusala vipāka and one is kusala vipāka. Sampaṭicchana-citta is ahetuka vipāka; there are no akusala hetus (unwholesome roots) or sobhana hetus (beautiful roots) arising with this type of citta. Sampaṭicchana-citta succeeds seeing-consciousness; seeing-consciousness is a condition for the arising of sampaṭicchana-citta. Likewise, when there is hearing-consciousness which hears sound, sampaṭicchana-citta succeeds hearing-consciousness. It is the same with regard to the other sense-doors.

Sampaṭicchana-citta always arises with upekkhā (indifferent feeling), no matter whether the sampaṭicchana-citta is akusala vipāka or kusala vipāka.

After the sampaṭicchana-citta has arisen and fallen away, the process of cittas experiencing an object is not yet over. The sampaṭicchana-citta is succeeded by another ahetuka vipākacitta which is still the result of kamma. This type of citta is called investigating-consciousness, santīraṇa-citta. Santīraṇa-citta investigates or considers the object which was experienced by one of the dvi-pañca-viññāṇas ("the five pairs"), and which was "received" by the sampaṭicchana-citta. Santīraṇa-citta succeeds sampaṭicchana-citta in a process of cittas experiencing an object through one of the five sense-doors; sampaṭicchana-citta is a condition for the arising of santīraṇa-citta. When seeing has arisen, sampaṭicchana-citta succeeds the seeing-consciousness, and santīraṇa-citta succeeds the sampaṭicchana-citta in the process of cittas which experience visible object. It is the same with the santīraṇa-citta which arises in the process of cittas experiencing an object through one of the other sense-doors; it succeeds the sampaṭicchana-citta. We cannot choose whether santīraṇa-citta should arise or not; cittas arise because of conditions, they are beyond control.

Santīraṇa-citta is also an ahetuka vipākacitta. When the object is unpleasant, the santīraṇa-citta is akusala vipāka and it is accompanied by upekkhā (indifferent feeling). As regards santīraṇa-citta which is kusala vipāka, there are two kinds. When the object is pleasant but not extraordinarily pleasant, santīraṇa-citta is accompanied by upekkhā. When the object is extraordinarily pleasant, the santīraṇa-citta is accompanied by somanassa, pleasant feeling. Thus, there are three kinds of santīraṇa-citta in all. It depends on conditions which kind of santīraṇa-citta arises.

Thus, there are fifteen types of ahetuka citta which are vipāka. Summarising them, they are:

- 10 cittas which are dvi-pañca-viññāṇa (five pairs)
- 1 sampaṭicchana-citta (receiving-consciousness) which is akusala vipāka
- 1 sampaṭicchana-citta which is kusala vipāka
- 1 santīraṇa-citta (investigating-consciousness) which is akusala vipāka, accompanied by upekkhā (indifferent feeling)
- 1 santīraṇa-citta which is kusala vipāka, accompanied by upekkhā
- 1 santīraṇa-citta which is kusala vipāka, accompanied by somanassa (pleasant feeling)

Seven types of the ahetuka vipākacittas are akusala vipāka and eight types are kusala vipāka, since there are two types of santīraṇa-citta which are kusala vipāka.

There are altogether eighteen ahetuka cittas. Of these eighteen ahetuka cittas fifteen are vipākacittas and three are *kiriyacittas*. Kiriyacittas are different from akusala cittas and kusala cittas and from vipākacittas. Akusala cittas and kusala cittas are cittas which are cause; they can motivate ill deeds and good deeds which are capable of producing their appropriate results. Vipākacittas are cittas which are the result of akusala kamma and kusala kamma. Kiriyacittas are cittas which are neither cause nor result.

One type of ahetuka kiriyacitta is the five-door-adverting-consciousness, in Pāli: pañca-dvārāvajjana-citta[1]. When an object impinges on one of the five senses, there has to be a citta which adverts or turns towards the object through that sense-door. When visible object impinges on the eyesense, there has to be the adverting-consciousness which adverts to visible object through the eye-door, the eye-door-adverting-consciousness (cakkhu-dvārāvajjana-citta; "cakkhu" means "eye"), before there can be seeing-consciousness (cakkhu-viññāṇa). When sound impinges on

[1] "Pañca" is five, "dvāra" is door, "āvajjana" is adverting or turning towards.

the earsense, the ear-door-adverting-consciousness (sota-dvārāvajjana-citta; "sota" means "ear") has to advert to the sound through the ear-door before there can be hearing-consciousness (sota-viññāṇa). The pañca-dvārāvajjana-citta merely turns towards the object which impinges on one of the five senses. It turns, for example, towards the visible object or sound which impinges on the corresponding sense-organ, but it does not see or hear. The pañca-dvārāvajjana-citta is an ahetuka kiriyacitta, it arises without hetu (root); there is not yet like or dislike when this citta arises. The pañca-dvārāvajjana-citta is succeeded by one of the dvi-pañca-viññāṇas, which is vipākacitta. Each citta which arises in the process of cittas experiencing an object has its own function.

The cittas which experience an object through one of the sense-doors do not know anything else but that object. When one, for example, is reading, the citta which sees experiences only visible object and it does not know the meaning of the letters. After the eye-door process has been completed visible object is experienced through the mind-door and then there can be other mind-door processes of cittas which know the meaning of what has been written and which think about it. Thus, there are processes of cittas which experience an object through one of the senses and processes of cittas which experience an object through the mind-door.

Another type of ahetuka kiriyacitta is the mind-door-adverting-consciousness, in Pāli: mano-dvārāvajjana citta. This type of citta arises both in the sense-door process and in the mind-door process but it performs two different functions according as it arises in each of those two kinds of processes, as we will see.

When an object contacts one of the sense-doors, the pañca-dvārāvajjana-citta (five-sense-door-adverting consciousness) turns towards the object, one of the dvi-pañca-viññāṇas experiences it, sampaṭicchana-citta receives the object and santīraṇa-citta investigates it. The process of cittas experiencing the object through that sense-door is, however, not yet over. The santīraṇa-citta is succeeded by an ahetuka kiriyacitta which experiences the object through that sense-door and "determines" that object, the determining-consciousness, in Pāli: votthapana-citta[2]. It is actually the same type of citta as the mano-dvārāvajjana-citta (mind-door-adverting-consciousness, the first citta of the mind-door process), but when it arises in a sense-door process it can be called votthapana-citta, since it performs the function of votthapana, determining the object, in the sense-door process. The votthapana-citta, after it has determined the object, is followed by akusala cittas or by kusala cittas[3]. The votthapana-citta itself is neither akusala citta nor kusala citta; it is kiriyacitta. This citta which determines the object is anattā, non-self. There is no self who can determine whether there will be akusala cittas or kusala cittas. The akusala cittas or kusala cittas which succeed the votthapana-citta are non-self either; it depends on one's accumulations of akusala and kusala whether the votthapana-citta will be succeeded by akusala cittas or by kusala cittas.

The cittas arising in a sense-door process which experience a sense object such as colour or sound, arise and fall away, succeeding one another. When the sense-door

---

[2] Votthapana can be translated as "fixing", "establishing" or "determining".

[3] Except in the case of arahats who have neither kusala cittas nor akusala cittas, but kiriyacittas instead.

process of cittas is finished, the sense object experienced by those cittas has also fallen away. Cittas arise and fall away extremely rapidly and very shortly after the sense-door process is finished, a mind-door process of cittas starts, which experience the sense object which has just fallen away. Although it has fallen away, it can be object of cittas arising in a mind-door process. The mano-dvārāvajjana-citta is the first citta of the mind-door process, it adverts through the mind-door to the object which has just fallen away. In the sense-door process the pañca-dvārāvajjana-citta adverts to the object which has not fallen away yet. For example, it adverts to visible object or sound which is still impinging on the appropriate sense-door. The mano-dvārāvajjana-citta which arises in the mind-door process, however, can experience an object which has fallen away already. It adverts, for example, to visible object which has been experienced through the eye-door or to sound which has been experienced through the ear-door. After the mano-dvārāvajjana-citta has adverted to the object it is succeeded by either kusala cittas or akusala cittas (in the case of non-arahats), which experience that same object. The mano-dvārāvajjana-citta is neither akusala citta nor kusala citta; it is kiriyacitta. It depends on one's accumulations by which types of cittas the mano-dvārāvajjana-citta is succeeded: by akusala cittas or by kusala cittas. All cittas arise because of their own conditions; they are anattā, not a person, not self.

The ahetuka kiriyacitta which is classified as mano-dvārāvajjana-citta can perform two functions: in the mind-door process it performs the function of āvajjana or adverting, it adverts to the object through the mind-door; in the sense-door process this citta performs the function of votthapana or determining the object. The citta which determines the object in the sense-door process can be called, after its function, the votthapana-citta[4].

When sound impinges on the earsense it can be experienced by cittas arising in the ear-door process and after that it is experienced by cittas arising in a mind-door process. Processes of cittas which experience an object through one of the five senses and through the mind-door succeed one another time and again.

How can there be akusala cittas or kusala cittas in the process of cittas which experience an object through one of the sense-doors, when one does not even know yet what is experienced? There can be akusala cittas or kusala cittas before one knows what it is. One can compare this situation with the case of a child who likes a brightly coloured object such as a balloon before it knows that the object is a balloon. We can have like or dislike of an object before we know what it is.

Another ahetuka kiriyacitta is the hasituppāda-citta, the smile-producing-consciousness of the arahat. Only arahats have this type of citta. When they smile the hasituppāda-citta may arise at that moment. Smiling can be motivated by different types of cittas. When people who are not arahats smile, it may be motivated by lobha or by kusala citta. Arahats do not have any defilements; they do not have akusala cittas. Neither do they have kusala cittas; they do not accumulate any more kamma. Instead of kusala cittas they have kiriyacittas accompanied by sobhana (beautiful) roots, sobhana kiriyacittas. Arahats do not laugh aloud, be-

---

[4] Among the 89 types of citta there is no special type of citta which is votthapana-citta; the mano-dvārāvajjana-citta serves the function of votthapana.

cause they have no accumulations for laughing; they only smile. When they smile the smiling may be motivated by sobhana kiriyacitta or by the ahetuka kiriyacitta which is called hasituppāda-citta.

Thus, of the eighteen ahetuka cittas, fifteen are ahetuka vipākacittas and three are ahetuka kiriyacittas. The three ahetuka kiriyacittas are:

- 1 Pañca-dvārāvajjana-citta (five-door-adverting-consciousness).
- 2 Mano-dvārāvajjana-citta (mind-door-adverting-consciousness), which performs the function of adverting to the object through the mind-door when it arises in the mind-door process and which performs the function of votthapana (determining the object) when it arises in the sense-door process.
- 3 Hasituppāda-citta (smile-producing-consciousness).

Those who are not arahats can have only seventeen of the eighteen types of ahetuka citta. These seventeen types of ahetuka citta arise in our daily life. When an object impinges on one of the five senses, the pañca-dvārāvajjana-citta (the five-door-adverting-consciousness) turns towards the object through that sense-door. This citta is followed by pañca-viññāṇa (one of the ten cittas which are the "five pairs") which experiences the object, by sampaṭicchana-citta which receives it, by santīraṇa-citta which investigates it and by votthapana-citta which determines the object and then by akusala cittas or kusala cittas. When the cittas of the sense-door process have fallen away the object is experienced through the mind-door. The mano-dvārāvajjana-citta adverts to the object through the mind-door and is then followed by akusala cittas or kusala cittas. There is "unwise attention" (ayoniso manasikāra) to the object which is experienced if akusala cittas arise, and there is "wise attention" (yoniso manasikāra) to the object if kusala cittas arise. For example, when we see insects there may be dislike and then there are dosa-mūla-cittas, cittas rooted in aversion. Thus there is unwise attention. The dosa may be so strong that one wants to kill the insects; then there is akusala kamma. If one realizes that killing is akusala and one abstains from killing, there are kusala cittas and thus there is wise attention. If one studies the Dhamma and develops vipassanā, insight, it is a condition for wise attention to arise more often. When we are mindful of the nāma or rūpa which appears through one of the sense-doors or through the mind-door, there is wise attention at that moment.

When there are two people in the same situation, one person may have unwise attention and the other may have wise attention, depending on their accumulations. We read in the Kindred Sayings (IV, Saḷāyatana-vagga, Kindred Sayings on Sense, Fourth Fifty, chapter V, paragraph 202, Lustful) about the monk, who, after he has experienced an object through one of the six doors, has unwise attention, and about the monk who has wise attention. We read that Mahā-Moggallāna said to the monks:

> Friends, I will teach you the way of lusting and also of not lusting. . .
>
> And how, friends, is one lustful?
>
> Herein, friends, a monk, seeing an object with the eye, feels attachment for objects that charm, feels aversion from objects that displease, abides without having established mindfulness of the body, and his thoughts are mean. He realizes not, in its true nature, that emancipation of heart, that

emancipation of wisdom, wherein those evil, unprofitable states that have arisen cease without remainder.

This monk, friends, is called "lustful after objects cognizable by the eye, nose, tongue. . . objects cognizable by the mind." When a monk so abides, friends, if Māra[5] come upon him by way of the eye, Māra gets an opportunity. If Māra come upon him by way of the tongue. . . by way of the mind, Māra gets access, gets opportunity. . .

So dwelling, friends, objects overcome a monk, a monk overcomes not objects. Sounds overcome a monk, a monk overcomes not sounds. Scents, savours, tangibles and mind-states overcome a monk, a monk overcomes not sounds, scents, savours, tangibles and mind-states. This monk, friends, is called "conquered by objects, sounds, scents, savours, tangibles and mind-states, not conqueror of them." Evil, unprofitable states, passion-fraught, leading to rebirth overcome him, states unhappy, whose fruit is pain, whose future is rebirth, decay and death. Thus, friends, one is lustful.

And how, friends, is one free from lust?

Herein, friends, a monk, seeing an object with the eye, is not attached to objects that charm, nor averse from objects that displease. . .

Tasting a savour with the tongue. . . with mind cognizing a mind-state, he is not attached to mind-states that charm, nor is he averse from mind-states that displease, but dwells, having established mindfulness of the body and his thought is boundless. So that he realizes in its true nature that emancipation of heart, that emancipation of wisdom, wherein those evil, unprofitable states that have arisen come to cease without remainder.

This monk, friends, is called "not lustful after objects cognizable by the eye. . . not lustful after mind-states cognizable by the mind." Thus dwelling, friends, if Māra come upon him by way of the eye, of the tongue, of the mind. . . Māra gets no access, gets no opportunity. . .

Moreover, friends, so dwelling a monk conquers objects, objects do not conquer him. He conquers sounds, scents, savours, tangibles, mind-states. They do not conquer him. Such a monk, friends, is called, "conqueror of objects, sounds, scents, savours, tangibles and mind-states." He is conqueror, not conquered. He conquers those evil, unprofitable states, passion-fraught, inciting to lust, leading to rebirth, states unhappy, whose fruit is pain, rebirth, decay and death. Thus, friends, is one free from lust.

Questions

1. What is kiriyacitta?
2. When we smile, is it always motivated by lobha, attachment?
3. Can akusala cittas and kusala cittas arise in a sense-door process?

[5] The "Evil One". Māra stands for everything which is unwholesome and dukkha, suffering.

10 The First Citta in Life

Time and again there are cittas arising which experience different objects through the senses and through the mind-door. There are seeing or hearing, there are cittas with attachment to what is seen or heard. These cittas arise because of different conditions. Seeing and the citta with attachment to visible object do not arise at the same time, they are different and they perform different functions. We will understand more about cittas if we know in what order they arise and which function they perform. Each citta has its own function (in Pāli: kicca). There are fourteen functions of citta in all.

The citta arising at the first moment of life must also have a function. What is birth, and what is it actually that is born? We speak about the birth of a child, but in fact, there are only nāma and rūpa which are born. The word "birth" is a conventional term. We should consider what birth really is. Nāma and rūpa arise and fall away all the time and thus there is birth and death of nāma and rūpa all the time. In order to understand what causes birth we should know what conditions the nāma and rūpa which arise at the first moment of a new lifespan.

What arises first at the beginning of our life, nāma or rūpa? At any moment of our life there have to be both nāma and rūpa. In the planes of existence where there are five khandhas (four nāmakkhandhas and one rūpakkhandha), nāma cannot arise without rūpa; citta cannot arise without the body[1]. What is true for any moment of our life is also true for the first moment of our life. At the first moment of our life nāma and rūpa have to arise at the same time. The citta which arises at that moment is called the rebirth-consciousness or *paṭisandhi-citta*[2]. Since there isn't any citta which arises without conditions, the paṭisandhi-citta must also have conditions. The paṭisandhi-citta is the first citta of a new life and thus its cause can only be in the past. One may have doubts about past lives, but how can people be so different if there were no past lives? We can see that people are born with different accumulations. Can we explain the character of a child only by the parents? What we mean by "character" is actually nāma. Could parents transfer to another being nāma which falls away as soon as it has arisen? There must be other factors which are the condition for a child's character. Cittas which arise and fall away succeed one another and thus each citta conditions the next one. The last citta of the previous life (dying-consciousness) is succeeded by the first citta of this life. That is why tendencies one had in the past can continue by way of accumulation from one citta to the next one and from past lives to the present life. Since people accumulated different tendencies in past lives, they are born with different tendencies and inclinations.

We do not only see that people are born with different characters, we also see that they are born in different surroundings; some people are born in pleasant

---

1 There are different planes of existence where one can be born and not in all of them are both nāma and rūpa. In some planes there is only nāma and in one plane there is only rūpa.

2 Paṭisandhi means relinking, it "links" the previous life to the present life. It is usually translated as rebirth-consciousness, but, since there is no person who is reborn, birth-consciousness would be more correct.

surroundings and some people are born in miserable surroundings. In order to understand this we should not cling to conventional terms such as "person" or "surroundings". If we think in terms of paramattha dhammas we will see that being in pleasant or miserable surroundings is nothing else but the receiving of pleasant or unpleasant objects through eyes, ears, nose, tongue and bodysense. It is kusala vipāka or akusala vipāka. Vipāka (result) does not arise without conditions; it is caused by good or bad deeds, by kamma. Different people perform different kamma and each deed brings its own result. The fact that people are born in different surroundings must have a condition: it is conditioned by kamma performed in a previous life. Kamma causes one to be born. The paṭisandhi-citta is the result of kamma; it is vipāka.

In this world we see different births of people and of animals. When we compare the life of an animal with the life of a human being, we notice that being born an animal is sorrowful; it is akusala vipāka. Being born a human being is kusala vipāka, even if one is born poor or if one has to experience many unpleasant things during one's life. The paṭisandhi-cittas of different people are of many different degrees of kusala vipāka because the kusala kammas which produced them were of different degrees.

At the first moment of our life kamma produces the paṭisandhi-citta and then rūpa has to arise at the same time. One may wonder what the cause is of the rūpa arising at the first moment of life. We see that people are born with different bodily features: some are strong, some are weak, some are handicapped from birth. This must have a cause. It is kamma which causes both nāma and rūpa to be born.

Could the rūpa we call "dead matter" and the rūpa we call "plant" be produced by kamma? A plant is not "born" because a plant cannot perform good and bad deeds; it has no kamma that could cause its birth. Temperature is the condition for the life of a plant. As regards human beings, kamma produces rūpa at the moment the paṭisandhi-citta arises. There couldn't be life if kamma did not produce rūpa from the first moment of life. There are four factors which produce different rūpas of the body. As we have seen kamma is one factor. The other factors are: citta, temperature and nutrition. Kamma produces rūpa at the moment the paṭisandhi-citta arises and after that the other factors also start to produce rūpas. Temperature produces rūpa; if there were not the right temperature the new life could not develop. Temperature produces rūpa throughout our life. As soon as the paṭisandhi-citta has fallen away, at the moment the next citta arises, citta too starts to produce rūpa, and it produces rūpa throughout our life. Furthermore, nutrition produces rūpa so that the body can grow. It produces rūpa throughout our life. Thus we see that there are four factors which produce rūpas of the body.

As regards rūpas which are not of the body but rūpas outside, such as rūpas in dead matter or in plants, these are produced solely by temperature.

Kamma produces rūpa not only at the first moment of life but throughout our life. Kamma does not only produce the vipākacittas which experience pleasant and unpleasant objects through the sense-doors, it also produces throughout our life the rūpas which can function as the sense-doors through which these objects are received. Could we for instance create our own eyesense? It could not be produced by temperature, only by kamma. Transplantation of the eye cannot be successful unless kamma produces eyesense in the body of the receiver.

Birth by way of the mother's womb is not the only way of birth. We learn from the teachings that there can be birth in four different ways: by way of the womb, by way of eggs, by way of moisture and by way of spontaneous birth.

People would like to know when life starts in the mother's womb. We cannot determine the exact moment. Life starts at the moment the paṭisandhi-citta arises together with the rūpa which is at the same time produced by kamma. A lifespan ends when the last citta, the dying-consciousness (cuti-citta) falls away. So long as the dying-consciousness has not fallen away there is still life. One cannot know the moment the dying-consciousness of someone else arises and falls away unless one has cultivated the knowledge of the cittas of other people. A Buddha or someone else who has cultivated this special kind of knowledge could know the exact moment of someone's death.

We may wonder which kamma in our life will produce the paṭisandhi-citta of the next life. Some people believe that by doing many good deeds in this life they can be assured of a happy rebirth. But the kamma which produces rebirth will not necessarily be from this life. We have in past lives as well as in this life performed both akusala kamma and kusala kamma and these kammas are of different degrees. Some kammas produce results in the same life in which they have been performed, some produce result in the form of rebirth-consciousness of a future life, or they produce result in the course of a future life. We have performed deeds in past lives which could produce rebirth but which have not yet come to fruition. We cannot know which kamma will produce our next rebirth.

If akusala kamma produces the rebirth of the next life there will be an unhappy rebirth. In that case the cittas which arise shortly before the dying-consciousness are akusala cittas and they experience an unpleasant object. The paṭisandhi-citta of the next life which succeeds the cuti-citta (the dying-consciousness), experiences that same unpleasant object. If kusala kamma produces the rebirth there will be a happy rebirth. In that case kusala cittas arise shortly before the cuti-citta and they experience a pleasant object. The paṭisandhi-citta of the next life experiences that same pleasant object.

People want to know whether they can ensure a happy rebirth for themselves by controlling the last cittas before the cuti-citta, by inducing them to be kusala. Some people invite monks to chant at the deathbed of a dying person in order to help him to have kusala cittas. However, nobody can be sure that his rebirth will be a happy one, unless he has attained one of the stages of enlightenment. One cannot have power over one's cittas. Can we control our thoughts now, at this moment? Since we cannot do this, how could we control our thoughts at the time shortly before dying? There is no self who can decide about his rebirth in a next life. After the last akusala cittas or kusala cittas in life have fallen away, the cuti-citta arises. The cuti-citta is succeeded by the paṭisandhi-citta of the next life. When the paṭisandhi-citta arises a new lifespan starts. So long as there is kamma there will be future lives.

The paṭisandhi-citta performs the function of rebirth or relinking. It "links" the past to the present. Since only the first citta of a lifespan performs the function of rebirth there is only one paṭisandhi-citta in a life. There is no self who transmigrates from one life to the next life; there are only nāma and rūpa arising and falling away. The present life is different from the past life but there is continuity in so far as the present life is conditioned by the past. Since the paṭisandhi-citta succeeds the cuti-citta of the previous life, the accumulated tendencies of past lives go on to the paṭisandhi-citta. Thus, inclinations one has in the present life are conditioned by the past.

The paṭisandhi-citta is the result of a previous good deed or bad deed committed in the past. The object the paṭisandhi-citta experiences is, as we have seen, the same as the object experienced by the last akusala cittas or kusala cittas which arose before the cuti-citta of the previous life. The Visuddhimagga (XVII, 164-168) explains by way of similes that although the present is different from the past there is continuity. The being who is born is not the same as the being of the past life, but it is conditioned by the past. There is "neither absolute identity nor absolute otherness", as the Visuddhimagga explains. We read with regard to the paṭisandhi-citta:

> An echo, or its like, supplies
> The figures here; connectedness
> By continuity denies
> Identity and otherness.

> And here let the illustration of this consciousness be such things as an echo, a light, a seal impression, a looking glass image, for the fact of its not coming here from the previous becoming and for the fact that it arises owing to causes that are included in past becomings. For just as an echo, a light, a seal impression, and a shadow, have respectively sound, etc., as their cause and come into being without going elsewhere, so also this consciousness.
>
> And with the stream of continuity there is neither identity nor otherness. For if there were absolute identity in a stream of continuity, there would be no forming of curd from milk. And yet if there were absolute otherness, the curd would not be derived from milk. And so too with all causally arisen things. . . So neither absolute identity nor absolute otherness should be assumed here.

One is glad to be born if one does not realize that birth is the result of kamma and that one will go forth in the cycle of birth and death so long as there is kamma. Not seeing the dangers of birth is ignorance. At this moment we are in the human plane of existence but so long as we have not attained any stage of enlightenment we cannot be sure that there will not be rebirth in one of the woeful planes. We all have performed both akusala kamma and kusala kamma in different lives. Who knows which of those deeds will produce the paṭisandhi-citta of the next life, even if we continue doing good deeds? Some people think that birth in a heavenly plane is desirable, but they do not realize that life in a heavenly plane does not last and that, after a lifespan in heaven is over, an ill deed previously performed could produce a paṭisandhi-citta in a woeful plane.

We read in the "Discourse on Fools and the Wise" (Middle Length Sayings III, 129) that the Buddha, when he was staying in the Jeta Grove, in Anāthapiṇḍika monastery, spoke to the monks about the sufferings in hell and about the anguishes of animal birth. The Buddha said:

> "In many a disquisition could I, monks, talk a talk about animal birth, but it is not easy to describe in full, monks, so many are the anguishes of animal birth.
>
> Monks, it is like a man who might throw a yoke with one hole into the sea. An easterly wind might take it westwards, a westerly wind might take it eastwards, a northerly wind might take it southwards, a southerly wind might take it northwards. There might be a blind turtle there who came to the surface once in a hundred years. What do you think, monks? Could that blind turtle push his neck through that one hole in the yoke?"
>
> "If at all, revered sir, then only once in a very long while."
>
> "Sooner or later, monks, could the blind turtle push his neck through the one hole in the yoke; more difficult than that, do I say, monks, is human status once again for the fool who has gone to the Downfall. What is the cause of that? Monks, there is no dhamma-faring there, no even-faring, no doing of what is skilled, no doing of what is good. Monks, there is devouring of one another there and feeding on the weak. Monks, if some time or other once in a very long while that fool came to human status (again), he would be born into those families that are low: a family of low caste or a family of hunters or a family of bamboo-plaiters or a family of cartwrights or a family of refuse-scavengers, in such a family as is needy, without enough to drink or to eat, where a covering for the back is with difficulty obtained. Moreover, he would be ill-favoured, ugly, dwarfish, sickly, blind or deformed or lame or paralysed; he would be unable to get food, drink, clothes, vehicles, garlands, scents and perfumes, bed, dwelling and lights; he would fare wrongly in body, wrongly in speech, wrongly in thought. Because he had fared wrongly in body, speech and thought, at the breaking up of the body after dying he would arise in the sorrowful ways, a bad bourn, the Downfall, Niraya Hell...
>
> ...This, monks, is the fool's condition, completed in its entirety..."

The Buddha spoke about the dangers of birth in many different ways. He said that birth is dukkha (sorrow); it is followed by old age, sickness and death. He pointed out the foulness of the body and he reminded people that also at this very moment the body is dukkha, impermanent and non-self. If we continue taking mind and body for self there will be no end to the cycle of birth and death.

We read in the Kindred Sayings (II, Nidāna-vagga, chapter XV, Kindred Sayings on the Incalculable Beginning, paragraph 10, A Person) that the Buddha, when he was in Rājagaha, on Vulture's Peak, said to the monks:

> Incalculable is the beginning, monks, of this faring on. The earliest point is not revealed of the running on, faring on of beings, cloaked in ignorance, tied by craving. . .
> The bones of one single person, monks, running on, faring on for an aeon would be a cairn, a pile, a heap as great as Mount Vepulla, were there a collector of those bones and the collection were not destroyed.
> How is this? Incalculable is the beginning, monks, of this faring on. The earliest point is not revealed of the running on, faring on of beings, cloaked in ignorance, tied by craving. . .
> Thus spoke the Exalted One. After the Wellfarer had said this, he spoke further:
>
> The pile of bones (of all the bodies of) one man
> Who has alone one aeon lived,
> Were heaped a mountain high – so said the mighty seer –
> Yes, reckoned high as Vipula
> To north of Vulture's Peak, crag-fort of Magadha.
> When he with perfect insight sees
> The Ariyan Truths: – what dukkha is and how it comes
> And how it may be overpassed,
> The Ariyan Eightfold Path, the way all ill to abate –
> Seven times at most reborn, a man
> Yet running on, through breaking every fetter down,
> Endmaker does become of dukkha.

It is fortunate to be born in the human plane where we can cultivate insight. When the first stage of enlightenment (the stage of the sotāpanna) has been attained, the four noble Truths have been directly understood. Then we will not be reborn more than seven times and we can be sure that there will eventually be an end to rebirth.

Questions

1. How many functions of citta are there in all?
2. The four classes, jātis, of citta are: akusala, kusala, vipāka and kiriya. Of which jāti is the paṭisandhi-citta?
3. Is birth as a human being always the result of kusala kamma?
4. When does human life start?
5. Why is birth sorrow (dukkha)?

11 Different Types of Rebirth-Consciousness

We see many different beings in this world, men and animals, all with a different appearance and with a different character. They must have been different from the first moment of their lives, from the moment of rebirth-consciousness, paṭisandhi-citta. We may be inclined to think that there must be many types of paṭisandhi-citta, but, on the other hand, beings who are born in this world also have many things in common. We share the same world and we receive impressions through the senses, no matter whether we are rich or poor. On account of the objects which we experience through the six doors, kusala cittas and akusala cittas arise. All these cittas, arising in daily life, are cittas of the sense-sphere, kāmāvacara cittas. "*Kāma*" means "sensual enjoyment" or "object of sensual enjoyment". However, kāmāvacara cittas are not only cittas rooted in attachment, lobha; they are all the cittas pertaining to the sense sphere.

Human birth is the result of kusala kamma. The paṭisandhi-citta arising in the human plane of existence where there are sense impressions is the result of kusala kamma performed by kāmāvacara cittas, cittas pertaining to the "sense-sphere". It cannot be the result of jhānacittas which are not kāmāvacara cittas. The jhānacittas arising when there is calm to the degree of "absorption" do not experience objects which present themselves through the five senses. Jhānacittas cannot cause birth in this world. Thus, beings born in the human plane of existence have in common that their paṭisandhi-citta is the result of kusala kamma performed by kāmāvacara cittas. As regards the many varieties of human birth, this is due to the degree of kusala kamma which produced the paṭisandhi-citta.

One could divide human beings as regards their birth into two classes, but each of these two classes includes many degrees of vipāka. The two classes are:

1. Those who are born with a paṭisandhi-citta which is ahetuka kusala vipāka (which means that the kusala vipākacitta is not accompanied by beautiful roots: by alobha or non-attachment, by adosa or non-aversion, or by paññā or wisdom)
2. Those who are born with a paṭisandhi-citta which is sahetuka kusala vipāka (kusala vipāka accompanied by beautiful roots)

When a human being is born with a paṭisandhi-citta which is ahetuka, his birth is the result of kāmāvacara kusala kamma (kamma performed by kusala cittas of the sense-sphere), but the degree of the kusala kamma is less than the kusala kamma which produces a sahetuka paṭisandhi-citta, a paṭisandhi-citta with "beautiful" roots (sobhana hetus). People who are born with an ahetuka paṭisandhi-citta are handicapped from the first moment of life. Eyesense or earsense does not develop or they have other defects. However, when we see someone who is handicapped we cannot tell whether there was at the first moment of his life an ahetuka paṭisandhi-citta or a sahetuka paṭisandhi-citta. We cannot tell whether someone was handicapped from the first moment of his life or whether he became handicapped later on, even while he was still in his mother's womb, and thus we do not know which type of paṭisandhi-citta he was born with. The fact that a person is handicapped has not happened by chance; it is due to one's kamma.

There is only one type of paṭisandhi-citta which is ahetuka kusala vipāka, but there are many degrees of this vipāka depending on the kamma which produces it: there can be birth in different surroundings, in unpleasant surroundings, though not in woeful planes, and in pleasant surroundings. This type of paṭisandhi-citta can even arise in the lowest heavenly plane.

There is also an ahetuka paṭisandhi-citta which is akusala vipāka. This type of citta does not arise in the human plane, but in a woeful plane. Only one type of paṭisandhi-citta is akusala vipāka, but it is of many degrees. There are many varieties of akusala kamma and thus there must be many varieties of unhappy rebirth. The unhappy rebirth we can see in this world is birth as an animal. There are three more classes of woeful planes, which we cannot see; they are the world of petas (ghosts), the world of asuras (demons), and the hell planes. There are different kinds of hell planes because there are many degrees of akusala kamma which produce different kinds of unhappy rebirth.

The function of paṭisandhi can be performed by different types of vipākacittas which are the results of different kammas. It depends on kamma which type of vipākacitta performs the function of paṭisandhi in the case of a particular being. The paṭisandhi-citta, the first citta in life, does not arise within a sense-door process or a mind-door process of cittas experiencing an object which impinges on one of the six doors. It merely performs the function of rebirth.

There are two ahetuka vipākacittas which can perform the function of paṭisandhi, namely: santīraṇa akusala vipākacitta and santīraṇa kusala vipākacitta. As we have seen (in chapter 9), santīraṇa-citta is an ahetuka vipākacitta. When santīraṇa-citta arises in a sense-door process of cittas experiencing an object through one of the five senses, it performs the function of investigating (santīraṇa) the object. However, santīraṇa-citta can also perform the function of rebirth, and this is the case when the paṭisandhi-citta is ahetuka vipāka. The same type of citta can perform more than one function, but at different moments and at different occasions. When santīraṇa-citta performs the function of paṭisandhi it does not arise in a sense-door process and it does not investigate an object.

As we have seen (in chapter 9), there are three kinds of santīraṇa-citta:

1. Santīraṇa-citta which is akusala vipāka, accompanied by upekkhā (indifferent feeling)
2. Santīraṇa-citta which is kusala vipāka, accompanied by upekkhā
3. Santīraṇa-citta which is kusala vipāka, accompanied by somanassa (pleasant feeling)

The santīraṇa-citta which is akusala vipāka, accompanied by upekkhā, can perform the function of paṭisandhi in woeful planes. This means that the type of paṭisandhi-citta arising in woeful planes is of the same type as the akusala vipākacitta which is santīraṇa-citta performing the function of investigating in a sense-door process of cittas.

The santīraṇa-citta which is kusala vipāka, accompanied by upekkhā, can, apart from the function of investigating in a sense-door process, also perform the function of paṭisandhi in the human plane and in the lowest heavenly plane.

The santīraṇa-citta which is kusala vipāka, accompanied by somanassa, does not perform the function of paṭisandhi.

Akusala kamma and kusala kamma of different beings can produce nineteen different types of paṭisandhi-citta in all, arising in different planes of existence. One of these types is akusala vipāka and eighteen types are kusala vipāka. Of the types of citta which are kusala vipāka, one type is ahetuka kusala vipāka and seventeen types are sahetuka kusala vipāka (accompanied by beautiful roots). There are many degrees of each of these nineteen types of paṭisandhi-citta because kamma can be of many degrees. It is due to kamma that people are born ugly or beautiful and that they are born in unpleasant or in pleasant surroundings. The fact that one is born into miserable circumstances does not mean that one's next birth will also be into miserable circumstances. It all depends on the kamma which has been accumulated and which produces result. As regards people who are born into happy circumstances, if akusala kamma produces their next birth, this will be an unhappy one.

We read in the Gradual Sayings (Book of the Fours, chapter IX, paragraph 5, Darkness):

> Monks, these four persons are found existing in the world. What four?
>
> He who is in darkness and bound for darkness; he who is in darkness but bound for light; he who is in light but bound for darkness; he who is in light and bound for light.
>
> And how, monks, is a person in darkness bound for darkness?
>
> In this case a certain person is born in a low family, the family of a scavenger or a hunter or a basket-weaver or wheelwright or sweeper, or in the family of some wretched man hard put to it to find a meal or earn a living, where food and clothes are hard to get. Moreover, he is ill-favoured, ugly, dwarfish, sickly, purblind, crooked, lame or paralysed, with never a bite or sup, without clothes, vehicle, without perfumes or flower-garlands, bed, dwelling or lights. He lives in the practice of evil with body, speech and thought; and so doing, when body breaks up, after death, he is reborn in the waste, the way of woe, the downfall, in hell. Thus, monks, is the person who is in darkness and bound for darkness.
>
> And how, monks, is a person in darkness but bound for light?
>
> In this case a certain person is born in a low family. . . without bed, dwelling or lights. He lives in the practice of good with body, speech and thought. . . and so doing, when body breaks up, after death he is reborn in the happy bourn, in the heaven-world.
>
> And how, monks, is a person in light but bound for darkness?
>
> In this case a certain person is born in a high family. . .
>
> And that man is well-built, comely and charming, possessed of supreme beauty of form. He is one able to get clothes, vehicle, perfumes and flower-garlands, bed, dwelling and lights. But he lives in the practice of evil with body, speech and thought. So doing, when body breaks up, after death he is reborn in the waste, the way of woe, the downfall, in hell. Thus, monks, is the person who is in light but bound for darkness.

And how, monks, is a person who is in light and bound for light?

In this case a person is born in a high family. . . able to get clothes. . . bed, dwelling and lights. He lives in the practice of good with body, speech and thought. So doing, when body breaks up after death, he is reborn in the happy bourn, in the heaven-world. Thus, monks, is one who is in light and bound for light.

These, monks, are the four persons found existing in the world.

The kusala kamma producing a paṭisandhi-citta which is sahetuka vipāka (with beautiful roots) is of a higher degree than the kusala kamma producing an ahetuka paṭisandhi-citta. Kāmāvacara kusala kammas (kusala kammas of the "sense sphere") can produce eight different types of sahetuka vipākacittas which can perform the function of paṭisandhi. Which type of vipākacitta performs this function in the case of a particular being depends on the kusala kamma which produces it.

People are born with different characters and with different capacities; they are born with different degrees of wisdom or without wisdom. The paṭisandhi-cittas of people are different. When the paṭisandhi-citta is sahetuka, it is always accompanied by alobha (non-attachment or generosity) and adosa (non-aversion or kindness), but not always by wisdom. It can be accompanied by wisdom or it can be without wisdom, depending on the kamma which produces it. When the paṭisandhi-citta is accompanied by wisdom, one is born with three sobhana hetus (beautiful roots): alobha, adosa and paññā. Someone who is born with wisdom is more inclined to develop wisdom in the course of his life than someone who is born without wisdom. Those who are born with a paṭisandhi-citta accompanied by wisdom can attain enlightenment if they cultivate the eightfold Path. If one is born without wisdom one can still develop right understanding, but in that life one cannot attain enlightenment. Thus we see that everything in our life depends on conditions.

Apart from the difference in the number of roots (two hetus or three hetus) which accompany the sahetuka paṭisandhi-citta there are other differences. Kusala kamma which produces the paṭisandhi-citta can be kamma performed by kusala citta with somanassa, pleasant feeling, or with upekkhā, indifferent feeling; by kusala citta which is "unprompted" (not induced, asaṅkhārika) or by kusala citta which is "prompted" (induced, sasaṅkhārika)[1]. Several factors determine the nature of kusala kamma which produces its result accordingly. The sahetuka paṭisandhi-cittas which are the results of kāmāvacara kusala kammas can be classified as eight different types in all. Summing them up they are:

1. Accompanied by pleasant feeling, with wisdom, unprompted. (Somanassa-sahagataṃ, ñāṇa-sampayuttaṃ, asaṅkhārikam ekaṃ[2]).
2. Accompanied by pleasant feeling, with wisdom, prompted. (Somanassa-sahagataṃ, ñāṇa-sampayuttaṃ, sasaṅkhārikam ekaṃ).

---

[1] See Ch. 4. Kusala cittas can arise unprompted, spontaneously, or prompted, induced either by someone else or by one's own deliberation.

[2] Ñāṇa is wisdom (paññā).

3. Accompanied by pleasant feeling, without wisdom, unprompted. (Somanassa-sahagataṃ, ñāṇa-vippayuttaṃ, asaṅkhārikam ekaṃ).
4. Accompanied by pleasant feeling, without wisdom, prompted. (Somanassa-sahagataṃ, ñāṇa-vippayuttaṃ, sasaṅkhārikam ekaṃ).
5. Accompanied by indifferent feeling, with wisdom, unprompted. (Upekkhā-sahagataṃ, ñāṇa-sampayuttaṃ, asaṅkhārikam ekaṃ).
6. Accompanied by indifferent feeling, with wisdom, prompted. (Upekkhā-sahagataṃ, ñāṇa-sampayuttaṃ, sasaṅkhārikam ekaṃ).
7. Accompanied by indifferent feeling, without wisdom, unprompted. (Upekkhā-sahagataṃ, ñāṇa-vippayuttaṃ, asaṅkhārikam ekaṃ). Accompanied by indifferent feeling, without wisdom, prompted. (Upekkhā-sahagataṃ, ñāṇa-vippayuttaṃ, sasaṅkhārikam ekaṃ).

It is useful to know more details about paṭisandhi-citta, because it can help us to understand why people are so different. The eight types of sahetuka paṭisandhi-citta which are the results of kāmāvacara kusala kammas do not arise only in the human plane, but they also arise in those heavenly planes of existence which are "sensuous" planes of existence, *kāma-bhūmi*.

Eleven planes are kāma-bhūmis (or kāma-lokas), sensuous planes of existence, and of these one is the plane of human beings, six are heavenly planes and four are woeful planes. Beings born in one of the kāma-bhūmis receive sense impressions, they have kāmāvacara cittas. There are also higher heavenly planes which are not kāma-bhūmi. There are thirty-one classes of planes of existence in all[3].

If one is born in one of the kāma-bhūmis and cultivates jhāna, absorption, one can, besides kāmāvacara cittas, also have rūpa-jhānacittas and arūpa-jhānacittas[4]. If one cultivates the eightfold Path one can have lokuttara cittas, supramundane cittas which directly experience nibbāna.

When someone attains jhāna, the kusala kamma he performs is not kāmāvacara kusala kamma; at the moment of jhāna there are no sense impressions. The kusala kamma which is jhāna does not produce result in the same lifespan one attains it, but it can produce result in the form of paṭisandhi-citta, the paṭisandhi-citta of the next life. In that case there are jhānacittas arising shortly before death and the paṭisandhi-citta of the next life experiences the same object as those jhānacittas.

The result of rūpāvacara kusala citta (kusala citta which is rūpa-jhānacitta) is birth in a heavenly plane which is not kāma-bhūmi but a rūpa-brahma-plane (fine-material world). The result of an arūpāvacara kusala citta (kusala citta which is arūpa-jhānacitta) is birth in a heavenly plane which is an arūpa-brahma plane (immaterial world). There are different rūpa-brahma-planes and arūpa-brahma planes.

There are five stages of rūpa-jhāna and thus there are five types of rūpāvacara kusala citta which can produce five types of rūpāvacara vipākacitta. There are four stages of arūpa-jhāna and thus there are four types of arūpāvacara kusala citta which

---

3 This will be explained in chapter 20, Planes of Existence.

4 For the difference between rūpa-jhāna, fine-material jhāna, and arūpa-jhāna, immaterial jhāna, see chapter 22.

can produce four types of arūpāvacara vipākacitta. Therefore, there are five types of paṭisandhi-citta which are the results of rūpāvacara kusala cittas and four types of paṭisandhi-citta which are the results of arūpāvacara kusala cittas. Altogether there are nine types of paṭisandhi-citta which are the results of the different types of jhānacittas. They are sahetuka vipākacittas and they are always accompanied by paññā.

Summarising the nineteen types of paṭisandhi-citta:

- 1 akusala vipāka santīraṇa-citta (ahetuka, result of akusala kamma)
- 1 kusala vipāka santīraṇa-citta (ahetuka, result of kāmāvacara kusala kamma)
- 8 mahā-vipākacittas (sahetuka, results of kāmāvacara kusala kammas)[5]
- 5 rūpāvacara vipākacittas (sahetuka, results of rūpa-jhānacittas)
- 4 arūpāvacara vipākacittas (sahetuka, results of arūpa-jhānacittas)

We do not know which of our deeds will produce the paṭisandhi-citta of our next life. Even a deed performed in a former life can produce the paṭisandhi-citta of the next life. The Buddha encouraged people to perform many kinds of kusala kamma. Each good deed is very valuable; it is certain to bear its fruit sooner or later. We read in As it was said (Khuddaka Nikāya, "Itivuttaka", the Ones, chapter III, paragraph 6) about the value of generosity. The Buddha said to the monks:

> Monks, if beings knew, as I know, the ripening of sharing gifts they would not enjoy their use without sharing them, nor would the taint of stinginess obsess the heart and stay there. Even if it were their last bit, their last morsel of food, they would not enjoy its use without sharing it, if there were anyone to receive it. . .

Kusala kamma can cause a happy rebirth, but the end of birth is to be preferred to any kind of rebirth. If one cultivates the eightfold Path and attains arahatship there will be no more rebirth. The dying-consciousness (cuti-citta) of the arahat is not succeeded by a paṭisandhi-citta. The Buddha reminded people of the dangers of birth and encouraged them to be mindful, in order to attain the "deathless" which is nibbāna. We read in the Gradual Sayings (Book of the Eights, chapter VIII, paragraph 4) that the Buddha, when he was staying at Nādika, in the Brick Hall, said to the monks:

> Mindfulness of death, monks, when made become, when developed is very fruitful, of great advantage, merging and ending in the deathless.
>
> And how, monks, is it so. . . ?
>
> Take the case of a monk, who, when the day declines and night sets in, reflects thus: "Many indeed are the chances of death for me. A snake or scorpion or a centipede might bite me and might cause my death; that would be a hindrance to me. I might stumble and fall; the food I have eaten might make me ill; bile might convulse me; phlegm choke me; winds (within me) with their scissor-like cuts give me ache; or men or non-humans might attack me and might cause my death. That would be a hindrance to me."

---

[5] The terms mahā-kusala, mahā-vipāka and mahā-kiriya are used for kāmāvacara cittas.

Monks, that monk must reflect thus: "Are there any evil and wrong states within me that have not been put away and that would be a hindrance to me were I to die tonight?" If, monks, on consideration he realize that there are such states. . . then to put away just those evil and wrong states, an intense resolution, effort, endeavour, exertion, struggle, mindfulness and self-possession must be made by that monk.

Monks, just as a man whose turban is on fire, or whose hair is burning, would make an intense resolution, effort, endeavour, exertion, struggle, mindfulness and self-possession to put out his (burning) turban or hair; even so, monks, an intense resolution, effort, endeavour, exertion, struggle, mindfulness and self-possession must be made by that monk to put away just those evil and wrong states.

But if that monk, on review, realize that there are no such states within him that have not been put away which would be a hindrance to him, were he to die that night – then let that monk live verily in joy and gladness, training himself day and night in the ways of righteousness.

Take the case, monks, of a monk who reflects likewise. . . when the night is spent and day breaks. He must reflect in the same way. . .

Monks, mindfulness of death when so made become, so developed is very fruitful, of great advantage, merging and ending in the deathless.

Questions

1. Can the paṭisandhi-citta be ahetuka?
2. How many types of paṭisandhi-citta are there?
3. How many types of paṭisandhi-citta are akusala vipāka?
4. When the paṭisandhi-citta is accompanied by wisdom, by which factor is this conditioned?

12 The Function of Bhavanga (Life-Continuum)

There are moments when there are no sense-impressions, when one does not think, when there are no akusala cittas or kusala cittas. Is there at those moments still citta? Even when there are no sense-impressions and no thinking there must be citta; otherwise there would be no life. The type of citta which arises and falls away at those moments is called bhavanga-citta. *Bhavanga* literally means "factor of life"; bhavanga is usually translated into English as "life-continuum". The bhavanga-citta keeps the continuity in a lifespan, so that what we call a "being" goes on to live from moment to moment. That is the function of the bhavanga-citta.

One may wonder whether bhavanga-cittas often arise. There must be countless bhavanga-cittas arising at those moments when there are no sense-impressions, no thinking, no akusala cittas or kusala cittas. When we are asleep and dreaming akusala cittas and kusala cittas arise, but even when we are in a dreamless sleep there still has to be citta. There are bhavanga-cittas at such moments. Also when we are awake countless bhavanga-cittas arise; they arise in between the different processes of citta. It seems that hearing, for example, can arise very shortly after seeing, but in reality there are different processes of citta and in between these processes bhavanga-cittas arise.

The bhavanga-citta succeeds the first citta in life, the paṭisandhi-citta, rebirth-consciousness. When the rebirth-consciousness falls away it conditions the arising of the next citta, the second citta in that life and this is the first bhavanga-citta in life.

The bhavanga-citta is vipākacitta; it is the result of the same kamma which produced the paṭisandhi-citta. There is only one paṭisandhi-citta in a life, but there are countless bhavanga-cittas. Not only the first bhavanga-citta, but all bhavanga-cittas arising during a lifespan are the result of the kamma which produced the paṭisandhi-citta.

The bhavanga-citta is the same type of citta as the paṭisandhi-citta. There are nineteen types of paṭisandhi-citta and thus there are nineteen types of bhavanga-citta. If the paṭisandhi-citta is akusala vipāka, which is the case when there is birth in a woeful plane, all bhavanga-cittas of that life are akusala vipāka as well. If the paṭisandhi-citta is ahetuka kusala vipāka, in which case one is handicapped from the first moment of life, all bhavanga-cittas of that life are ahetuka kusala vipāka as well. If the paṭisandhi-citta is sahetuka (arising with sobhana hetus, beautiful roots), the bhavanga-citta is sahetuka as well. All bhavanga-cittas during a lifespan are of the same type as the paṭisandhi-citta of that life, they arise with the same hetus, they are accompanied by the same cetasikas, mental factors. If one is born with two hetus, with alobha (non-attachment) and adosa (non-aversion), but without wisdom, then all bhavanga-cittas have only two hetus. Such a person can cultivate wisdom, but he cannot become enlightened during that life. If one is born with three hetus, which means that one is born with alobha, adosa and paññā (wisdom), all bhavanga-cittas are accompanied by these three sobhana hetus as well. Thus that person is more inclined to cultivate wisdom and, if he develops the eightfold Path, he can attain enlightenment during that life. If one is born with somanassa, happy feeling, all bhavanga-cittas of that life are accompanied by somanassa.

Every citta must experience an object and thus the bhavanga-citta too experiences an object. Seeing has what is visible as object; hearing has sound as object. The bhavanga-citta does not arise within a process of cittas and thus it has an object which is different from the objects which present themselves time and again and are experienced through the sense-doors and through the mind-door. The bhavanga-citta which is of the same type of citta as the paṭisandhi-citta also experiences the same object as the paṭisandhi-citta.

As we have seen (in chapter 10), the paṭisandhi-citta experiences the same object as the akusala cittas or kusala cittas which arose shortly before the dying-consciousness, cuti-citta, of the previous life. If akusala kamma produces the rebirth of the next life there will be an unhappy rebirth. In that case akusala cittas arise shortly before the dying-consciousness and they experience an unpleasant object. The paṭisandhi-citta of the next life which succeeds the cuti-citta (the dying-consciousness), experiences that same unpleasant object. If kusala kamma produces the rebirth there will be a happy rebirth. In that case kusala cittas arise shortly before the cuti-citta and they experience a pleasant object. The paṭisandhi-citta of the next life experiences that same pleasant object. Whatever object is experienced by the last kusala cittas or akusala cittas of the previous life, the paṭisandhi-citta experiences that same object. The paṭisandhi-citta is succeeded by the first bhavanga-citta of that life and this citta experiences the same object as the paṭisandhi-citta. Moreover, all bhavanga-cittas of that life experience that same object.

The Visuddhimagga (XIV, 114) states with regard to the bhavanga-citta:

When the paṭisandhi-citta has ceased, then, following on whatever kind of rebirth-consciousness it may be, the same kinds, being the result of the same kamma whatever it may be, occur as bhavanga-citta with that same object; and again those same kinds. And as long as there is no other kind of arising of consciousness to interrupt the continuity, they also go on occurring endlessly in periods of dreamless sleep, etc., like the current of a river.

The bhavanga-cittas are like the current of a river and this current is interrupted when an object presents itself through one of the senses or through the mind-door. When the cittas of the sense-door process or the mind-door process have fallen away, the current of bhavanga-cittas is resumed.

When an object contacts one of the five senses the stream of bhavanga-cittas is interrupted and there is a sense-cognition. However, there cannot be a sense-cognition immediately. When sound, for example, impinges on the earsense, there is not immediately hearing. There are still some bhavanga-cittas arising and falling away before the pañca-dvārāvajjana-citta (five-door-adverting consciousness) adverts to the sound through the ear-door and hearing arises. The bhavanga-cittas do not perform the function of adverting to the sound which contacts the earsense, they do not experience the sound. They have their own function which is keeping the continuity in a lifespan, and they experience their own object which is the same as the object of the paṭisandhi-citta. Although the bhavanga-citta does not experience the sound which contacts the earsense, it can be affected, "disturbed" by it and then the stream of bhavanga-cittas will be interrupted and sound will be experienced by cittas which arise in the ear-door process. One may wonder how the bhavanga-citta which experiences its own object can still be "affected" by an object which impinges on one of the doorways. Each citta can experience only one object at a time but the bhavanga-citta can still be affected by an object which impinges on one of the doorways. A commentary to the Visuddhimagga, the Paramattha-Mañjūsa, (478; see Visuddhimagga XIV, 115, footnote 46) explains this by way of a simile:

...But how does there come to be disturbance (movement) of the bhavanga that has a different support? Because it is connected with it. And here the example is this: when grains of sugar are put on the surface of a drum and one of the grains of sugar is tapped, a fly sitting on another grain of sugar moves.

When a rūpa which is one of the sense objects contacts one of the senses, there is first one moment of bhavanga-citta arising and falling away which is denoted by the name atīta-bhavanga or "past bhavanga". This citta is succeeded by the bhavanga-calana or "vibrating bhavanga". It is called "vibrating bhavanga" because it is disturbed by the object, although it does not experience that object. The last bhavanga-citta which arises before the stream of bhavanga-cittas is interrupted and the pañca-dvārāvajjana-citta adverts to the object, is the bhavangupaccheda or "arrest-bhavanga", so called because the stream of bhavanga-cittas is arrested after this citta.

The different names which denote these bhavanga-cittas do not represent different functions; bhavanga-cittas have as their only function to keep the continuity in the life of a being. The different names only indicate that these bhavanga-cittas are the last ones before the stream is interrupted and a new object which impinges on one of the doorways is experienced by a process of cittas. When the bhavangupaccheda, the arrest-bhavanga, has arisen and fallen away, a sense-door process of cittas which experience an object through one of the sense-doors can begin. When the sense-door process is over, the stream of bhavanga-cittas is resumed, so that the series of cittas succeeding one another in our life is not interrupted. The object which impinged on one of the senses is then experienced through the mind-door. In between the sense-door process and the mind-door process, however, there are bhavanga-cittas. When the cittas of the mind-door process have fallen away, the stream of bhavanga-cittas is resumed.

A sense object which is experienced through one of the five senses is rūpa. Rūpa arises and falls away, but it does not fall away as rapidly as nāma. One rūpa which impinges on one of the senses, can be experienced by several cittas succeeding one another in a process. When, for example, the rūpa which is sound impinges on the earsense, it can be experienced by cittas arising in the ear-door process. Before the process starts there are bhavanga-cittas. The last bhavanga-cittas which arise before the sound can be experienced by the cittas of the ear-door process are:

- atīta-bhavanga (past bhavanga)
- bhavanga-calana (vibrating bhavanga)
- bhavangupaccheda (arrest-bhavanga)

When the stream of bhavanga-cittas has been arrested, the ear-door-adverting-consciousness (sota-dvārāvajjana-citta) adverts to the object through the ear-door.

The following cittas in that process which each perform their own function can experience the sound before it falls away. The duration of one material unit, a rūpa, has been determined by the commentaries as seventeen moments of citta. The number seventeen should be seen as a comparative notion which is expressed here[1]. The cittas in a complete sense-door process of cittas, including three bhavanga-cittas which arise before the impinging rūpa is experienced, are seventeen in number. Later on (in chapter 15) I will deal in more detail with all the cittas arising in a process. Within this process each citta performs its own function while they experience a rūpa which has not fallen away yet. Therefore, the duration of a rūpa has been counted as seventeen moments of citta which succeed one another in a process[2]. We cannot count these moments, we cannot imagine the shortness of time of a process of cittas; one citta lasts shorter than a flash of lightning.

A process of cittas does not always run its full course. When a rūpa impinges on one of the senses, it may happen that more than one moment of bhavanga-citta passes before the bhavanga-calana, which precedes the bhavangupaccheda; in that case the rūpa which has impinged on one of the senses does not survive until the process is completed since it cannot last longer than seventeen moments of citta. A process can, after it has started, be interrupted, for example, after the votthapana-citta (determining-consciousness), and then there are no kusala cittas or akusala cittas in that process[3]. It may also happen that the atīta-bhavanga is succeeded by the bhavanga-calana which is "disturbed" by the object, but that the rūpa then falls away. In that case there is no bhavangupaccheda (arrest-bhavanga); the stream of bhavanga-cittas is not interrupted and the sense-door process cannot start. Sound may, for example, impinge on the earsense and then the atīta-bhavanga is succeeded by the bhavanga-calana. However, the bhavangupaccheda does not arise and thus the current of bhavanga-cittas is not interrupted and the ear-door process cannot start. In that case the sound cannot be heard.

When a sense-door process of cittas begins, the rūpa which has impinged on that sense-door is experienced. When the sense-door process of cittas which experience a rūpa such as visible object or sound is over, that object has also fallen away. Cittas succeed one another extremely rapidly and very shortly after the sense-door process of cittas is over, a mind-door process of cittas begins. The cittas of the mind-door process which follows upon the sense-door process experience through the mind-door the rūpa which has just fallen away. Before the mind-door process begins, however, there are bhavanga-cittas. Bhavanga-cittas arise in between the different processes of cittas. The last two bhavanga-cittas arising before the mano-dvārāvajjana-citta, the mind-door-adverting consciousness, are the bhavanga-

---

[1] See Ven. Nyanaponika, "Abhidhamma Studies", The Problem of Time.

[2] The commentaries count the duration of rūpa as sixteen or seventeen moments of citta. Although the scriptures do not expressively mention these numbers, they refer to the different cittas in processes which each perform their own function while they experience an object, as I explained in my preface.

[3] According to the Atthasālinī II, Book I , Part X, Ch 2, 269, the object is in that case weak.

calana (vibrating bhavanga) and the bhavangupaccheda (arrest-bhavanga)[4]. Then the mano-dvārāvajjana-citta adverts to the object through the mind-door and it is succeeded by seven kusala cittas or akusala cittas (in the case of non-arahats)[5].

Summarising these cittas, they are:

1. bhavanga-calana (vibrating bhavanga), bhavangupaccheda (arrest-bhavanga)
2. mano-dvārāvajjana-citta (mind-door-adverting-consciousness)
3. seven akusala or kusala cittas (or, for the arahat: kiriyacittas)

When the mind-door process is over, the stream of bhavanga-cittas is resumed until there is again a process of cittas experiencing an object through one of the sense-doors or through the mind-door. There are countless bhavanga-cittas arising throughout our life in between the processes of cittas experiencing an object through one of the sense-doors or through the mind-door.

What is the mind-door? It is different from the sense-doors. A "doorway" is the means through which citta experiences an object. The sense-doors are the following rūpas: eyesense, earsense, smellingsense, tastingsense and bodysense. Bodysense is all over the body. These rūpas are the means through which a sense object is experienced. The mind-door is not one of these rūpas. In order to understand what the mind-door is we should consider what the first citta of the mind-door process is. This citta which performs the function of adverting to the object is the mano-dvārāvajjana-citta, the mind-door-adverting-consciousness. It does not advert to the object through one of the five senses but through the mind-door. The mind-door must be nāma, it is a citta. The citta which precedes the mano-dvārāvajjana-citta is the mind-door, it is the means through which the cittas of the mind-door process, beginning with the mano-dvārāvajjana-citta, receive the object. The citta which precedes the mano-dvārāvajjana-citta is the bhavangupaccheda and this citta is the mind-door. It is the mind-door through which the mano-dvārāvajjana-citta adverts to the object and it is also the doorway for the succeeding cittas of that process.

The study of the different sense-door processes and mind-door processes which take their course according to conditions will help us to see realities as elements which are devoid of self, beyond control. We may, for example, be infatuated with a beautiful sound we hear. What we take for a long time of hearing are many different moments of citta which do not last. Even when we do not know yet the origin of the sound, what kind of sound it is, sound has already been experienced through the mind-door since cittas succeed one another extremely rapidly, arising and falling away. Sound does not stay either, it falls away.

We read in the Kindred Sayings (IV, Saḷāyatana-vagga, Kindred Sayings on Sense, Fourth Fifty, chapter V, paragraph 205, The Lute) that the Buddha said to the monks:

> ...Suppose, monks, the sound of a lute has never been heard by a rājah or royal minister. Then he hears the sound of a lute and says: "Good

[4] The atīta bhavanga, which is merely one moment of bhavanga which elapses before the bhavanga calana and the subsequent bhavangupaccheda preceding a sense-door process, is not counted again before the mind-door process starts.

[5] I will explain in more detail about these cittas in Chapter 14.

men, pray, what is that sound so entrancing, so delightful, so intoxicating, so ravishing, of such power to bind?"

Then they say to him: "That, lord, is the sound of what is called a lute, that sound so entrancing, so delightful, so intoxicating, so ravishing, of such power to bind."

Then he says: "Go, my men. Fetch me that lute."

So they fetch him that lute and say to him: "This, lord, is that lute, the sound of which is so entrancing. . . of such power to bind."

Then he says: "Enough of this lute, my men. Fetch me that sound."

They say to him: "This lute so called, lord, consists of divers parts, a great number of parts. It speaks because it is compounded of divers parts, to wit, owing to the belly, owing to the parchment, the handle, the frame, the strings, owing to the bridge and proper effort of a player. Thus, lord, this lute, so called, consists of divers parts, of a great number of parts. It speaks because it is compounded of divers parts."

Then that rājah breaks up that lute into ten or a hundred pieces. Having done so, he splinters and splinters it again. Having done so, he burns it in fire, then makes it a heap of ashes and winnows the heap of ashes in a strong wind or lets them be borne down by the swift stream of a river.

Then he says: "A poor thing is what you call a lute, my men, whatever a lute may be. Herein the world is exceeding careless and led astray."

Even so, monks, a monk investigating body as far as there is scope for body, investigating feeling, perception, the activities (saṅkhārakkhandha), investigating consciousness, so far as there is scope for consciousness – in all of these investigations, whatever there be of "I" or "I am" or "Mine", there is none of that for him.

Questions

1. At which moments do bhavanga-cittas arise?
2. When did the first bhavanga-citta in life arise?
3. Can bhavanga-citta be ahetuka?
4. Can bhavanga-citta be accompanied by wisdom?

13 Functions of Citta

Each citta has its own function to perform; no citta arises without performing a function. For example, seeing and hearing are functions performed by citta. We are not used to considering seeing and hearing as functions, because we cling to a self. If we want to know more about cittas we should learn about their different functions (in Pāli: *kicca*).

The function performed by the first citta in life is the function of paṭisandhi (rebirth or "relinking"). The paṭisandhi-citta is succeeded by the bhavanga-citta (life-continuum). The function of bhavanga, life-continuum, is the second function of citta. The bhavanga-citta keeps the continuity in a lifespan. So long as one is still alive bhavanga-cittas arise and fall away during the time there is no sense-door process or mind-door process of cittas. Bhavanga-cittas arise in between the different processes of cittas which experience an object through one of the six doors. For example, seeing and thinking about what was seen arise in different processes of citta and there have to be bhavanga-cittas in between the different processes.

When a rūpa impinges on one of the senses the current of bhavanga-cittas is interrupted; there are a few more bhavanga-cittas arising and falling away, and then the five-door-adverting consciousness, the pañca-dvārāvajjana-citta, arises. The pañca-dvārāvajjana-citta is the first citta in the process of cittas experiencing the rūpa which has come into contact with one of the senses.

The pañca-dvārāvajjana-citta performs the function of āvajjana or adverting to the object which impinges on one of the five senses; it adverts to the object through that sense-door. The pañca-dvārāvajjana-citta is an ahetuka kiriyacitta.

The Visuddhimagga (XIV, 107) states concerning the pañca-dvārāvajjana-citta (mind-element):

> Herein, the mind-element has the characteristic of being the forerunner of eye-consciousness, etc., and cognizing visible data, and so on. Its function is to advert. It is manifested as confrontation of visible data, and so on. Its proximate cause is the interruption of (the continued occurrence of consciousness as) life-continuum (bhavanga). It is associated with equanimity (upekkhā) only.

The pañca-dvārāvajjana-citta is the "forerunner" because it arises before seeing, hearing and the other sense-cognitions (pañca-viññāṇa). When it adverts to an object which has contacted the eye-sense, it adverts through the eye-door and it is eye-door-adverting-consciousness (cakkhu-dvārāvajjana-citta). When it adverts to an object which has contacted the ear-sense it is the ear-door-adverting-consciousness (sota-dvārāvajjana-citta). The pañca-dvārāvajjana-citta is named after the sense-door through which it adverts to the object. The pañca-dvārāvajjana-citta arises countless times a day, but we do not notice it. Whenever there is seeing, the eye-door-adverting-consciousness has adverted already to the visible object which has impinged on the eyesense, and it has fallen away already. Whenever there is hearing or any one of the other pañca-viññāṇas, the pañca-dvārāvajjana-citta has adverted to the object already and it has fallen away.

The pañca-dvārāvajjana-citta is succeeded by the other cittas of the sense-door process which experience that same object. When that process is over, the object is experienced through the mind-door. First there are bhavanga-cittas and then the mano-dvārāvajjana-citta (mind-door-adverting-consciousness) performs the function of āvajjana, adverting, through the mind-door.

Thus there are two types of citta which perform the function of adverting (āvajjana-kicca) these are: the pañca-dvārāvajjana-citta which adverts to the object through one of the five sense-doors and the mano-dvārāvajjana-citta which adverts to the object through the mind-door. The mano-dvārāvajjana-citta is an ahetuka kiriyacitta; it is not accompanied by unwholesome roots (akusala hetus) or beautiful roots (sobhana hetus). After it has adverted to the object it is followed by kusala cittas or by akusala cittas.

When visible object contacts the eye-sense the eye-door-adverting-consciousness (cakkhu-dvārāvajjana-citta) adverts to visible object through the eye-door. When the eye-door-adverting-consciousness has fallen away it is succeeded by seeing-consciousness (cakkhu-viññāṇa). The function of seeing (in Pāli: dassana-kicca) is performed by seeing-consciousness. Seeing is vipāka; it is the result of kusala kamma or akusala kamma. We are born to receive the results of our deeds: we see, hear and experience objects through the other senses.

The citta which performs the function of seeing only sees visible object. This citta does not like or dislike, it is an ahetuka vipākacitta. Neither does it think about the object. If one does not develop right understanding one does not realize that the citta which only sees visible object is a reality different from the citta which likes or dislikes the visible object and different from the citta which pays attention to shape and form. Because of our accumulated ignorance and wrong view we do not realize the impermanence of citta which falls away as soon as it has arisen and which is succeeded by another citta which is a different reality.

There are only two kinds of citta which can perform the function of seeing: one is akusala vipāka and one is kusala vipāka.

When sound has impinged on the earsense and the ear-door-adverting-consciousness has arisen and fallen away, hearing-consciousness arises. The function of hearing (in Pāli: savana-kicca) is another function of citta. Hearing is ahetuka vipāka. Two kinds of citta can perform the function of hearing: one is akusala vipāka and one is kusala vipāka.

Another function of citta is the function of smelling (in Pāli: ghāyana-kicca). Two kinds of citta which are both ahetuka vipāka can perform this function: one is akusala vipāka and one is kusala vipāka.

There are two kinds of ahetuka vipākacitta which can perform the function of tasting (in Pāli: sāyana kicca): one is akusala vipāka and one is kusala vipāka. When the citta which performs this function tastes, for example, a sweet or a salty flavour, it merely experiences that flavour; it does not know the name of the flavour. The cittas which know the conventional name of the flavour arise later on.

The function of experiencing tangible object through the bodysense (in Pāli: phusana-kicca) is another function of citta. When an object contacts the bodysense, the pañca-dvārāvajjana-citta adverts to the object through the doorway of the bodysense. It is succeeded by body-consciousness (kāya-viññāṇa) which performs the function of experiencing tangible object through the bodysense. Two kinds of citta which are both ahetuka vipāka can perform this function: one is akusala vipāka and one is kusala vipāka. The objects experienced by kāya-viññāṇa are the following rūpas:

- solidity (experienced as hardness or softness)
- temperature (experienced as heat or cold)
- motion (experienced as oscillation or pressure)

These objects are experienced through the doorway of the bodysense, which is rūpa. This rūpa, which has the capacity to receive bodily impressions, is all over the body, except in those parts where there is no sensitivity.

Thus, summarising the functions performed by the cittas which are the pañca-viññāṇas, they are:

- the function of seeing (dassana-kicca)
- the function of hearing (savana-kicca)
- the function of smelling (ghāyana-kicca)
- the function of tasting (sāyana-kicca)
- the function of experiencing tangible object (phusana kicca)

Seeing, hearing, smelling, tasting and experiencing tangible object are different functions, not performed by a self but by citta. These cittas arise because of their appropriate conditions. In order to remind people of this truth the Buddha explained how cittas experience objects through the five senses and through the mind-door. He pointed out the different conditions for the arising of cittas and the impermanence of these conditions. Since the conditions for the arising of cittas are impermanent, cittas cannot be permanent.

We read in the Kindred Sayings (IV, Saḷāyatana-vagga, Kindred Sayings on Sense, Second Fifty, chapter IV, paragraph 93, Duality II) that the Buddha said to the monks:

> Owing to a dual (thing), monks, consciousness comes into being. And what, monks, is that dual owing to which consciousness comes into being?
>
> Owing to the eye and objects arises eye-consciousness. The eye is impermanent, changing, its state is "becoming otherness". So also are objects. Thus this dual, mobile and transitory, impermanent, changing, – its state is "becoming otherness".
>
> Eye-consciousness is impermanent, changing, its state is "becoming otherness". That condition, that relation of the uprising of eye-consciousness, – they also are impermanent, changing, their state is "becoming otherness". This eye-consciousness, arising as it does from an impermanent relation, – how could it be permanent?
>
> Now the striking together, the falling together, the meeting together of these three things[1], – this, monks, is called "eye-contact". Eye-contact is impermanent, changing, its state is "becoming otherness". That

[1] That is: eye, visible object and eye-consciousness.

> condition, that relation of the uprising of eye-contact – they also are impermanent... This eye-contact, arising as it does from an impermanent relation,-how could it be permanent?
>
> Contacted, monks, one feels. Contacted, one is aware. Contacted, one perceives. Thus these states also are mobile and transitory, impermanent and changing. Their state is "becoming otherness"...

The same is said with regard to the other doorways.

In the process of citta, the pañca-viññāṇa is succeeded by sampaṭicchana-citta. This citta which performs the function of sampaṭicchana, receiving the object, receives the object after the pañca-viññāṇa has fallen away. Sampaṭicchana-citta is ahetuka vipāka. Two kinds of citta can perform this function: one is akusala vipāka and one is kusala vipāka.

Kamma does not only produce the dvi-pañca-viññāṇas (the five pairs) and sampaṭicchana-citta, it also produces santīraṇa-citta (investigating-consciousness) which succeeds sampaṭicchana-citta. Santīraṇa-citta performs in the sense-door process the function of investigating the object, santīraṇa; it is ahetuka vipākacitta. The function of investigating the object is another function of citta, different from seeing, hearing, smelling, tasting, experiencing tangible object through the bodysense and sampaṭicchana, receiving.

As we have seen (in chapter 9), there are three kinds of santīraṇa-citta which can perform the function of investigating:

1. santīraṇa-citta which is akusala vipāka, accompanied by upekkhā
2. santīraṇa-citta which is kusala vipāka, accompanied by upekkhā
3. santīraṇa-citta which is kusala vipāka, accompanied by somanassa (when the object is extraordinarily pleasant)

Santīraṇa-citta is succeeded by votthapana-citta, determining-consciousness. *Votthapana* is another function of citta; the votthapana-citta determines the object in the sense-door process. After it has determined the object it is succeeded by kusala cittas or by akusala cittas. Votthapana-citta is not vipāka, it is not kusala or akusala but it is an ahetuka kiriyacitta. The conditions for its arising are different from the conditions for santīraṇa-citta which is produced by kamma. As we have seen (in Chapter 9), the citta which performs the function of votthapana is the ahetuka kiriyacitta which is classified as mano-dvārāvajjana-citta. The mano-dvārāvajjana-citta performs two functions: in the mind-door process it performs the function of adverting to the object through the mind-door, and in the sense-door process it performs the function of votthapana and then it can be called, after its function, votthapana-citta.

Cittas experience pleasant or unpleasant objects through the senses and through the mind-door. If someone has accumulated a great deal of lobha and dosa, lobha-mūla-cittas are likely to arise when the object is pleasant and dosa-mūla-cittas are likely to arise when the object is unpleasant. At such moments there is "unwise attention" to the object. These cittas arise because of conditions, they are not self, and beyond control.

We are inclined to think that in the process of cittas, akusala vipākacittas which experience an unpleasant object should necessarily be followed by akusala cittas, since we let ourselves be ruled by the objects we experience. However, if there is "wise attention" there is no aversion towards unpleasant objects. Kusala cittas and akusala cittas arise because of conditions which are entirely different from the conditions for vipākacittas. Akusala vipāka and kusala vipāka are the result of kamma. We wish to control our vipāka, but this is impossible. When it is time for akusala vipāka, we cannot prevent it from arising. We should understand that our life is nāma and rūpa, which arise because of conditions and fall away immediately. If we would truly understand vipāka as it is: as only a moment of citta which falls away as soon as it has arisen, we would be less likely to have aversion towards unpleasant objects we experience.

One may wonder whether it is necessary to know in detail about cittas and their functions. Is it not enough to know only about kusala cittas and akusala cittas? Apart from kusala cittas and akusala cittas we should know also about other kinds of cittas which perform different functions in the processes of cittas and which arise because of different conditions. Then there will be more understanding of the fact that there is no self who can direct the arising of particular cittas at particular moments. There is no self who can choose to have kusala cittas. People have different accumulations and thus, when an object presents itself, kusala cittas or akusala cittas will arise in the process of cittas which experience that object, according to one's accumulations. When, for example, different people smell delicious food, some people may have akusala cittas whereas others may have kusala cittas. Those who are attached to food are likely to have lobha-mūla-cittas. In the case of someone who has accumulations for dāna (generosity), kusala cittas may arise when he has smelled the food; he may wish to offer food to the monks. In the case of others again, there may be kusala cittas with paññā which realizes odour, for example, as only a kind of rūpa, not some "thing", impermanent and devoid of a "self".

Through the study of the Dhamma and above all through the development of "insight", right understanding of realities, there can be conditions for kusala cittas and then there is "wise attention" to the object. No matter whether the object is pleasant or unpleasant, in the sense-door process the votthapana-citta can be succeeded by kusala cittas and in the mind-door process the mano-dvārāvajjana-citta can, after it has adverted to the object, be succeeded by kusala cittas. If there can be "wise attention" at this moment, there will be more conditions for "wise attention" in the future.

Kusala cittas and akusala cittas are bound to arise because we have accumulated both kusala and akusala. People are inclined to blame the world for the arising of their defilements because they do not know that defilements are accumulated in the citta; defilements are not in the objects around ourselves. One might wish to be without the six doors in order to have no defilements. However, the only way to eradicate defilements is: knowing the realities which appear through the six doors. We read in the Kindred Sayings (IV, Saḷāyatana-vagga, Kindred Sayings on Sense, Fourth Fifty, chapter III, paragraph 194, On fire) that the Buddha said to the monks:

> I will teach you, monks, a discourse (illustrated) by fire, a Dhamma-discourse. Do you listen to it. And what, monks, is that discourse?
>
> It were a good thing, monks, if the organ of sight were seared with a red-hot iron pin, on fire, all ablaze, a glowing mass of flame. Then would there be no grasping of the marks or details of objects cognizable by the eye. The consciousness might stand fast, being firmly bound by the satisfaction either of the marks or details (of the objects). Should one die at such a time, there is the possibility of his winning one of two destinies, either hell or rebirth in the womb of an animal. Seeing this danger, monks, do I so declare.
>
> It were a good thing, monks, if the organ of hearing were pierced with an iron spike, on fire. . . if the organ of smell were pierced with a sharp claw, on fire. . . if the organ of taste were seared with a sharp razor, on fire. . . if the organ of touch were seared with a sword, on fire. . .
>
> It were a good thing, monks, to be asleep. For sleep, I declare, is barren for living things. It is fruitless for living things, I declare. It is dull for living things, I declare. For (if asleep) one would not be applying his mind to such imaginations as would enslave him, so that (for instance) he would break up the Order. Seeing this danger (of being awake), monks, do I so declare.
>
> As to that, monks, the well-taught ariyan disciple thus reflects:
>
> "Let alone searing the organ of sight with an iron pin, on fire, all ablaze, a glowing mass of flame; what if I thus ponder: Impermanent is the eye, impermanent are objects, impermanent is eye-consciousness, eye-contact, the pleasant or unpleasant or neutral feeling which arises owing to eye-contact, – that also is impermanent. . ."
>
> So seeing, the well-taught ariyan disciple is repelled by the eye, by objects, by eye-consciousness, by eye-contact. He is repelled by that pleasant or unpleasant or neutral feeling that arises owing to eye-contact. . . Being repelled he is dispassionate. Dispassionate, he is set free. By freedom comes the knowledge, "I am freed", so that he realizes: "Destroyed is rebirth. Lived is the righteous life. Done is the task. For life in these conditions there is no hereafter."
>
> Such, monks, is the Dhamma-discourse (illustrated) by fire.

This sutta reminds us to be mindful at this moment, when we are seeing, hearing, smelling, tasting, experiencing objects through the bodysense or through the mind-door. All these moments are functions, performed by different cittas which do not last.

Questions

1. Which citta in a sense-door process determines the object before it is succeeded by akusala cittas or by kusala cittas? Is it accompanied by hetus (roots) or is it ahetuka?
2. Which citta in the mind-door process precedes the kusala cittas or akusala

cittas arising in that process? What is its function?

3. Is the citta which in the mind-door process precedes the kusala cittas or akusala cittas the first citta in that process experiencing the object?
4. Can this citta be accompanied by wisdom?
5. Sound is experienced through the ear-door and through the mind-door. Has the sound fallen away when it is experienced through the mind-door?
6. How many types of citta can perform the function of adverting to the object, āvajjana ?

14 The Function of Javana

When we see, hear, smell, taste, experience an object through the bodysense or through the mind-door, there is not only one citta experiencing the object through the appropriate doorway, but a series or process of cittas. A rūpa which impinges on one of the senses is experienced by a process of cittas. When that sense-door process is over, the object is experienced by cittas arising in a mind-door process. Cittas in sense-door processes and in mind-door processes arise and fall away continuously.

We may not know that both in a sense-door process and in a mind-door process there are akusala cittas or kusala cittas arising. Because of our accumulated ignorance we do not clearly know our different cittas and we do not recognize our more subtle defilements.

In a sense-door process the object is experienced first by cittas which are not kusala cittas or akusala cittas; it is experienced by kiriyacittas and by vipākacittas. The five-door-adverting-consciousness (pañca-dvārāvajjana-citta) is an ahetuka kiriyacitta (without beautiful roots or unwholesome roots). It is succeeded by one of the dvi-pañca-viññāṇas (the five pairs of seeing-consciousness, hearing-consciousness, etc.) and this citta is ahetuka vipāka. Then there are two more ahetuka vipākacittas: the sampaṭicchana-citta which receives the object and the santīraṇa-citta which investigates the object. The santīraṇa-citta is succeeded by the votthapana-citta (determining-consciousness) which is an ahetuka kiriyacitta. The votthapana-citta determines the object and is then succeeded by kusala cittas or by akusala cittas. In the case of those who are arahats there are no kusala cittas or akusala cittas succeeding the votthapana-citta but kiriyacittas. When the cittas of the sense-door process have fallen away, cittas of the mind-door process experience the object. First there are bhavanga-cittas and then the mano-dvārāvajjana-citta arises which has the function of adverting to the object through the mind-door. The mano-dvārāvajjana-citta is succeeded by kusala cittas or by akusala cittas in the case of those who are not arahats. The mano-dvārāvajjana-citta is not kusala or akusala, it is ahetuka kiriyacitta.

Since cittas arise and fall away very rapidly it is hard to know the different cittas which arise. Often we may not even know when we have kusala cittas or akusala cittas. For example, after there has been seeing we may not realize when there is attachment to the object, when there is aversion towards it, or when there is ignorance of realities. If we study the Dhamma we will learn about our cittas in detail and we will also come to know our more subtle defilements. Ignorance of our akusala cittas is dangerous. If we do not know when we have akusala cittas we will continue to accumulate akusala.

The kusala cittas and akusala cittas which arise perform a function; they perform the function of *javana* or "running through the object"[1]. In the sense-door process the votthapana-citta has determined the object already when the javana-cittas arise. Thus, the kusala cittas or akusala cittas which follow have as their only function to "run through" the object. There is not just one moment of citta which performs the function of javana, but usually there are seven cittas in succession which perform

[1] Javana is sometimes translated as "impulsion" or as "apperception".

this function[2]. As we have seen (in chapter 12) one material unit, a sense-object which is experienced by cittas in a process, equals sixteen or seventeen mental units. Such numbers should be seen as a comparative notion. Within a process of cittas the duration of javana occupies seven moments. Since cittas arise and fall away extremely rapidly we cannot count these seven moments, it all takes place in a flash.

The javana-cittas arising in one process are a sequence of seven cittas of the same type. If the first javana-citta is kusala, the succeeding six cittas are also kusala cittas; if the first javana-citta is akusala, the succeeding six cittas are also akusala cittas. Do we know when the javana-cittas are akusala cittas rooted in lobha, dosa or moha, or when they are kusala cittas? We are ignorant most of the time, even of javana-cittas.

There are fifty-five kinds of citta which can perform the function of javana. There are twelve akusala cittas performing the function of javana, namely: eight lobha-mūla-cittas, two dosa-mūla-cittas and two moha-mūla-cittas[3].

There are eight kāmāvara kusala cittas[4], which are called mahā-kusala cittas, performing the function of javana.

There are eight mahā-kiriyacittas of the arahat (kiriyacittas, "inoperative cittas", which are not ahetuka, but accompanied by sobhana hetus) performing the function of javana. The arahat has mahā-kiriyacittas instead of mahā-kusala cittas since he does not accumulate any more kamma. Mahā-kiriyacittas are of the sensuous plane of consciousness; they are not jhānacittas or lokuttara cittas.

Arahats also have kāmāvacara cittas; they see, hear or think of objects experienced through the senses. However, there are no kusala cittas or akusala cittas arising on account of what is experienced.

For the arahat there is also an ahetuka kiriyacitta performing the function of javana, which may arise when he smiles: the hasituppāda-citta or the smile-producing consciousness.

Those who attain rūpa-jhāna (fine-material jhāna) can have five types of rūpāvacara kusala cittas performing the function of javana, since there are five stages of rūpa-jhāna. Arahats who attain rūpa-jhāna can have five types of rūpāvacara kiriyacittas which perform the function of javana.

---

[2] In the "Book of Conditional Relations" it has been explained under "repetition condition" that kusala khandhas are followed by kusala khandhas and akusala khandhas by akusala khandhas. The commentaries, the Visuddhimagga (XIV, 121) and the Atthasālinī (II, Book I, Part X, chapter II, 270) state that there are six or seven moments of javana. The number of seven is not expressively stated in the scriptures, but when we consider the number of cittas in the mind-door process during which enlightenment is attained, as we will see in chapter 24, we have an indication that the number of javana-cittas as given by the commentaries is based on canonical tradition. In different parts of the scriptures the javana-cittas of this process are denoted by particular names and in this way we can know the number of these cittas.

[3] See Ch 4, 6 and 7.

[4] Kāmāavacara cittas are cittas of the sensuous plane of consciousness, not jhānacittas or lokuttara cittas. Details will be given in Ch 19.

For those who attain arūpa-jhāna (immaterial jhāna) there can be four types of arūpāvacara kusala cittas performing the function of javana, since there are four stages of arūpa-jhāna. Arahats who attain arūpa-jhāna can have four types of arūpāvacara kiriyacittas performing the function of javana.

Those who directly experience nibbāna have lokuttara cittas. There are four stages of enlightenment and at each of these stages lokuttara kusala citta or magga-citta ("path-consciousness; "magga" means path) and lokuttara vipākacitta or phala-citta ("fruit-consciousness"; "phala" means fruit) arise. Thus there are for the four stages of enlightenment four pairs of lokuttara cittas: four magga-cittas and four phala-cittas[5]. Lokuttara magga-citta produces result immediately, in the same process of cittas. The phala-citta citta succeeds the magga-citta in the same process. Kusala kamma that is not lokuttara, supramundane, does not produce vipāka in the same process but it does so later on. The magga-citta performs the function of javana, "running through the object" which is nibbāna, and the phala-cittas also perform the function of javana. The vipākacittas other than the lokuttara vipākacitta do not perform the function of javana. Thus, all eight lokuttara cittas perform the function of javana.

There are fifty-five cittas in all which perform the function of javana. Summarising them, they are:

- 8 lobha-mūla-cittas (cittas rooted in attachment)
- 2 dosa-mūla-cittas (cittas rooted in aversion)
- 2 moha-mūla-cittas (cittas rooted in ignorance)

- 8 mahā-kusala cittas (kāmāvacara kusala cittas)
- 8 mahā-kiriyacittas
- 1 hasituppāda-citta (ahetuka kiriyacitta of the arahat which may arise when he smiles)
- 5 rūpāvacara kusala cittas (rūpa-jhānacittas)
- 5 rūpāvacara kiriyacittas (rūpa-jhānacittas of the arahat)
- 4 arūpāvacara kusala cittas (arūpa-jhānacittas)
- 4 arūpāvacara kiriyacittas (arūpa-jhānacittas of the arahat)
- 4 magga-cittas (lokuttara kusala cittas)
- 4 phala-cittas (lokuttara vipākacittas)

It is useful to know that when akusala cittas arise on account of an object, not merely one akusala citta, but seven akusala cittas arise in one process and this process of cittas can be followed by other processes with akusala javana-cittas. Each time we dislike something there are processes of cittas which experience the object, and in each of these processes there are seven akusala javana-cittas. Countless akusala cittas may arise on account of something we dislike or are attached to.

There is no self who can prevent akusala cittas from arising; as soon as the votthapana-citta in the sense-door process has determined the object, this citta is

[5] Lokuttara cittas will be explained in chapter 23 and 24.

succeeded by akusala cittas already, and as soon as the mano-dvārāvajjana-citta has adverted to the object in the mind-door process, this citta is succeeded by akusala cittas already. The cittas which arise in processes do so in a fixed order. When the first javana-citta has arisen it has to be succeeded by the following javana-cittas. The first javana-citta conditions the second one and this again the following one; each subsequent javana-citta is conditioned by the preceding one.

Processes with kusala javana-cittas and processes with akusala javana-cittas can arise shortly one after the other. For instance, people have the intention to offer food to the monks. However, when someone has bought the ingredients for the food he is going to offer, he may find the cost rather high. At that moment there may be cittas with stinginess and then the javana-cittas are akusala cittas. Thus we see that accumulated defilements can appear at any time when there are conditions, even if one has the intention to do a good deed.

It is during the time of the javana-cittas that we accumulate wholesomeness or unwholesomeness. There is no self who can control javana-cittas, but knowing the conditions for wholesomeness will help us to have kusala cittas.

The Buddha, out of compassion, taught people the way to have less akusala. He encouraged them to perform all kinds of kusala, no matter whether it is dāna (generosity), sīla (morality) or bhāvanā (mental development). He taught the development of the wisdom which can eradicate all kinds of akusala. There are different degrees of wisdom, paññā. If there is understanding of what is kusala and what is akusala, there is paññā, but it is not of the degree that it can eradicate akusala. When paññā has been developed to the degree of "insight-wisdom", it will become clearer that there is no self who develops wholesomeness and abstains from ill deeds. However, only the paññā of the sotāpanna has eradicated the wrong view of self. So long as there is the concept of self, defilements cannot be eradicated.

The person who is not an ariyan (noble person who has attained enlightenment) may be able to observe the five precepts, but there is a difference between him and the sotāpanna, the ariyan who has attained the first stage of enlightenment, who does not transgress them. The non-ariyan may transgress the five precepts when there are conditions for it, whereas for the sotāpanna there are no more conditions for transgressing them. Moreover, the sotāpanna who observes sīla does not take the observing of sīla for self any more, since he has eradicated the latent tendency of wrong view. Thus his sīla is purer. He is on the way leading to the eradication of all defilements.

When we are not mindful of realities, we take the objects we experience for "self". When paññā realizes the objects which are experienced as nāma and rūpa, elements which do not last and which are devoid of self, there is less opportunity for akusala javana-cittas.

In the Visuddhimagga (I, 55) we read about the "Elder" Mahā-Tissa:

> ...It seems that as the Elder was on his way from Cetiyapabbata to Anurādhapura for alms, a certain daughter-in-law of a clan, who had quarrelled with her husband and had set out early from Anurādhapura all dressed up and tricked out like a celestial nymph to go to her relatives' home, saw him on the road, and being low-minded, she laughed a loud

laugh. (Wondering) "What is that?", the Elder looked up, and finding in the bones of her teeth the perception of foulness, he reached Arahatship. Hence it was said:

```
''He saw the bones that were her teeth,
And kept in mind his first perception;
And standing on that very spot,
The Elder became an Arahat.''

But her husband who was going after her saw the Elder
and asked ''Venerable sir, did you by any chance
see a woman?'' The Elder told him:

''Whether it was a man or woman
That went by I noticed not;
But only that on this high road
There goes a group of bones.''
```

Mahā-Tissa was not absorbed in the object he experienced, nor entranced by the details. He realized when he perceived the woman's teeth the "foulness of the body" and he did not take what he perceived for "self". The perception of the "foulness of the body" can remind us not to see the self in the body, but to realize bodily phenomena as rūpas which do not stay. Mahā-Tissa saw things as they are; the paññā arising at that moment was to the degree that it could eradicate all defilements.

There are countless javana-cittas in a day with lobha, dosa and moha, and therefore we should not be heedless. We read in the Kindred Sayings (IV, Saḷāyatana-vagga, Kindred Sayings on Sense, Second Fifty, chapter V, paragraph 97, Dwelling heedless) :

> At Sāvatthī was the occasion (of this discourse)...
>
> "I will teach you, monks, of the one who dwells heedless, and of the one who dwells earnest. Do you listen to it.
>
> And how, monks, does one dwell heedless?
>
> In him, monks, who dwells with the faculty of sight uncontrolled, the heart is corrupted by objects cognizable by the eye. In him whose heart is corrupted there is no delight. Without delight there is no joy. Where joy is not, there is no calm. Without calm one dwells in sorrow. The sorrowful man's heart is not composed. When the heart is not composed, one has not clear ideas. Through not having clear ideas he is reckoned as one who dwells heedless.
>
> (And it is the same with regard to the faculties of taste, touch and mind.)
>
> And how, monks, does one dwell earnest?
>
> In him, monks, who dwells with the faculty of sight controlled the heart is not corrupted by objects cognizable by the eye. In him whose heart is not corrupted delight is born. In one delighted joy is born. When one is joyful

the body is calmed. He whose body is calmed feels at ease. Composed is the heart of him who is at ease. When the heart is composed one's ideas are clear. Through having clear ideas one is reckoned as one who dwells earnest.
(And it is the same with regard to the faculty of taste, touch and mind) Thus, monks, is one a dweller in earnestness."

Questions

1. Are there for the arahat only lokuttara cittas performing the function of javana, or can he also have kāmāvacara cittas (cittas of the sense sphere) performing the function of javana?
2. Are there vipākacittas which can perform the function of javana?

15 The Functions of Tadārammaṇa and Cuti

An object which impinges on one of the senses can be visible object, sound, odour, flavour or tangible object. Each of these objects is rūpa. They arise and fall away, but they do not fall away as rapidly as nāma. As we have seen (in chapter 12), rūpa lasts as long as seventeen moments of citta. When a sense object which is rūpa impinges on one of the senses, a process of cittas occurs which arise in a particular order and perform each their own function while they experience that sense object. The first citta of that process, the pañca-dvārāvajjana-citta, five-door-adverting-consciousness, does not arise immediately. First there have to be bhavanga-cittas and these are: atīta-bhavanga, past bhavanga, bhavanga-calana, vibrating bhavanga, and bhavangupaccheda, arrest-bhavanga or last bhavanga before the current of bhavanga-cittas is arrested. These bhavanga-cittas do not experience the rūpa which impinges on one of the senses. The pañca-dvārāvajjana-citta, which is a kiriyacitta, adverts to the object and is then succeeded by one of the dvi-pañca-viññāṇas (seeing-consciousness, hearing-consciousness, etc.) which is vipāka, the result of a good deed or a bad deed. There is, however, not only one moment of vipāka in a process, but several moments. The pañca-viññāṇa (sense-cognition) is succeeded by sampaṭicchana-citta (receiving-consciousness) which is vipāka and this citta is succeeded by santīraṇa-citta (investigating-consciousness) which is also vipāka. The santīraṇa-citta is succeeded by the votthapana-citta (determining-consciousness) which is kiriyacitta. This citta is succeeded by seven javana-cittas[1] which are, in the case of non-arahats, akusala cittas or kusala cittas. All cittas, starting with the pañca-dvārāvajjana-citta, experience the object which impinges on one of the senses. Counting from the atīta-bhavanga, fifteen moments of citta have elapsed when the seventh javana-citta has fallen away. If the rūpa which has impinged on one of the senses and atīta-bhavanga arose at the same time, that rūpa can survive two more moments of citta, since the duration of rūpa equals seventeen moments of citta. Thus, after the javana-cittas there can be two more moments of citta which directly experience the object. These cittas, which are vipākacittas, are tadārammaṇa-cittas or tadālambana-cittas. They perform the function of *tadārammaṇa* or tadālambana, which is translated as "registering" or "retention". Tadārammaṇa literally means "that object"; the citta "hangs on" to that object. When the tadārammaṇa-cittas have fallen away the sense-door process has run its full course. There is, however, not always a complete sense-door process. When a rūpa which impinges on one of the senses, more than three moments of bhavanga-cittas may pass before a process starts and then the process cannot run its full course. Since rūpa does not last longer than seventeen moments of citta, it falls away before the tadārammaṇa-cittas could arise. Thus, in that case there are no tadārammaṇa-cittas[2].

---

[1] See chapter 14.

[2] The "Abhidhammattha Sangaha", Ch 4, Analysis of Thought Processes, calls sense objects "very great" when the process runs its full course; it calls them "great" when the process is interrupted after the javana-cittas; it calls them "slight" when the process is interrupted after the votthapana-citta; it calls them very slight when the process does not start.

Only in the sensuous plane of existence kamma can, after kāmāvacara javana-cittas (of the sense-sphere), produce the vipākacittas which are the tadārammaṇa-cittas, "hanging on" to the sense object[3]. For those who are born in rūpa-brahma-planes where there are less conditions for sense-impressions, and for those who are born in arūpa-brahma planes where there are no sense-impressions, there are no tadārammaṇa-cittas[4].

Summarising the cittas which succeed one another when a rūpa impinges on one of the senses and becomes the object of cittas of a sense-door process which runs its full course:

1. Atīta-bhavanga (past bhavanga)
2. Bhavanga-calana (vibrating bhavanga)
3. Bhavangupaccheda (arrest-bhavanga)
4. Pañca-dvārāvajjana-citta (five-door-adverting-consciousness)
5. Dvi-pañca-viññāṇa (the five pairs of seeing-consciousness, etc.)
6. Sampaṭicchana-citta (receiving-consciousness)
7. Santīraṇa-citta (investigating-consciousness)
8. Votthapana-citta (determining-consciousness)
9. Javana-cittas
10. ditto kusala cittas or akusala cittas
11. ditto (in the case of non-arahats)
12. ditto "running through the object"
13. ditto
14. ditto
15. ditto
16. Tadārammaṇa-citta (registering-consciousness)
17. ditto

The tadārammaṇa-citta experiences an object not only through the five sense-doors but also through the mind-door. In the sense-door process tadārammaṇa-citta can arise only when the object has not fallen away yet. If tadārammaṇa-cittas arise in a sense-door process they can also arise in the succeeding mind-door process. The tadārammaṇa-citta is a vipākacitta which can experience an object through six doors. For example, when visible object contacts the eyesense and the process runs its full course, the tadārammaṇa-cittas arising in that process experience the object through the eye-door. The tadārammaṇa-cittas of the mind-door process which

[3] See Visuddhimagga XIV, 122.

[4] Birth in a rūpa-brahma plane is the result of rūpāvacara kusala citta (rūpa-jhānacitta) and birth in an arūpa-brahma-plane is the result of arūpāvacara kusala citta (arūpa-jhānacitta). Those who develop jhānacitta see the disadvantage of sense impressions, they want to be freed from them.

succeeds the eye-door process experience that object through the mind-door[5]. When the object which contacts the sense-door is unpleasant, all the vipākacittas in that process and thus also the tadārammaṇa-cittas, if they arise, are akusala vipāka. The tadārammaṇa-cittas of the succeeding mind-door process are also akusala vipāka. When the object which contacts the sense-door is pleasant, all vipākacittas of that process, including the tadārammaṇa-cittas, are kusala vipāka. It is the same with the tadārammaṇa-cittas of the subsequent mind-door process.

The function of tadārammaṇa can be performed by eleven different types of vipākacitta: by three ahetuka vipākacittas (unaccompanied by hetus, roots) and by eight sahetuka vipākacittas (accompanied by sobhana hetus, beautiful roots).

If the tadārammaṇa-citta is ahetuka, the function of tadārammaṇa is performed by the ahetuka vipākacitta which is classified as santīraṇa-citta. As we have seen (in chapter 9), there are three kinds of santīraṇa-citta: one type is akusala vipāka accompanied by upekkhā (indifferent feeling), one type is kusala vipāka, accompanied by upekkhā, and one type is kusala vipāka, accompanied by somanassa (pleasant feeling). As stated before (in chapter 11), santīraṇa-citta can perform more than one function at different occasions. Santīraṇa-citta performs the function of santīraṇa (investigating the object) when it arises in a sense-door process and succeeds sampaṭicchana-citta. Apart from the function of investigating the object, santīraṇa-citta can also perform the functions of paṭisandhi (rebirth), bhavanga and cuti (dying). In those cases santīraṇa-citta does not arise within a process of cittas. Moreover, santīraṇa-citta can perform the function of tadārammaṇa. Apart from the three ahetuka vipākacittas which can perform the function of tadārammaṇa, there are eight sahetuka vipākacittas or mahā-vipākacittas which can perform the function of tadārammaṇa.

All the time cittas arise and fall away, performing different functions. The last function of citta in life is the function of *cuti* (dying). When we say in conventional language that a person has died, the cuti-citta (dying-consciousness), which is the last citta of that life, has fallen away. The cuti-citta is succeeded by the paṭisandhi-citta (rebirth-consciousness) of the following life.

Death is unavoidable. Everybody, no matter whether he is in one of the unhappy planes, in the human plane or in one of the heavenly planes, has to have cuti-citta. We read in the teachings about birth, old age, sickness and death. Old age is mentioned immediately after birth, before sickness is mentioned. The reason is that as soon as we are born, we are already ageing, we are already on our way to death. We read in the Sutta-Nipāta (The Group of Discourses, chapter III, paragraph 8, The Barb, vs. 574-587, Khuddaka Nikāya):

> The life of mortals here cannot be predicted by any sign, and (its duration) is uncertain. (It is) difficult and brief, and it is combined with misery.
> For there is no means whereby those born do not die. Even (for one) arriving at old age there is death, for of such a nature are living creatures.

[5] The "Abhidhammattha Sangaha", in Ch 4, Analysis of Thought Processes, calls the object, experienced through the mind-door, when the process runs its full course, a "clear object". If the mind-door process is interrupted after the javana-cittas, the object is called "obscure".

> Just as for ripe fruit there is constantly fear of falling, so for mortals who are born there is constantly fear of death.
>
> Just as vessels made of clay by a potter all have breaking as their end, so is the life of mortals.
>
> Young and old, those who are foolish and those who are wise, all go into the power of death, all have death as their end.
>
> When they are overcome by death, going from here to the next world, the father does not protect the son, nor the relatives the (other) relatives.
>
> See, while the relatives are actually looking on, (and) wailing much, each one of the mortals is led away like a cow to be slaughtered.
>
> Thus the world is smitten by death and old age. Therefore wise men do not grieve, knowing the way of the world.
>
> Whose path you do not know, whether come or gone, not seeing both ends you lament (him) uselessly.
>
> If lamenting (and) harming himself a deluded person should pluck out any advantage (from his action), a wise man would do that too.
>
> For not by weeping and grief does one obtain peace of mind. His misery arises all the more, his body is harmed.
>
> He becomes thin and discoloured, harming himself by himself. The departed ones do not fare well thereby. Lamentation is useless.
>
> Not abandoning grief a person goes all the more to misery. Bewailing the dead man he goes under the influence of grief...

If one is not wise, one grieves, but for those who develop the eightfold Path, there will be less sorrow. For him who has attained the stage of the arahat, there will be cuti-citta, but it will not be succeeded by paṭisandhi-citta. Then the end to birth, old age, sickness and death has been reached.

We read in the Gradual Sayings (Book of the Threes, chapter VII, paragraph 62, Terror, V and VI):

> Monks, these three terrors part mother and son. What three?
>
> A mother cannot bear to see her son grow old. She says, "I am growing old. Let not my son grow old." The son likewise cannot bear to see his mother grow old. He says, "I am growing old. Let not my mother grow old." And it is the same with regard to getting sick and dying. These are the three terrors that part mother and son.
>
> But, monks, there is a way, there is a practice that leads to the abandoning, to the overpassing of these three terrors that part mother and son, a way which joins mother and son. What is that way, what is that practice which so leads?
>
> It is just this Eightfold Way, to wit: Right view, right thinking, right speech, right action, right livelihood, right effort, right mindfulness, right concentration. That is the way, that is the practice...

The eightfold Path eventually leads to the end of birth, old age, sickness and death. If one is not an arahat, there will be a paṭisandhi-citta succeeding the cuti-citta. Before the cuti-citta arises, there are only five javana-cittas instead of seven, because the javana process is weaker due to the nearness of death (Vis. chapter XVII, 143). These are the last javana-cittas of that lifespan. If akusala kamma produces the rebirth of the next life there will be an unhappy rebirth. In that case the last javana-cittas are akusala cittas and they experience an unpleasant object. If kusala kamma produces the rebirth there will be a happy rebirth. In that case the last javana-cittas are kusala cittas and they experience a pleasant object[6]. These javana-cittas experience an object through one of the sense-doors or through the mind-door. The object that presents itself to the dying person may be the past kamma that will condition his rebirth, a sign of past kamma, a sign of his future destiny or any object that is experienced through one of the senses (Vis. XVII, 136-146). The tadārammaṇa-citta which has as function to register the object may or may not follow. Then the cuti-citta arises, the last citta of this present life. The cuti-citta is succeeded by the paṭisandhi-citta of the following life and this citta experiences the same object as the last javana-cittas arising before the cuti-citta of the previous life. Whatever that object may have been, the paṭisandhi-citta of the new life and also all bhavanga-cittas arising in the course of that new life and finally the cuti-citta of that life experience that object. There is sometimes a misunderstanding that the cuti-citta of the previous life determines one's rebirth, but this is not so. The only function of the cuti-citta is being the last moment of a lifespan. The cuti-citta is vipākacitta produced by the kamma which produced the paṭisandhi-citta and the bhavanga-cittas of the life which is just ending; it is of the same type as these cittas and it experiences the same object. Past kusala kamma or akusala kamma which will produce one's rebirth conditions the last javana-cittas to experience a pleasant object or an unpleasant object.

The paṭisandhi-citta, the bhavanga-cittas and the cuti-citta in one lifespan are the same type of vipākacitta and they experience the same object. There are nineteen types of citta which can perform the function of paṭisandhi[7] and the function of bhavanga, and these same nineteen types of citta can perform the function of cuti.

If someone suffers great pains before he dies because of an accident or sickness, the last javana-cittas arising before the cuti-citta will not necessarily be akusala cittas. There may be akusala cittas with aversion when he feels the pain, but the last javana-cittas may be kusala cittas, depending on the kamma which will produce his next birth.

We read in the Gradual Sayings (Book of the Sixes, chapter VI, paragraph 2, Phagguna) that the Buddha visited the venerable Phagguna who was very ill. Phagguna had attained the second stage of enlightenment (the stage of the sakadāgāmī, once-returner); he was not yet completely freed from the "five lower fetters". We read in the sutta that the Buddha said to Phagguna:

> "I hope, Phagguna, you're bearing up, keeping going; that your aches and pains grow less, not more; that there are signs of their growing less, not more?"

---

[6] See chapter 10.

[7] See chapter 11.

"Lord, I can neither bear up nor keep going; my aches and pains grow grievously more, not less; and there are signs of their growing more, not less.

Lord, the violent ache that racks my head is just as though some lusty fellow chopped at it with a sharp-edged sword; lord, I can neither bear up nor keep going; my pains grow more, not less. . ."

So the Exalted One instructed him, roused him, gladdened him and comforted him with Dhamma-talk, then rose from his seat and departed.

Now not long after the Exalted One's departure, the venerable Phagguna died; and at the time of his death his faculties were completely purified.

Then went the venerable Ānanda to the Exalted One, saluted him, and sat down at one side. So seated, he said:

"Lord, not long after the Exalted One left, the venerable Phagguna died; and at that time his faculties were completely purified."

"But why, Ānanda, should not the faculties of the monk Phagguna have been completely purified? The monk's mind, Ānanda, had not been wholly freed from the five lower fetters; but, when he heard that Dhamma teaching, his mind was wholly freed.

There are these six advantages, Ānanda, in hearing Dhamma in time, in testing its goodness in time. What six?

Consider, Ānanda, the monk whose mind is not wholly freed from the five lower fetters, but, when dying, is able to see the Tathāgata: the Tathāgata teaches him Dhamma, lovely in the beginning, lovely in the middle, lovely in the end, its goodness, its significance; and makes known the brahman-life[8], wholly fulfilled, perfectly pure. When he has heard that Dhamma teaching, his mind is wholly freed from the five lower fetters[9]. This, Ānanda, is the first advantage in hearing Dhamma in time.

Or. . .though not just able to see the Tathāgata, sees his disciple, who teaches him Dhamma. . .and makes known the brahman-life. . .Then is his mind wholly freed from the five lower fetters. This, Ānanda, is the second advantage. . .

Or. . .though not able to see the Tathāgata or his disciple, continues to reflect in mind on Dhamma, as heard, as learnt, ponders on it, pores over it. Then is his mind wholly freed from the five lower fetters. This, Ānanda, is the third advantage in testing its goodness in time. . ."

The same is said with regard to the monk who has attained the third stage of enlightenment (the stage of the anāgāmī), and who, after hearing Dhamma in time and testing its goodness in time, can attain the stage of the arahat.

Summary of functions (kicca) of citta:

---

[8] In Pāli: brahma-cariya: pure or holy life. This term is not only used for the monk's life, but also with regard to all those who develop the eightfold Path which leads to the eradication of all defilements.

[9] Those who have attained the third stage of enlightenment, the stage of the anāgāmī, non-returner, are completely free from the five "lower fetters".

1. Paṭisandhi (rebirth)
2. Bhavanga (life-continuum)
3. Āvajjana (adverting, through the sense-doors and through the mind- door)
4. Seeing
5. Hearing
6. Smelling
7. Tasting
8. Experiencing tangible object through the bodysense
9. Sampaṭicchana (receiving)
10. Santīraṇa (investigating)
11. Votthapana (determining)
12. Javana (impulsion, or "running through the object")
13. Tadārammaṇa (or tadālambana, registering)
14. Cuti (dying)

Questions

1. Why can tadārammaṇa-citta not arise in the rūpa-brahma planes and in the arūpa-brahma planes?
2. By how many types of citta can the function of cuti (dying) be performed?

16 Objects and Doors

Citta knows or experiences something, it experiences an object. There cannot be any citta without an object. When an object presents itself through one of the five senses or through the mind-door, do we realize that it is citta which experiences an object? So long as we do not see things as they really are, we think that a self experiences objects, and, moreover, we take objects for permanent and for self. For example, when we see a log of wood, we are used to thinking that the object which is seen at that moment is a log of wood; we do not realize that only visible object is the object which can be seen. When we touch the log of wood, hardness or cold, for example, can be experienced through the bodysense. We take the log of wood for a thing which lasts, but what we call "log of wood" are many different rūpas which arise and fall away. Only one characteristic of rūpa can be experienced at a time, when it presents itself. If we develop understanding of the different characteristics which appear through different doorways we will be able to see things as they really are.

The ariyan sees life in a way which is different from the way the non-ariyan sees it. What the non-ariyan takes for happiness (in Pāli: sukha), is for the ariyan sorrow (dukkha); what for the non-ariyan is sorrow, is for the ariyan happiness. In the Kindred Sayings (IV, Saḷāyatana-vagga, Third Fifty, chapter IV, paragraph 136) it is said in verse:

```
Things seen and heard, tastes, odours, what we touch,
Perceive—all, everything desirable,
Pleasant and sweet, while one can say ''it is'',
These are deemed ''sukha'' by both gods and men.
And when they cease to be they hold it woe.
The dissolution of the body-self
To ariyans seems ''sukha''. Everything
The world holds good, sages see otherwise.

What other men call ''sukha'', that the saints
Call ''dukkha''; what the rest so name,
That do the ariyans know as happiness.
Behold a Dhamma that's hard to apprehend.
Hereby are baffled they that are not wise.
Darkness is theirs, enmeshed by ignorance:
Blindness is theirs, who cannot see the light...
```

The Buddha taught about objects, experienced by cittas through different doors, in order to cure people of their blindness. When we study the teachings we learn that there are six classes of objects (in Pāli: ārammaṇa), which can be known by citta.

1. The first class is: visible object or rūpārammaṇa. The object which is experienced through the eye-door can only be the kind of rūpa which is visible object. We can call it visible object or colour, it does not matter how we name

it; but we should know that it is just that which is visible, that which appears through the eyes. Visible object is not a thing or a person we may think of. When we think that we see a tree, animal or man, we think of concepts and such moments are different from seeing, the experience of what is visible.

2. The second class of ārammaṇa, is sound (saddārammaṇa).
3. The third class is smell (gandhārammaṇa).
4. The fourth class is taste (rasārammaṇa).
5. The fifth class is tangible object, experienced through the bodysense (phoṭṭhabbārammaṇa). Tangible object comprises the following rūpas:
   - the Element of Earth[1] (in Pāli: paṭhavi-dhātu) or solidity, which can be experienced as hardness or softness
   - the Element of Fire (in Pāli: tejo-dhātu) or temperature, which can be experienced as heat or cold
   - the Element of Wind (in Pāli: vāyo-dhātu) or motion, which can be experienced as motion or pressure
     - Solidity (earth), cohesion (water), temperature (fire) and motion (wind or air) are the four principle rūpas (mahā-bhūta-rūpas). Rūpas arise in groups or units of several kinds of rūpas and the four principle rūpas always have to arise together with any other kind of rūpa, no matter whether it is in the body or external. Cohesion or fluidity (the Element of Water, in Pāli: apo-dhātu) cannot be experienced through the bodysense. When we touch water the characteristics of hardness or softness, heat or cold, motion or pressure can be directly experienced through the bodysense. The characteristic of cohesion can be experienced only through the mind-door; it is, as we will see, included in the sixth class of ārammaṇa, the dhammārammaṇa.
6. Dhammārammaṇa comprises all objects other than those included in the first five classes of objects, as will be explained later on. Dhammārammaṇa can be experienced only through the mind-door.

If one has not developed "insight", right understanding of realities, one does not clearly know which object presents itself through which doorway, one is confused as to objects and doors; thus, one is confused about the world. The ariyan is not confused about the world; he knows the objects which appear through the six doors as nāma and rūpa, not self.

The Discourse on the Six Sixes (Middle Length Sayings III, no. 148) is very helpful for the understanding of realities which present themselves through the six doors. When the Buddha was staying in the Jeta Grove in Anāthapiṇḍika's monastery, he explained to the monks about the six "internal sense-fields" and the six "external sense-fields" (in Pāli: āyatana). The six "internal sensefields" are the five senses and the mind. The six "external sense-fields" are the objects, experienced through six doors. The Buddha explained about six classes of consciousness (seeing,

---

[1] Here earth, water, fire and wind do not denote conventional ideas; in Buddhism they are names for characteristics of realities.

hearing, etc.) which arise in dependence on six doors and on the objects experienced through these doors. He also explained about six kinds of contact (phassa), six kinds of feeling conditioned by the six kinds of contact, and six kinds of craving conditioned by the six kinds of feeling. Thus there are "Six Sixes", six groups of six realities.

The Buddha then explained about the person who has attachment, aversion and ignorance with regard to what he experiences through the six doors. We read:

> "Monks, visual consciousness arises because of eye and visible object, the meeting of the three is sensory impingement[2] ; an experience arises conditioned by sensory impingement that is pleasant or painful or neither painful nor pleasant. He, being impinged on by a pleasant feeling, delights, rejoices and persists in cleaving to it; a tendency to attachment is latent in him. Being impinged on by a painful feeling, he grieves, mourns, laments, beats his breast and falls into disillusion; a tendency to repugnance is latent in him. Being impinged on by a feeling that is neither painful nor pleasant, he does not comprehend the origin nor the going down nor the satisfaction nor the peril of that feeling nor the escape from it as it really is; a tendency to ignorance is latent in him..."

The same is said with regard to the other doorways. We then read about the person who has developed the wisdom which can eradicate attachment, aversion and ignorance:

> "...He, being impinged on by pleasant feeling, does not delight, rejoice or persist in cleaving to it; a tendency to attachment is not latent in him. Being impinged on by a painful feeling, he does not grieve, mourn, lament, beat his breast or fall into disillusion; a tendency to repugnance is not latent in him. Being impinged on by a feeling that is neither painful nor pleasant, he comprehends the origin and the going down and the satisfaction and the peril of that feeling and the escape as it really is, a tendency to ignorance is not latent in him. That he, monks, by getting rid of any tendency to attachment to a pleasant feeling, by driving out any tendency to repugnance for a painful feeling, by rooting out any tendency to ignorance concerning a feeling that is neither painful nor pleasant, by getting rid of ignorance, by making knowledge arise, should here and now be an end-maker of dukkha – this situation exists.
>
> Seeing this thus, monks, the instructed disciple of the ariyans turns away from eye, turns away from material shapes, turns away from visual consciousness, turns away from impact on the eye, turns away from feeling, turns away from craving. He turns away from ear, he turns away from sounds...He turns away from nose, he turns away from smells...He turns away from tongue...he turns away from tastes...He turns away from body, he turns away from touches...He turns away from mind, he turns away from mental states, he turns away from mental consciousness, he turns away from impact on the mind, he turns away from feeling, he turns away from craving. Turning away he is dispassionate; by dispassion

[2] Contact

> he is freed; in freedom is the knowledge that he is freed, and he comprehends: Destroyed is birth, brought to a close the Brahma-faring, done is what was to be done, there is no more of being such or so."
> Thus spoke the Lord. Delighted, these monks rejoiced in what the Lord had said. And while this exposition was being given the minds of as many as sixty monks were freed from the cankers without grasping.

While the Buddha explained to the monks about the objects appearing through the six doors, the monks were mindful of nāma and rūpa while they listened; they developed right understanding and several among them could even attain arahatship.

As we have seen, dhammārammaṇa, the sixth class of objects, can be experienced only through the mind-door. It includes all objects other than the sense objects. Dhammārammaṇa can again be subdivided into six classes. They are:

1. The five sense-organs (pasāda-rūpas)
2. The subtle rūpas (sukhuma-rūpas)
3. Citta
4. Cetasika
5. Nibbāna
6. Concepts and conventional terms (paññatti)

The first class of dhammārammaṇa comprises the five sense-organs (pasāda-rūpas); they are the rūpas which have the capacity to receive sense-impressions. The pasāda-rūpas themselves do not experience anything, they are rūpa, not nāma; they function as the doors through which cittas experience objects. The pasāda-rūpas can only be known through the mind-door, not through the sense-doors. For example, we know that there is eyesense, because there is seeing, but we cannot experience eyesense through the eyes.

The five sense-organs are classified as gross (olārika) rūpas. Altogether there are twenty-eight kinds of rūpa of which twelve are classified as gross and sixteen as subtle (sukhuma). The gross rūpas include, besides the five sense-organs, the sense objects which can be experienced through the five sense-doors; these are seven rūpas, that is to say: four rūpas which can respectively be experienced through the four sense-doors of eyes, ears, nose and tongue, and the three rūpas of solidity, temperature and motion which can be experienced through the door of the bodysense. Thus, there are altogether twelve gross rūpas. As we have seen, the sense objects have been classified separately, they are not included in dhammārammaṇa.

There are sixteen kinds of subtle rūpa and these have been classified as the second class of dhammārammaṇa. They include, for example, nutritive essence (ojā), bodily intimation, kāya-viññatti, the rūpa which is the physical condition for expression through the body, such as gestures or facial expression, and vocal intimation, vacīviññatti, the rūpa which is the physical condition for speech or other ways of vocal intimation.

Citta is another class of dhammārammaṇa. Cittas experience different objects, ārammaṇas, but citta itself can be ārammaṇa as well. Kusala cittas, akusala cittas and many other types of citta can be the object experienced by another citta.

The class of dhammārammaṇa which is cetasika comprises all fifty-two cetasikas. Feeling is a cetasika. Painful feeling, for example, can be known by citta; then the object of citta is dhammārammaṇa. When one experiences hardness the object is not dhammārammaṇa but tangible object (phoṭṭhabbārammaṇa), which is included in the fifth class of objects. Hardness and painful feeling can appear closely one after the other. If one does not realize that hardness and painful feeling are different ārammaṇas and if one is ignorant of the different characteristics of nāma and rūpa, one will continue taking them for self.

Citta can experience all objects. Also nibbāna can be experienced by citta. Nibbāna is dhammārammaṇa, it can only be experienced through the mind-door. Thus, citta can experience both conditioned dhammas and the unconditioned dhamma, which is nibbāna. The citta which experiences conditioned dhammas is lokiya citta, "mundane"[3]. The citta which, at the attainment of enlightenment, directly experiences nibbāna is lokuttara citta, "supramundane citta".

Another class of dhammārammaṇa is concepts(paññatti), that is to say, both ideas and conventional terms . Thus we see that citta can know both paramattha dhammas, absolute realities, and concepts which are not real in the absolute sense.

A concept or a conventional truth is not a paramattha dhamma. We can think of a person, an animal or a thing because of remembrance of past experiences, but these are not paramattha dhammas, realities which each have their own unchangeable characteristic, no matter how one names them. When there is thinking about a concept, it is nāma which thinks; thinking is a paramattha dhamma but the concept which is the object of thinking is not real in the absolute sense.

Paññatti can mean a concept or idea which is not real in the absolute sense as well as a conventional term. Conventional terms can denote both realities and things which are not real. A term which in itself is not a paramattha dhamma, can denote a paramattha dhamma. For instance, the terms "nāma" and "rūpa" are paññatti, but they denote paramattha dhammas. It is essential to know the difference between paramattha dhamma and paññatti. If we cling to the terms "nāma" and "rūpa" and continue thinking about nāma and rūpa, instead of being aware of their characteristics when they appear, we will know only paññattis instead of realities.

Summarising the objects which citta can experience: five classes of objects which are rūpas, namely, visible object, sound, smell, taste and tangible object ; the sixth class, dhammārammaṇa, which is again subdivided into six classes, including: citta, cetasika, the rūpas which are the five senses, subtle rūpas, nibbāna and also paññatti.

Different objects can be experienced through different doorways (in Pāli: dvāra). For example, the eyesense, the pasāda-rūpa which has the capacity to receive visible object, is a necessary condition for citta to experience visible object. If there were no pasāda-rūpa in the eye, citta could not experience visible object. This rūpa is the means, the doorway, through which citta experiences visible object.

---

[3] This does not mean "worldly" as it is understood in conventional language.

Cittas arising in the sense-door processes know their objects through the doors of the eye, the ear, the nose, the tongue and the bodysense. As regards the door of the bodysense, the pasāda-rūpa which has the capacity to receive tangible object such as hardness, softness, heat, cold, motion or pressure, is any part of the body where there is sensitivity for such impressions. Thus, any part of the body can be body-door, except those parts which have no sensitivity.

Five doors are rūpa and one door is nāma. The mind-door is nāma. The cittas of the mind-door process experience an object through the mind-door. Before the mind-door-adverting-consciousness, mano-dvārāvajjana-citta, arises, there are the bhavanga-calana (vibrating bhavanga) and the bhavangupaccheda (arrest-bhavanga). The bhavangupaccheda, the citta preceding the mano-dvārāvajjana-citta, is the mind-door. It is the "doorway" through which the mano-dvārāvajjana-citta and the succeeding cittas of the mind-door process experience the object. It is useful to know through which door cittas experience different objects. For example, visible object, rūpārammaṇa, can be experienced both through the eye-door and through the mind-door. It is experienced through the eye-door when it has not fallen away yet. When it is experienced by the cittas in the mind-door process following upon that eye-door process, it has just fallen away. When visible object is experienced through the mind-door the cittas only know visible object, they do not pay attention to shape and form or think of a person or a thing. But time and again there are also mind-door processes of cittas which think of people or things and then the object is a concept, not visible object. The experience of visible object conditions the thinking of concepts which arises later on.

In both the sense-door process and the mind-door process javana-cittas arise[4]; these javana-cittas are, if one is not an arahat, either kusala cittas or akusala cittas. When visible object is experienced through the eye-door, one does not yet perceive a person or a thing, but, already in the sense-door process, attachment to what is seen can arise, or aversion towards it, or ignorance. Defilements are deeply rooted, they can arise in the sense-door processes and in the mind-door processes. We may think that the enslavement to objects which are experienced through the different doorways is caused by the objects. Defilements, however, are not caused by objects, they are accumulated in the citta which experiences the object.

We read in the Kindred Sayings (IV, Saḷāyatana-vagga, Fourth Fifty, chapter III, paragraph 191, Koṭṭhika) that Sāriputta and Mahā-Koṭṭhika were staying near Vārānasi at Isipatana, in the Antelope Park. Koṭṭhika said to Sāriputta:

> "How now, friend? Is the eye the bond of objects, or are objects the bond of the eye? Is the tongue the bond of savours, or are savours the bond of the tongue? Is mind the bond of mind-objects[5], or are mind-objects the bond of the mind?"
>
> "Not so, friend Koṭṭhika. The eye is not the bond of objects, nor are objects the bond of the eye, but that desire and lust that arise owing to these two. That is the bond. And so with the tongue and the mind. . . it is

---

[4] See chapter 14.

[5] The Pāli text has dhammā, and the English text has here "mind-states".

the desire and lust that arise owing to savours and tongue, mind-objects and mind.

Suppose, friend, two oxen, one white and one black, tied by one rope or one yoke-tie. Would one be right in saying that the black ox is the bond for the white one, or that the white one is the bond for the black one?"

"Surely not, friend."

"No, friend. It is not so. But the rope or the yoke-tie which binds the two, – that is the bond that unites them. So it is with the eye and objects, with tongue and savours, with mind and mind-objects. It is the desire and lust which arise owing to them that form the bond that unites them. If the eye, friend, were the bond of objects, or if objects were the bond of the eye, then this righteous life for the utter destruction of dukkha could not be proclaimed. But since it is not so, but the desire and lust which arise owing to them are the bond, therefore is the righteous life for the utter destruction of dukkha proclaimed...

There is in the Exalted One an eye, friend. The Exalted One sees an object with the eye. But in the Exalted One is no desire and lust. Wholly heart-free is the Exalted One. There is in the Exalted One a tongue...a mind. But in the Exalted One is no desire and lust. Wholly heart-free is the Exalted One.

By this method, friend, you are to understand, as I said before, that the bond is the desire and lust that arise owing to things."

Questions

1. Through which doors can motion be experienced?
2. Through which door can bodysense be experienced?
3. What class of ārammaṇa (object) is cohesion?
4. What class of ārammaṇa is lobha-mūla-citta (citta rooted in attachment)?
5. Through which door can lobha-mūla-citta be experienced?
6. Through which doors can lobha-mūla-citta experience an object?
7. What class of ārammaṇa is cold?
8. What class of ārammaṇa is painful bodily feeling?
9. What class of ārammaṇa is unpleasant mental feeling?
10. What class of ārammaṇa is paññā (wisdom)?
11. Is the word "peace" an ārammaṇa? If so, what class?
12. How many doors are rūpa and how many nāma?
13. Can visible object be experienced through the mind-door?
14. Through how many doors does citta know dhammārammaṇa?
15. How many classes of ārammaṇa are known through the mind-door?

17 Doors and Physical Bases of Citta

The Buddha pointed out the dangers of being infatuated with the objects we experience through the six doors. He taught people to develop the wisdom which knows the realities experienced through the six doors as nāma and rūpa, phenomena which are impermanent and non-self. What is impermanent is "dukkha", it cannot be happiness. When we come to know things as they are, we will be less infatuated with objects.

We read in the Kindred Sayings (IV, Saḷāyatana-vagga, Kindred Sayings on Sense, Second Fifty, chapter III, paragraph 81, A brother) about the purpose of the Buddha's teachings. The text states:

> Then a number of monks came to see the Exalted One... Seated at one side those monks said to the Exalted One: –
>
> "Now here, lord, the wandering sectarians thus question us: 'What is the objective, friend, for which the holy life is lived under the rule of Gotama the recluse?' Thus questioned, lord, we thus make answer to those wandering sectarians: 'It is for the full knowledge of dukkha that the holy life is lived under the rule of the Exalted One.' Pray, lord, when, thus questioned, we so make answer, do we state the views of the Exalted One, without misrepresenting the Exalted One by stating an untruth? Do we answer in accordance with his teaching, so that no one who agrees with his teaching and follows his views could incur reproach?"
>
> "Truly, monks, when thus questioned you thus make answer, you do state my views... in stating that it is for the full knowledge of dukkha that the holy life is lived under my rule.
>
> But if, monks, the wandering sectarians should thus question you: 'But what, friend, is that dukkha, for the full knowledge of which the holy life is lived under the rule of Gotama the recluse?' – thus questioned you should answer thus: 'The eye, friend is dukkha. For the full knowledge of that the holy life is lived... Objects... that pleasant or unpleasant or indifferent feeling that arises through eye-contact... the mind... that pleasant or unpleasant or indifferent feeling that arises through mind-contact, – that also is dukkha. Fully to know that, the holy life is lived under the rule of the Exalted One.' Thus questioned, monks, by those wandering sectarians, thus should you make answer."

In being aware of nāma and rūpa which appear, such as seeing, visible object, feeling or thinking, we can prove to ourselves the truth of the Buddha's teachings; we can prove that the objects experienced through the six doors are impermanent and non-self. The truth will not be known if one follows other people blindly or if one speculates about the truth. We read in the Kindred Sayings (IV, Saḷāyatana-vagga, Third Fifty, chapter V, paragraph 152, Is there a method?) that the Buddha said:

> "Is there, monks, any method, by following which a monk, apart from belief, apart from inclination, apart from hearsay, apart from argument as to method, apart from reflection on reasons, apart from delight in spec-

ulation, could affirm insight thus: 'Ended is birth, lived is the righteous life, done is the task, for life in these conditions there is no hereafter' ?"

"For us, lord, things have their root in the Exalted One... Well indeed were it if the meaning of this that has been spoken were to manifest itself in the Exalted One. Hearing it from him the monks will remember it."

"There is indeed a method, monks, by following which a monk... could affirm insight... And what is that method?

Herein, monks, a monk, seeing an object with the eye, either recognizes within him the existence of lust, aversion and ignorance, thus: 'I have lust, aversion and ignorance', or recognizes the non-existence of these qualities within him, thus: 'I have not lust, aversion and ignorance.' Now as to that recognition of their existence or non-existence within him, are these conditions, I ask, to be understood by belief, or by inclination, or hearsay, or argument as to method, or reflection on reasons, or delight in speculation?"

"Surely not, lord."

"Are these states to be understood by seeing them with the eye of wisdom?"

"Surely, lord."

"Then, monks, this is the method by following which, apart from belief... a monk could affirm insight thus: 'Ended is birth... for life in these conditions there is no hereafter.' "

The same is said with regard to the doors of the ear, the nose, the tongue, the body and the mind.

When we study the Abhidhamma we should keep in mind the purpose of the Buddha's teachings: the eradication of defilements through the wisdom which realizes the phenomena appearing through the six doors as they are. The development of this wisdom is the "method" leading to the end to the cycle of birth and death.

We should remember that the Abhidhamma is not a theoretical textbook but an exposition of realities appearing in daily life. We learn about nāma and rūpa; we learn about cittas which each have their own function in the sense-door process and in the mind-door process. There are sense-door processes and mind-door processes time and again, and objects are experienced by cittas arising in these processes. If there is awareness of characteristics of nāma and rūpa when they appear, the paññā is developed which can eradicate defilements. This kind of wisdom is deeper than any kind of theoretical knowledge.

Nāma and rūpa which arise and fall away are conditioned realities, they arise because of different conditions. Through the study of the Abhidhamma we learn about different conditions for nāma and rūpa. Each reality which arises is dependent on several conditions. For instance, seeing is vipāka, produced by kamma. Visible object conditions seeing by being its object (ārammaṇa). If there is no visible object there cannot be seeing. Eyesense, the kind of rūpa in the eye (pasāda-rūpa) which is able to receive visible object, is another condition for seeing.

The rūpa which is eyesense can function as the door (in Pāli: dvāra) for seeing. A door or "*dvāra*" is the means through which citta experiences an object. There is eyesense arising and falling away all the time; throughout our life it is produced by kamma. However, eyesense is not a door all the time, because there is not all the time the experience of visible object. Eyesense is a door only when citta experiences visible object. It is the same with the pasāda-rūpas which are the other sense-organs. They are doors only when they are the means through which citta experiences an object.

The eye-door is the means through which citta experiences visible object. Not only the cittas which are eye-door-adverting-consciousness, cakkhu-dvārāvajjana-citta, and seeing-consciousness, cakkhu-viññāṇa, experience the object through the eye-door, the other cittas of that process, which are receiving-consciousness, sampaṭicchana-citta, investigating-consciousness, santīraṇa-citta, determining-consciousness, votthapana-citta, the javana-cittas and the tadārammaṇa-cittas (retention) are also dependent on the same door, in order to experience the object. All the cittas of that process experience the object through the eye-door while they each perform their own function. After the rūpa which is experienced by these cittas has fallen away, the object is experienced through the mind-door (mano-dvāra).

Cittas arising in a process which experience an object through one of the six doors are vīthi-cittas (vīthi means: way, course or process). Vīthi-cittas are named after the door through which they experience an object. For example, the cittas which experience an object through the eye-door are called cakkhu-dvāra-vīthi-cittas (cakkhu-dvāra means eye-door). The cittas which experience an object through the ear-door (sota-dvāra) are called sota-dvāra-vīthi-cittas. The cittas which experience an object through the mind-door (mano-dvāra) are called mano-dvāra-vīthi-cittas.

In between the different processes of citta there have to be bhavanga-cittas (life-continuum). Bhavanga-cittas are not vīthi-cittas. They are not part of the process of cittas experiencing objects which time and again throughout our life impinge on the six doors. They experience an object without being dependent on any doorway. As we have seen (in chapter 15), the paṭisandhi-citta, rebirth-consciousness, the bhavanga-cittas and the cuti-citta, dying consciousness, in one lifespan experience the same object as the last javana-cittas which arose before the cuti-citta of the previous life. The paṭisandhi-citta, the bhavanga-citta and the cuti-citta are "process-free cittas" (vīthi-mutta cittas), thus, they are different from the cittas arising in sense-door processes and mind-door processes.

Some cittas perform their function only through one door. For example, the two types of citta which are hearing-consciousness, sota-viññāṇa, which can be kusala vipāka or akusala vipāka, only perform their functions through one door, the ear-door. Some cittas can perform their function through more than one door. Sampaṭicchana-citta, receiving-consciousness, performs its function of receiving the object through five doors, depending on the doorway which is contacted by the object. Santīraṇa-citta, investigating-consciousness, performs different functions through different doorways. It performs the function of investigating the object through the five sense-doors, and it can perform the function of tadārammaṇa (retention or registering, occurring after the javana-cittas) through six doorways[1]. It also performs functions without being dependent on any doorway and this is the case when it performs the functions of paṭisandhi, bhavanga and cuti[2].

In the processes of citta the doorway (dvāra) is the means through which citta experiences its object. The physical base or vatthu is another factor which conditions citta by being its place of origin. In the planes of existence where there are nāma and rūpa, cittas do not arise independently of the body; a citta which arises has a rūpa as its place of origin. Cittas such as seeing, hearing or thinking could not arise without the body. Where does seeing arise? It needs the eye as its physical base. The eyesense, cakkhuppasāda-rūpa, the rūpa in the eye which can receive visible object, is the physical base for the citta which sees. The physical base or vatthu is not the same as dvāra or doorway. Although the five sense-organs can serve as dvāra and vatthu, dvāra and vatthu have different functions. For example, the cakkhuppasāda-rūpa functions as the eye-door (cakkhu-dvāra), the means through which cittas of the eye-door process experience an object, and also as the eye-base (cakkhu-vatthu), the physical base, the place of origin for seeing-consciousness. This rūpa is the base only for seeing-consciousness, not for the other cittas of that process. Thus, one and the same rūpa, the eyesense, serves as both doorway and base only for seeing-consciousness. Regarding the other cittas of the eye-door process, they have the eyesense as doorway, but they have a different base, as I shall explain later. It is the same in the case of the other pañca-viññāṇas (sense-cognitions). The vatthu for hearing-consciousness is the earsense (sotappasāda-rūpa), the vatthu for smelling-consciousness the smelling-sense (ghānappasāda-rūpa), the vatthu for tasting-consciousness the tasting-sense (jivhāppasāda-rūpa), the vatthu for body-consciousness the bodysense (kāyappasāda-rūpa).The bodysense can arise all over the body. Any part of the body which has sensitivity can be vatthu for the kāya-viññāṇa. Thus, the five kinds of pasāda-rūpa, the sense-organs, are the vatthus of the pañca-viññāṇas.

There is a sixth vatthu which is not one of the pasāda-rūpas, sense- organs. This is the rūpa which is the material support, the physical base for all cittas other than the pañca-viññāṇas, the sense-cognitions of seeing, hearing, etc. This rūpa is called in the commentaries the heart-base or hadaya-vatthu[3]. We should know its function, but there is no need to specify its exact location. The hadaya-vatthu, heart-base, is different from the mind-door. The mind-door is a citta, the bhavangupaccheda (arrest-bhavanga) which is the last bhavanga-citta arising before the mind-door-adverting-consciousness (mano-dvārāvajjana-citta). The hadaya-vatthu is rūpa, not nāma.

---

[1] See chapter 15.

[2] See chapter 11, 12 and 15.

[3] The name "heart-base" cannot be found in the scriptures. The "Book of Conditional Relations", the seventh book of the Abhidhamma, refers, under "support condition" (nissaya paccaya), to the heart-base as "that rūpa" which is the material support for the "mind-element" and the "mind-consciousness element". These "elements" are the cittas other than the pañca-viññāṇas.

When sound contacts the ear-sense, the five-door-adverting-consciousness (pañca-dvārāvajjana-citta) which arises has as its place of origin the hadaya-vatthu, but the hearing-consciousness has the earsense, the sotappasāda-rūpa, as its vatthu. All succeeding cittas of that process, however, have the hadaya-vatthu as their place of origin. All cittas of the mind-door process too have the hadaya-vatthu as their place of origin.

The paṭisandhi-citta, the bhavanga-citta and the cuti-citta are, as we have seen, "process-free cittas" (vīthi-mutta cittas), cittas which do not arise within a process and which experience an object without dependence on any door. The "process-free cittas" also need, in the planes where there are both nāma and rūpa, a vatthu, a physical base. A new life begins when the paṭisandhi-citta arises; however, there is not only nāma, there has to be rūpa as well. The hadaya-vatthu is the rūpa which is the vatthu of the paṭisandhi-citta. Also all bhavanga-cittas and the cuti-citta have the hadaya-vatthu as their physical base.

The vatthu is the place of origin not only of citta, but also of cetasikas arising together with the citta. Thus, except in the planes of existence where there is only nāma there has to be rūpakkhandha as well when the four nāmakkhandhas, which include citta and cetasikas, arise.

The sense-bases, citta and the objects experienced by citta can be classified as twelve āyatanas, translated sometimes as "sense-fields" (Vis. XV, 1-17)[4]. There are six inward āyatanas and six outward āyatanas. They are classified as follows:

six inward āyatanas	**six outward āyatanas**
eyesense	visible object
earsense	sound
smelling-sense	odour
tasting-sense	taste
bodysense	tangible object
mind-base (manāyatana)	mind-object (dhammāyatana)

Mind-base, manāyatana, includes all cittas; mind-object, dhammāyatana, includes cetasikas, subtle rūpas and nibbāna. When we see, hear or think we believe that a self experiences objects, but in reality there is the association of the inward āyatana and the outward āyatana, the objects "outside". This classification can remind us that all our experiences are dependent on conditions. We read in the Visuddhimagga (XV, 15), in the section on the āyatanas, about conditioned realities:

> ...they do not come from anywhere previous to their arising, nor do they go anywhere after their falling away. On the contrary, before their arising they had no individual essence, and after their falling away their individual essences are completely dissolved. And they occur without

[4] See also Book of Analysis, Vibhaṅnga, II, Analysis of Bases. Also in other parts of the scriptures, including the suttas, there is reference to this classification.

power (being exercisable over them)[5] since they exist in dependence on conditions. . .

Likewise they should be regarded as incurious and uninterested. For it does not occur to the eye and visible object, etc., "Ah, that consciousness might arise from our concurrence". And as door, physical basis, and object, they have no curiosity about, or interest in, arousing consciousness. On the contrary, it is the absolute rule that eye-consciousness, etc., come into being with the union of eye with visible object, and so on. So they should be regarded as incurious and uninterested. . .

It is useful to become familiar with different classifications of realities, such as the classification by way of kicca, function, ārammaṇa, object, dvāra, doorway, vatthu, physical base, āyatana, sensefield, and other classifications. In this way we will have a clearer understanding of citta and of the conditions for its arising. We should, however, remember that this kind of understanding is not yet the wisdom which eradicates lobha, dosa and moha. In the Kindred Sayings (III, Khandhavagga, Kindred Sayings about Rādha, chapter I, paragraph 4, To be understood) we read:

At Sāvatthī. . .

As the venerable Rādha thus sat at one side the Exalted One addressed him thus: –

"I will show you the things to be understood, and the understanding, and the person who has understood. Do you listen to it."

The Exalted One thus spoke: "And what, Rādha, are the things to be understood? Body, Rādha, is a thing to be understood; so is feeling, perception, the activities (saṅkhārakkhandha). Consciousness is a thing to be understood. These, Rādha, are the things to be understood.

And what, Rādha, is understanding?

The destruction of lust, the destruction of hatred, the destruction of ignorance, – this, Radhā, is called 'understanding'.

And who, Rādha, is the person who has understood?

'Worthy', should he be called, that venerable one of such and such a name, of such and such a clan: – that, Rādha, is the meaning of 'the person who has understood'."

Sometimes the Buddha reminded people of the purpose of the teachings in a longer discourse, sometimes in a shorter discourse, but one has to be often reminded of the goal. What is the purpose of understanding if it does not lead to the eradication of defilements?

Questions

1. Can citta know an object, ārammaṇa, without being dependent on any doorway?
2. Through how many doors can citta know an ārammaṇa?

[5] There is no self who could control them.

3. Through how many doors does the five-door-adverting-consciousness (pañca-dvārāvajjana-citta) experience an object?
4. Through how many doors does mind-door-adverting-consciousness mano-dvārāvajjana-citta) experience an object?
5. Through how many doors does hearing-consciousness (sota-viññāṇa) experience an object?
6. Through how many doors does santīraṇa-citta perform the function of investigating, santīraṇa?
7. Does santīraṇa-citta perform the function of paṭisandhi in dependence on a doorway?
8. Of how many cittas is the eye-base (cakkhu-vatthu) the place of origin?
9. Can the earsense (sotappasāda-rūpa) be door, dvāra, or base, vatthu, or both?
10. What are the respective functions of dvāra and vatthu?

18 Elements

The Buddha spoke about realities as elements, dhātus[1], in order to remind us that they are non-self. When we speak about elements we usually think of elements in chemistry or physics. In chemistry and physics matter is analysed into elements, but it may seem strange to us to regard the eye or seeing as elements. We are not used to considering them as elements because we are inclined to take them for self.

What we take for self are only nāma-elements and rūpa-elements which arise because of their appropriate conditions and then fall away again. Eyesense is only an element which has its own characteristic and is devoid of self; it is rūpa which arises because of conditions and then falls away again. Seeing is only an element which has its own characteristic and is devoid of self; it is nāma which arises because of conditions and falls away again.

In the Buddha's teachings realities are classified as elements, *dhātus*, some of which are rūpa and some of which are nāma. There are different ways of classifying realities as elements. When they are classified as eighteen elements, they are as follows:

The five senses:

1. Eye-element (cakkhu-dhātu)
2. Ear-element (sota-dhātu)
3. Nose-element (ghāna-dhātu)
4. Tongue-element (jivhā-dhātu)
5. Body-element (kāya-dhātu, which is the bodysense)

The five objects (experienced through the five senses):

6. Visible object-element (rūpa-dhātu)
7. Sound-element (sadda-dhātu)
8. Smell-element (gandha-dhātu)
9. Taste-element (rasa-dhātu)
10. Element of tangible objects (phoṭṭhabba-dhātu), comprising the following three kinds of rūpa: earth-element (solidity), appearing as hardness or softness, fire-element (temperature), appearing as heat or cold, wind-element, appearing as motion or pressure

The dvi-pañca-viññāṇas (the "five pairs" of sense-cognitions, experiencing the five sense-objects):

11. Seeing-consciousness-element (cakkhu-viññāṇa-dhātu)
12. Hearing-consciousness-element (sota-viññāṇa-dhātu)
13. Smelling-consciousness-element (ghāna-viññāṇa-dhātu)
14. Tasting-consciousness-element (jivhā-viññāṇa-dhātu)
15. Body-consciousness-element (kāya-viññāṇa-dhātu)

---

[1] Dhātu is derived from dharati, to hold or to bear. Dhātu is that which bears its own intrinsic nature; it is a reality which has its own characteristic.

In addition, there are three more elements:

16. Mind-element (mano-dhātu)
17. Dhamma-dhātu
18. Mind-consciousness-element (mano-viññāṇa-dhātu)

Thus, in this classification there are eighteen elements in all. The five elements which are the five senses are rūpa and the five elements which are the sense objects experienced through the sense-doors are rūpa as well. The five elements which are the dvi-pañca-viññāṇas, experiencing these objects, are nāma. There are two cittas which are seeing-consciousness-element since seeing-consciousness is either kusala vipāka or akusala vipāka. It is the same with the other pañca-viññāṇas. Thus there are five pairs of citta which are collectively called the pañca-viññāṇa-dhātu.

The element which is mind-element or mano-dhātu is nāma. Mano-dhātu comprises the pañca-dvārāvajjana-citta, five-door-adverting-consciousness, and the two types of sampaṭicchana-citta, receiving-consciousness, which are kusala vipāka and akusala vipāka. Thus, three kinds of citta are mano-dhātu.

Dhamma-dhātu comprises cetasikas, the subtle rūpas (sukhuma rūpas) and nibbāna. Thus, dhamma-dhātu comprises both nāma and rūpa. Dhamma-dhātu is not identical with dhammārammaṇa, mind-objects. Cittas are included in dhammārammaṇa but not in dhamma-dhātu. Cittas have been classified separately as different dhātus. Concepts, which are included in dhammārammaṇa, are not classified as elements, because concepts are not paramattha dhammas; only paramattha dhammas are classified as elements.

Mind-consciousness-element, the mano-viññāṇa-dhātu, is nāma. Mind-consciousness-element includes all cittas except the dvi-pañca-viññāṇas and the three kinds of cittas classified as mind-element, mano-dhātu. For example, santīraṇa-citta (the investigating-consciousness), mano-dvārāvajjana-citta (the mind-door-advertingconsciousness), and cittas performing the function of javana[2] such as lobha-mūla-citta and also bhavanga-citta are included in mind-consciousness-element. Mind-element includes cittas which can experience an object through one of the five sense-doors, whereas mind-consciousness-element includes cittas which can experience an object through six doors as well as cittas which are not dependent on any doorway[3].

Viññāṇa-dhātu is a collective name for all cittas. When cittas are classified as elements, they are the seven classes of viññāṇa-dhātu, namely:

- pañca-viññāṇa-dhātu (which are five classes)
- mano-dhātu, mind-element
- mano-viññāṇa-dhātu, mind-consciousness-element

It is important to remember this classification of cittas, because in the teachings and the commentaries, and also in the Visuddhimagga, different types of cittas are often denoted as the elements which are classified above. If we do not remember

[2] See Chapter 14.

[3] The rebirth-consciousness, the bhavanga-citta (life-continuum) and the dying-consciousness.

which cittas are mind-element and which cittas are mind-consciousness-element, we will not know which citta is referred to in the texts.

Sometimes the Buddha spoke about six elements; or he classified realities as two elements. There are many different ways of classifying realities, but no matter in which way they are classified, as khandhas, by way of objects, ārammaṇas, as āyatanas, as dhātus, or in any other way, we should remember the purpose of classifying realities: understanding that what we take for self are only nāma-elements and rūpa-elements.

In the Satipaṭṭhāna-sutta (Discourse on the Applications of Mindfulness, Middle Length Sayings I, no. 10) we read in the section on "mindfulness of the body", that the Buddha spoke about the body in terms of elements. The text states:

> And again, monks, a monk reflects on this body according to how it is placed or disposed in respect of the elements, thinking: "In this body there is the element of extension[4], the element of cohesion, the element of heat, the element of motion." Monks, even as a skilled cattle-butcher, or his apprentice, having slaughtered a cow, might sit displaying its carcase at a cross-roads, even so, monks, does a monk reflect on this body itself according to how it is placed or disposed in respect of the elements, thinking: "In this body there is the element of extension, the element of cohesion, the element of heat, the element of motion". Thus he fares along contemplating the body in the body internally. . . and he fares along independently of and not grasping anything in the world. It is thus too, monks, that a monk fares along contemplating the body in the body. . .

The Visuddhimagga (XI, 30) states:

> What is meant? Just as the butcher, while feeding the cow, bringing it to the shambles, keeping it tied up after bringing it there, slaughtering it, and seeing it slaughtered and dead, does not lose the perception "cow" so long as he has not carved it up and divided it into parts; but when he has divided it up and is sitting there, he loses the perception "cow" and the perception "meat" occurs; he does not think "I am selling cow" or "They are carrying cow away", but rather he thinks "I am selling meat" or "They are carrying meat away"; so too this bhikkhu, while still a foolish ordinary person – both formerly as a layman and as one gone forth into homelessness – , does not lose the perception "living being" or "man" or "person" so long as he does not, by resolution of the compact into elements, review this body, however placed, however disposed, as consisting of elements. But when he does review it as consisting of elements, he loses the perception "living being" and his mind establishes itself upon elements. . .

It may not be appealing to see the body as elements. We think of people as "this man" or "that woman". We are not used to analysing what we take for a "person" just as we analyse matter, for example, in physics. We might find it crude to think of a body which is carved up and divided up into parts, just as a cow is carved up by a butcher. However, if we consider the body as it is, there are only elements.

[4] Solidity.

Isn't it true that there are solidity, cohesion, temperature and motion? Are these realities "self", or are they elements devoid of "self"?

Do the four elements of solidity, cohesion, temperature and motion have anything to do with our daily life? We can find out that these elements arise all the time. Temperature can appear either as heat or cold; do we not feel heat or cold very often? When we are stung by an insect we can experience the characteristic of heat. We can feel impact of hardness or softness on our body when we are lying down, sitting, walking or standing. That is the element of solidity appearing in our daily life. If we are mindful of the characteristics of the elements more often, we will see things as they are.

The Buddha reminded people of the truth in many different ways. Sometimes he spoke about the body as a corpse in different stages of dissolution. Or he spoke about the "parts of the body" and he explained that the body is full of impurities, in order to remind people that what they take for "my body" are only elements which are devoid of beauty, which are impermanent, dukkha and not self.

We read in the Satipaṭṭhāna-sutta, in the section on "mindfulness of the body":

> Monks, it is like a double-mouthed provision bag that is full of various kinds of grain such as hill-paddy, paddy, kidney beans, peas, sesamum, rice; and a keen-eyed man, pouring them out, were to reflect: "That's hill-paddy, that's paddy, that's kidney beans, that's peas, that's sesamum, that's rice." Even so, monks, does a monk reflect on precisely this body itself, encased in skin and full of various impurities, from the soles of the feet up and from the crown of the head down...

Not only the body, but also the mind should be considered as elements. There is nothing in our life which is not an element. Our past lives were only elements and our future lives will only be elements. We are inclined to think of our future life and wish for a happy rebirth. We should, however, realize that there is no self which in the future will have another existence; there are and will be only elements. We have learnt to classify citta in different ways and this can remind us that cittas are only elements. Not only cittas are elements, but cetasikas too are elements. We are attached to happy feeling and we dislike unpleasant feeling. Feelings, however, are only elements which arise because of conditions. When we are tired or sick we take tiredness and sickness for self and we have aversion. Why do we not accept unpleasant things as they come to us, since they are only elements? One might not be inclined to see realities as elements, but it is the truth. One might not like to remember that things are impermanent, that birth is followed by ageing, sickness and death, but it is the truth. Why do we not want to see the truth?

In the Discourse on the Manifold Elements (Middle Length Sayings III, no. 115) we read that the Buddha, while he was staying in the Jeta Grove, in Anāthapiṇḍika's monastery, said to the monks:

> "Whatever fears arise, monks, all arise for the fool, not the wise man. Whatever troubles arise, all arise for the fool, not the wise man. Whatever misfortunes arise, all arise for the fool, not the wise man...Monks, there is not fear, trouble, misfortune for the wise man. Wherefore, monks,

thinking, 'Investigating, we will become wise', this is how you must train yourselves, monks."

When this had been said, the venerable Ānanda spoke thus to the Lord: "What is the stage at which it suffices to say, revered sir: 'Investigating, the monk is wise'?"

"Ānanda, as soon as a monk is skilled in the elements and skilled in the sense-fields (āyatanas) and skilled in conditioned genesis[5] and skilled in the possible and the impossible[6], it is at this stage, Ānanda, that it suffices to say, 'Investigating, the monk is wise.' "

"But, revered sir, at what stage does it suffice to say, 'The monk is skilled in the elements'?"

"There are these eighteen elements, Ānanda: the element of eye, the element of visible object, the element of visual consciousness; the element of ear, the element of sound, the element of auditory consciousness; the element of nose, the element of smell, the element of olfactory consciousness; the element of tongue, the element of taste, the element of gustatory consciousness; the element of body, the element of tangible object, the element of body-consciousness; the element of mind, the element of mind-objects, the element of mental consciousness. When, Ānanda, he knows and sees these eighteen elements, it is at this stage that it suffices to say, 'The monk is skilled in the elements. ' "

"Might there be another way also, revered sir, according to which it suffices to say, 'The monk is skilled in the elements'?"

"There might be, Ānanda. There are these six elements, Ānanda: the element of extension, the element of cohesion, the element of radiation (heat), the element of mobility, the element of space, the element of consciousness. When, Ānanda, he knows and sees these six elements, it is at this stage that it suffices to say, 'The monk is skilled in the elements.' "

"Might there be another way also, revered sir, according to which it suffices to say, 'The monk is skilled in the elements'?"

"There might be, Ānanda. There are these six elements, Ānanda: the element of happiness, the element of anguish, the element of gladness, the element of sorrowing, the element of equanimity, the element of ignorance. When, Ānanda, he knows and sees these six elements, it is at this stage that it suffices to say, 'The monk is skilled in the elements'."

The Buddha then explained still other ways of being skilled in the elements and further on we read that Ānanda asked again:

"Might there be another way also, revered sir, according to which it suffices to say, 'The monk is skilled in the elements'?"

---

[5] Dependent Origination, the conditional arising of phenomena.

[6] Right understanding of what is possible according to conditions and what is impossible.

> "There might be, Ānanda. There are these two elements, Ānanda: the element that is constructed[7] and the element that is unconstructed[8]. When, Ānanda, he knows and sees these two elements, it is at this stage that it suffices to say, 'The monk is skilled in the elements'."

The element which is "constructed" (sankhata), is all conditioned realities (the five khandhas), and the element which is "unconstructed" (asaṅkhata), is nibbāna. Also nibbāna is an element, it is not a person, it is devoid of self, anattā. We read in this sutta about the monk who knows and sees the elements. Knowing and seeing the elements does not mean only knowing them in theory and thinking about them. One knows and sees the elements when there is paññā which realizes nāma and rūpa as they are: only elements, not self. This knowledge will lead to the end of fears, troubles and misfortunes, to the end of dukkha.

Questions

1. When realities are classified as eighteen elements, what element is cetasika?
2. Which paramattha dhammas are viññāṇa-dhātu (consciousness-element)?
3. Is mind-consciousness-element (mano-viññāṇa-dhātu) included in viññāṇa-dhātu?
4. Through how many doors can mind-element (mano-dhātu) experience an object?
5. Why is also nibbāna an element?

[7] saṅkhata
[8] asaṅkhata

19 The Sobhana Cittas in our Life

There are many different types of citta which arise in our life and they can be classified in different ways. When they are classified by way of four "jātis" (jāti means "birth" or "nature"), they are:

1. Kusala cittas (wholesome cittas)
2. Akusala cittas (unwholesome cittas)
3. Vipākacittas (cittas which are result)
4. Kiriyacittas (cittas which are "inoperative", neither cause nor result)

Another way of classifying cittas is as follows:

1. Sobhana cittas, cittas accompanied by sobhana (beautiful) cetasikas
2. Asobhana cittas, cittas unaccompanied by sobhana cetasikas.

Akusala cittas and ahetuka cittas are asobhana cittas, they are not accompanied by sobhana cetasikas. As we have seen, there are twelve types of akusala cittas. They are:

- 8 types of lobha-mūla-citta (cittas rooted in attachment)
- 2 types of dosa-mūla-citta (cittas rooted in aversion)
- 2 types of moha-mūla-citta (cittas rooted in ignorance)

Ahetuka cittas are cittas without roots and unaccompanied by sobhana cetasikas, and thus they are asobhana. As we have seen, there are eighteen types of ahetuka cittas. Summarising them, they are:

- 10 dvi-pañca-viññāṇas, which are ahetuka vipākacittas (the five pairs of seeing, hearing, etc.)
- 2 sampaṭicchana-cittas, receiving-consciousness, which are ahetuka vipāka cittas (one akusala vipāka and one kusala vipāka)
- 3 santīraṇa-cittas, investigating-consciousness, which are ahetuka vipāka cittas (one akusala vipāka, one kusala vipāka, accompanied by upekkhā, and one kusala vipāka, accompanied by somanassa)
- 1 pañca-dvārāvajjana-citta, five-door-adverting-consciousness, which is ahetuka kiriyacitta
- 1 mano-dvārāvajjana-citta, mind-door-adverting-consciousness, which is ahetuka kiriyacitta
- 1 hasituppāda-citta, an ahetuka kiriyacitta which can produce the smile of an arahat

Thus, there are thirty asobhana cittas: twelve akusala cittas and eighteen ahetuka cittas.

There are also sobhana cittas arising in our life, cittas which are accompanied by sobhana cetasikas. Three among the sobhana cetasikas are hetu, root. They are: alobha (non-attachment), adosa (non-aversion) and amoha or paññā, wisdom. Sobhana cittas are always accompanied by the two sobhana hetus of alobha and adosa and they may or may not be accompanied by paññā. Thus, sobhana cittas are sahetuka, accompanied by hetus. When we perform dāna (generosity), observe sīla (morality) or apply ourselves to bhāvanā (which comprises samatha, vipassanā and the study or teaching of Dhamma), there are kusala cittas, accompanied by sobhana cetasikas. Thus, kusala cittas are among the sobhana cittas.

The kusala cittas which perform dāna, observe sīla or apply themselves to bhāvanā are cittas belonging to the lowest plane of consciousness, the "sense sphere"; they are kāmāvacara cittas. Kāmāvacara cittas are the cittas we have in daily life, when, for example, we are seeing, thinking or wishing for something. Sometimes kāmāvacara cittas arise with sobhana hetus (beautiful roots), sometimes with akusala hetus, and sometimes without any hetus. Dāna, sīla and bhāvanā is performed by kāmāvacara kusala cittas; these kinds of kusala kamma can be performed in daily life, where there are sense-impressions. Kāmāvacara kusala cittas are called mahā-kusala cittas ("mahā" means "many" or "great").

For those who attain jhāna (absorption, developed in samatha, tranquil meditation) there is at that moment no seeing, hearing or any other sense-impression; then the citta is not kāmāvacara citta, but it is of a higher plane of consciousness. The jhānacittas can be rūpāvacara cittas (rūpa-jhānacittas) or arūpāvacara cittas (arūpa jhānacittas). However, while one is developing samatha the cittas are mahā-kusala cittas before one attains jhāna.

When enlightenment is attained and the citta experiences nibbāna, the citta is of the lokuttara bhūmi, the "supramundane" plane of consciousness (bhūmi is plane). However, lokuttara kusala cittas, magga-cittas, are preceded by mahā-kusala cittas in the process of cittas during which enlightenment is attained.

We would like to have kusala cittas more often. We may think that the circumstances of our life or other people hinder the arising of kusala citta, but this is not so. The real cause that kusala cittas seldom arise is our lack of development of what is wholesome. If we know the conditions for the development of kusala, there will be more kusala cittas in our life. Through the study of the Dhamma we will learn how to develop kusala. If we have not studied Dhamma we may think that we are performing kusala while we have, on the contrary, akusala cittas. For example, we may think that when we give something away, there are only kusala cittas. However, lobha-mūla-cittas may also arise. We may give something to friends and expect them to be kind to us in return. This is not kusala but lobha, attachment. When we study Dhamma we learn that the pure way of giving is giving without expecting anything in return. When we perform wholesome deeds our aim should be to have less selfishness, and this is beneficial both for ourselves and for others.

People have different accumulations and these are conditions for the arising of kusala cittas and akusala cittas. For example, when people visit a temple and see others presenting gifts to the monks, they may, because of their accumulations, react in different ways. Some people may appreciate someone else's good deeds; others may not be interested at all. If one would know the value of kusala and realize that appreciating the good deeds of others is a way of dāna, one would use more opportunities to develop kusala.

If the Buddha had not attained enlightenment and taught Dhamma we would not have any means of knowing ourselves thoroughly; we would not have a precise knowledge of our kusala cittas and akusala cittas and of the conditions for their arising. The Buddha taught people how to develop wholesomeness and eradicate defilements, and therefore, living according to the precepts and performing other kinds of wholesomeness is the way to pay respect to him. We read in the Mahā-Parinibbāna-sutta (Dialogues of the Buddha II, no. 16, chapter V, 137,138) that before the Buddha passed away, the twin Sāla trees, which were full of flowers although it was not the season, dropped their flowers all over his body, that heavenly Mandārava-flowers and sandalwood-powder descended on his body, and that heavenly music sounded, out of reverence for him. The Buddha said to Ānanda:

> Now it is not thus, Ānanda, that the Tathāgata is rightly honoured, reverenced, venerated, held sacred or revered. But the monk or the nun, the devout man or the devout woman, who continually fulfils all the greater and lesser duties, who is correct in life, walking according to the precepts –it is he who rightly honours, reverences, venerates, holds sacred, and reveres the Tathāgata with the worthiest homage. Therefore, O Ānanda, be constant in the fulfilment of the greater and of the lesser duties, and be correct in life, walking according to the precepts; and thus, Ānanda, should it be taught.

We all have in our daily life opportunities for dāna and sīla. As regards bhāvanā, this comprises samatha and vipassanā, and the studying of Dhamma or explaining it to others. Not only the monks but also laypeople can study and teach Dhamma. We read in the Mahā-Parinibbāna-sutta (chapter III, 112, 113) that the Buddha told Ānanda that Māra, the Evil One, had said to the Buddha after his enlightenment that it was now the time for him to pass away. The Buddha said:

> And when he had thus spoken, Ānanda, I addressed Māra, the Evil One, and said:- "I shall not pass away, O Evil One! Until not only the monks and nuns of the Order, but also the laydisciples of either sex shall have become true hearers, wise and well trained, ready and learned, carrying the teachings in their memory, masters of the lesser corollaries that follow from the larger doctrine, correct in life, walking according to the precepts–until they, having thus themselves learned the doctrine, shall be able to tell others of it, preach it, make it known, establish it, open it, minutely explain it and make it clear–until they, when others start vain doctrine easy to be refuted by the truth, shall be able in refuting it to spread the wonder-working truth abroad! I shall not die until this pure religion of mine shall have become successful, prosperous, widespread, and popular in all its full extent–until, in a word, it shall have been well proclaimed among men!"

The fact that we are able to perform wholesome deeds in our lives is due to conditions, it is not due to a self. We read in the Dialogues of the Buddha (III, no. 34, Tenfold Series, chapter IV, 276) about factors which are helpful conditions for kusala:

> Four. . .that help much:-four "wheels"[1], to wit, the orbit of a favourable place of residence, the orbit of association with the good, perfect adjustment of oneself, the cycle of merit wrought in the past.

As regards a favourable place of residence, living in a Buddhist country can be a helpful condition for kusala cittas. Then one has the opportunity to visit temples and listen to the preaching of Dhamma. The Dhamma can change our life, it is the condition for the performing of wholesome deeds, for dāna, sīla and bhāvanā.

As regards association with the good, this means association with the right friend in Dhamma. If one, even though living in a Buddhist country, does not meet the right friend in Dhamma who can help in the search for the truth, one lacks the condition which is most helpful for the development of wisdom and the eradication of defilements.

Perfect adjustment of oneself is "adjusting oneself" with kusala, becoming established in good qualities. There are many degrees of kusala. If one develops the wisdom of the eightfold Path in being mindful of nāma and rūpa, there will be less clinging to the concept of self. If there is mindfulness of nāma and rūpa while performing wholesome deeds, one will come to realize that no self, no person performs these deeds. In that way kusala kamma will be purer and eventually defilements will be eradicated.

The accumulation of kusala in the past is the fourth factor which is helpful. The kusala kammas which were accumulated in the past are the condition for us to go to the right place and meet the right people. It is kamma which causes one to be born in a Buddhist country or to live in a Buddhist country. The kusala accumulated in the past conditions our study and practice of the Dhamma at the present time. If we consider the factors in our life which are the conditions for kusala we will understand more clearly that it is not self who performs good deeds.

In the Abhidhamma we learn that there are eight types of mahā-kusala cittas, kusala cittas of the sensuous plane of consciousness. Why isn't there only one type? The reason is that each type has its own conditions for its arising. If we know about these different types and if we can be aware of them when their characteristics present themselves, it will help us not to take them for self. Four types of mahā-kusala cittas arise with somanassa (pleasant feeling) and four types arise with upekkhā (indifferent feeling). We would like to have kusala cittas with somanassa, because we cling to somanassa. However, we cannot force somanassa to arise. Sometimes we perform dāna with somanassa, sometimes with upekkhā. It depends on conditions whether somanassa or whether upekkhā arises with the mahā-kusala citta. Four types are accompanied by wisdom; four types are not accompanied by wisdom. We may, for example, help others without paññā or with paññā. When we realize that helping is kusala, or when we are aware of the nāma or rūpa appearing at that moment, there is paññā arising with the mahā-kusala citta. Four types are asaṅkhārika (unprompted, spontaneous, not induced by someone else or by one's own consideration) and four types are sasaṅkhārika (prompted, by someone else or by oneself). The eight types of mahā-kusala cittas are the following:

[1] Wheel means here: vehicle or means of success.

1. Accompanied by pleasant feeling, with wisdom, unprompted (Somanassa-sahagataṃ, ñāṇa sampayuttaṃ, asaṅkhārikam ekaṃ)
2. Accompanied by pleasant feeling, with wisdom, prompted (Somanassa-sahagataṃ, ñāṇa-sampayuttaṃ, sasaṅkhārikam ekaṃ)
3. Accompanied by pleasant feeling, without wisdom, unprompted (Somanassa-sahagataṃ, ñāṇa-vippayuttaṃ, asaṅkhārikam ekaṃ)
4. Accompanied by pleasant feeling, without wisdom, prompted (Somanassa-sahagataṃ, ñāṇa-vippayuttaṃ, sasaṅkhārikam ekaṃ)
5. Accompanied by indifferent feeling, with wisdom, unprompted (Upekkhā-sahagataṃ, ñāṇa-sampayuttaṃ, asaṅkhārikam ekaṃ)
6. Accompanied by indifferent feeling, with wisdom, prompted (Upekkhā-sahagataṃ, ñāṇa-sampayuttaṃ, sasaṅkhārikam ekaṃ)
7. Accompanied by indifferent feeling, without wisdom, unprompted (Upekkhā-sahagataṃ, ñāṇa-vippayuttaṃ, asaṅkhārikam ekaṃ)
8. Accompanied by indifferent feeling, without wisdom, prompted (Upekkhā-sahagataṃ, ñāṇa-vippayuttaṃ, sasaṅkhārikam ekaṃ)

Mahā-kusala cittas are not the only kind of kāmāvacara sobhana cittas (beautiful cittas of the sensuous plane of consciousness). Mahā-kusala cittas are cittas which are cause; they can motivate kusala kamma through body, speech or mind which is capable of producing results. There are also mahā-vipākacittas, which are results of kusala kamma performed with mahā-kusala cittas. Mahā-vipākacittas are sobhana cittas too, arising with sobhana cetasikas. There are several types of mahā-vipākacittas because the kusala kammas which produce them are of different kinds.

People's deeds are not the same and thus the results cannot be the same. People are born with different paṭisandhi-cittas (rebirth-consciousness). Paṭisandhi-cittas are vipākacittas; they are the result of kamma. As we have seen before (in chapter 11), human beings can be born with a paṭisandhi-citta which is ahetuka kusala vipāka (and in this case they are handicapped from the first moment of life), or with a paṭisandhi-citta which is sahetuka vipāka, accompanied by sobhana hetus. In the case of human beings, and of beings born in other sensuous planes of existence, the paṭisandhi-citta which is sahetuka vipākacitta is mahā-vipākacitta, the result of kāmāvacara kusala kamma (kamma performed by mahā-kusala cittas, kusala cittas of the sensuous plane of consciousness). Apart from mahā-vipākacitta there are other types of sahetuka vipākacitta which are not the result of kāmāvacara kusala kamma but of kusala kamma of higher planes of consciousness. These types will be dealt with later on.

There are eight types of mahā-vipākacittas. They can be accompanied by somanassa or by upekkhā, they can be with paññā or without paññā, they can be unprompted, asaṅkhārika, or prompted, sasaṅkhārika. They are classified in the same way as the eight types of mahā-kusala cittas mentioned above.

The bhavanga-citta (life-continuum) and the cuti-citta (dying-consciousness) are the same type of citta as the first citta in one's life, the paṭisandhi-citta. If the paṭisandhi-citta is mahā-vipākacitta, the bhavanga-citta and the cuti-citta of that life are the same type of mahā-vipākacitta. In that case the functions of paṭisandhi, bhavanga and cuti are performed by mahā-vipākacitta.

When we see a beautiful visible object or experience pleasant objects through the other sense-doors, the citta is kusala vipākacitta, the result of kusala kamma; however, that kind of vipākacitta is ahetuka vipāka (arising without hetu), it is not mahā-vipāka. The functions of seeing, hearing, smelling, tasting and experiencing tangible object through the bodysense, and also the functions of sampaṭicchana, receiving, and santīraṇa, investigating, cannot be performed by mahā-vipākacittas, they are performed by ahetuka vipākacittas. Tadārammaṇa-citta, a vipāka-citta which may arise after the javana-cittas and which performs the function of tadārammaṇa, registering or retention, can be ahetuka vipākacitta or mahā-vipākacitta[2].

There are still other kinds of kāmāvacara sobhana cittas: the mahā-kiriyacittas[3]. The arahat has mahā-kiriyacittas instead of mahā-kusala cittas. Since he has no conditions for rebirth he does not accumulate any more kamma. He has mahā-kiriyacittas (inoperative cittas) which perform the function of javana in the sense-door process and in the mind-door process. When we experience a pleasant object lobha may arise and when we experience an unpleasant object dosa may arise. The arahat has equanimity towards pleasant objects and unpleasant objects, he has no more defilements. The arahat can have mahā-kiriyacittas which are ñāṇa-vippayutta, not accompanied by wisdom. Arahats can have mahā-kiriyacittas which are ñāṇa-vippayutta, because paññā does not necessarily accompany the mahā-kiriyacittas when they are not preaching or discussing Dhamma.

The arahat has kiriyacittas which are sobhana cittas and also kiriyacittas which are asobhana cittas. The five sense-door-adverting consciousness, pañca-dvārāvajjana-citta, the mind-door-adverting consciousness, mano-dvārāvajjana-citta, the hasituppāda-citta, smile producing consciousness of the arahat which can perform the function of javana, are asobhana kiriyacittas. These types of citta are not accompanied by sobhana cetasikas, they are ahetuka.

There are eight types of mahā-kiriyacittas in all. They are accompanied by somanassa or by upekkhā, they are accompanied by paññā or not accompanied by paññā, they are asaṅkhārika or sasaṅkhārika. They are classified in the same way as the eight types of mahā-kusala cittas.

Altogether there are fifty-four cittas which are kāma-bhūmi[4], or kāmāvacara cittas, cittas of the sensuous plane of consciousness. They are:

---

[2] See chapter 15. Tadārammaṇa-citta is either ahetuka or sahetuka, accompanied by hetus. Tadārammaṇa-citta which is sahetuka is called mahā-vipākacitta, since it belongs to the sense sphere.

[3] Mahā-kusala cittas, mahā-vipākacittas and mahā-kiriya cittas are always kāmāvacara cittas, cittas of the sensuous plane of consciousness.

[4] Bhūmi is plane; in this case, plane of citta, not plane of existence. The difference between plane of citta and plane of existence will be explained in chapter 20.

30 asobhana cittas	**24 sobhana cittas**
12 akusala cittas	8 mahā-vipākacittas
18 ahetuka cittas	8 mahā-kusalacittas
	8 mahā-kiriyacittas

Thus, there are thirty asobhana cittas and twenty-four kāma-sobhana cittas (sobhana cittas of the sensuous plane of consciousness).

There are also sobhana cittas which are not kāma-sobhana cittas, namely:

- the sobhana cittas which are rūpa-bhūmi (rūpāvacara cittas, for those who attain rūpa-jhāna)
- the sobhana cittas which are arūpa-bhūmi (arūpāvacara cittas, for those who attain arūpa-jhāna)
- the sobhana cittas which are lokuttara bhūmi, (lokuttara cittas for those who attain enlightenment)

Only kāmāvacara cittas can include both sobhana cittas and asobhana cittas. Cittas which are rūpa-bhūmi, arūpa-bhūmi and lokuttara bhūmi can only be sobhana cittas.

Those who do not attain jhāna or attain enlightenment cannot know the cittas of other bhūmis, but they can verify the truth of the Buddha's teachings as regards the kāma-bhūmi, the cittas of the sensuous plane of consciousness. We can find out for ourselves whether it is beneficial to perform dāna, observe sīla and apply ourselves to bhāvanā. We can find out whether the development of these ways of kusala helps us to have less akusala cittas. Sometimes it is the right moment for dāna, sometimes for sīla or for bhāvanā. Vipassanā, right understanding of realities, can be developed at any time, no matter whether we perform dāna, observe sīla, study or teach Dhamma. Right understanding can also be developed when there is no opportunity for dāna, sīla or other ways of kusala. Through mindfulness of nāma and rūpa we come to know the different types of cittas which arise, also akusala cittas and eventually there will be less attachment to the concept of self. In being mindful we can verify the truth of the Buddha's teachings.

We read in the Gradual Sayings (Book of the Sevens, chapter VIII, paragraph 9, The message):

> Now the venerable Upāli came to the Exalted One, saluted and sat down at one side. So seated, he said: "Well were it for me, lord, if the Exalted One were to expound Dhamma briefly to me, so that, having heard it, I might abide resolute, alone, secluded, earnest and zealous."
>
> "The doctrines, Upāli, of which you may know: 'These doctrines lead one not to complete weariness (of the world), nor to dispassion, nor to ending, nor to calm, nor to knowledge, nor to awakening, nor to the cool'-regard them definitely as not Dhamma, not the discipline, not the word of the Teacher. But the doctrines of which you may know: 'These doctrines lead one to complete weariness, dispassion, ending, calm, knowledge, the awakening, the cool'-regard them unreservedly as Dhamma, the discipline, the word of the Teacher."

The Commentary to this sutta, the "Manorathapūraṇi", explains the word "knowledge" as the penetration of the three characteristics of conditioned realities, namely, impermanence, dukkha and anattā. The "awakening" refers to the attainment of enlightenment and the "cool" to nibbāna.

Questions

1. Which cittas are ahetuka (without hetu)? Are they always asobhana?
2. Do arahats have asobhana cittas?
3. Why is the jhānacitta not kāmāvacara citta?
4. Are mahā-kusala cittas always accompanied by somanassa (pleasant feeling)?
5. Can vipākacitta be sobhana citta?
6. Can kiriyacitta be sobhana citta?
7. Why has the arahat mahā-kiriyacittas instead of mahā-kusala cittas?
8. How many types of kāmāvacara cittas are there?

20 Planes of Existence

We are born, we die and then we are born again. It is beyond control in which plane of existence we will be reborn; it depends on the kamma which produces the paṭisandhi-citta (rebirth-consciousness) after the cuti-citta (dying-consciousness) has fallen away.

At this moment we are living in the human plane. Human life, however, is very short. When this life is over we do not know in which plane we will be reborn. Most people do not like to think of the shortness of human life; they are absorbed in what they experience through the sense-doors and on account of these experiences they are happy or unhappy. However, we should realize that happiness and unhappiness are only mental phenomena which arise because of conditions and fall away again. Our whole life is a sequence of phenomena which arise and fall away again.

Many religions teach about heaven and hell. In what respect are the Buddhist teachings different? Do we just have to believe in heaven and hell? Through the Buddhist teachings we learn to study realities, to study cause and effect in life. Each cause brings about its appropriate result. People perform good and bad deeds and these deeds bring different results; they can cause birth in different planes of existence. A plane of existence is the place where one is born. Birth in a woeful plane is the result of a bad deed and birth in a happy plane is the result of a good deed. Since the deeds of beings are of many different degrees of kusala and akusala, the results are of many different degrees as well. There are different woeful planes and different happy planes of existence.

The animal world is a woeful plane. We can see how animals devour one another and we find that nature is cruel. The animal world is not the only woeful plane. There are different hell planes. The akusala vipāka in hell is more intense than the sufferings which can be experienced in the human plane. The descriptions of hells in the Buddhist teachings are not merely allegories; the experience of unpleasant things through eyes, ears, nose, tongue and bodysense is akusala vipāka and akusala vipāka is reality. Life in a hell plane is not permanent; when one's lifespan in a hell plane is over there can be rebirth in another plane.

Apart from the animal plane and the hell planes, there are other woeful planes. Birth in the plane of petas (ghosts) is the result of akusala kamma. Beings in that plane have a deformed figure and they are always hungry and thirsty.

Furthermore, there is the plane of asuras (demons). The objects which are experienced in the asura plane are not as enjoyable as the objects which can be experienced in the human plane. There are four classes of woeful planes in all.

Birth as a human being is a happy rebirth. In the human plane there is opportunity for the development of kusala. One can study Dhamma and learn to develop the way leading to the end of defilements, to the end of birth and death. Birth in the human plane is kusala vipāka, but during one's lifespan in this plane there are both kusala vipāka and akusala vipāka. Each person experiences different results in life: there are gain and loss, honour and dishonour, praise and blame, happiness and misery. It is due to kamma whether someone is born into pleasant or unpleasant surroundings, whether he belongs to a family which is well-to-do or which is poor.

The experience of pleasant and unpleasant things through eyes, ears, nose, tongue and bodysense are the results of kamma.

Other happy planes, apart from the human plane, are the heavenly planes. In the heavenly planes there is more kusala vipāka than in the human plane and less akusala vipāka. There are several heavenly planes and although life in a heavenly plane lasts a very long time, it is not permanent. The woeful planes, the human plane and the six heavenly planes which are deva planes, are sensuous planes of existence. Sensuous planes of existence are planes where there is seeing, hearing, smelling, tasting, the experience of tangible object through the bodysense and other kāmāvacara cittas (cittas which are of the sensuous plane of consciousness). There are eleven classes of sensuous planes of existence in all.

Those who see the disadvantages of sense-impressions may cultivate jhāna; they can be reborn in higher heavenly planes which are not sensuous planes. Those who attain rūpa-jhāna can be reborn in rūpa-brahma-planes where there are less sense-impressions. There are sixteen rūpa-brahma planes in all. One of them is the asañña-satta plane[1] where there is only rūpa, not nāma. Those who have attained the highest stage of rūpa-jhāna and who wish to have no consciousness at all, can be reborn without citta; for them there is only a body. These beings have seen the disadvantages of consciousness; even happiness is a disadvantage, since it does not last.

Those who see the disadvantages of rūpa cultivate arūpa-jhāna. If they attain arūpa-jhāna they can be reborn in arūpa-brahma planes where there is no rūpa. There are four classes of arūpa-brahma planes. Beings born in these planes have only nāma, not rūpa. One may wonder how there can be beings which only have rūpa or beings which only have nāma. When right understanding of nāma and rūpa has been developed realities will be seen as only elements which arise because of conditions, not a being, not a person, no self. One will come to understand that, under the appropriate conditions, there can be rūpa without nāma and nāma without rūpa.

There are thirty-one classes of planes of existence in all, namely:

- 4 woeful planes
- 1 human plane
- 6 deva planes

The above are 11 sensuous planes

- 16 rūpa-brahma planes
- 4 arūpa-brahma planes

We read in the Gradual Sayings (Book of the Sevens, chapter VI, paragraph 9a, Amity) about the value of wholesome deeds. They can bring pleasant results for a long time and cause birth in different happy planes. We read that the Buddha told the monks about his births in different happy planes. The Buddha said:

[1] Asañña means: without saññā, perception or remembrance, and satta means: being.

Monks, be not afraid of deeds of merit. It is a name for happiness, that is, meritorious deeds. For well I know, monks, that deeds of merit done for a long time have a ripening, a blossoming, which is pleasing, joyous and lovely for a long time.

For seven years I fostered thoughts of amity, and then for seven ages of the world's rolling on and rolling back I came not again to this world. Then when the world rolled on, I reached the sphere of Radiance; then when the world rolled back, I won to Brahmā's empty palace. Then, monks, I became Brahmā, great Brahmā, the conqueror, unconquered, all-seeing, all-powerful. Thirty-six times I was Sakka, the deva-king. Many times seven was I a Wheel-turning rajah, just, righteous, conquering the four ends of the earth, bringing stability to the country, possessing the seven gems...

As we have seen, the fact that beings are born in different planes of existence is due to their accumulated kamma. Plane of existence is the place or world where one is born. Plane of existence is not the same as plane of citta. There are different planes of citta depending on the object (ārammaṇa) the citta experiences. There are four different planes of citta which are the following:

1. kāmāvacara cittas (sensuous plane of citta or kāma-bhūmi)
2. rūpāvacara cittas (plane of rūpa-jhānacittas)
3. arūpāvacara cittas (plane of arūpa-jhānacittas)
4. lokuttara cittas (plane of supramundane cittas experiencing nibbāna)

Kāmāvacara cittas can be classified as asobhana cittas (cittas not accompanied by sobhana cetasikas) and as kāma-sobhana cittas (cittas of the sensuous plane of consciousness, accompanied by sobhana cetasikas).

Kāmāvacara cittas arise in thirty planes of existence; they do not arise in the asañña-satta plane, where there is no nāma, only rūpa. Even in the arūpa-brahma-planes there are kāmāvacara cittas.

As regards kāma-sobhana cittas, they can arise even in woeful planes. Furthermore, they arise in the human plane, in the deva planes, in the rūpa-brahma planes and in the arūpa-brahma planes. They arise in thirty planes of existence, the asañña-satta plane excepted. Not all types, however, arise in all planes of existence.

As regards asobhana cittas, they can arise in thirty planes of existence, but not all types arise in all planes. Lobha-mūla-cittas (cittas rooted in attachment) can arise in thirty planes; even in the rūpa-brahma planes and arūpa-brahma planes lobha-mūla-cittas can arise. Dosa-mūla-cittas (cittas rooted in aversion) arise in the eleven sensuous planes of existence. It is clinging to sense objects which conditions dosa; when one does not obtain the pleasant object one likes, one has aversion. Dosa-mūla-cittas do not arise in the rūpa-brahma planes or in the arūpa-brahma planes. So long as beings live in the rūpa-brahma planes and in the arūpa-brahma planes there are no conditions for dosa. Moha-mūla-cittas (cittas rooted in ignorance) arise in thirty planes of existence; all those who are not arahats have moha and thus moha-mūla-cittas arise in all planes of existence, except in the asañña-satta plane.

As we have seen, not only akusala cittas, but also ahetuka cittas are asobhana cittas (cittas which are not accompanied by sobhana cetasikas). As regards the asobhana cittas which are ahetuka, the ahetuka cittas which arise in a process of cittas experiencing an object through one of the sense-doors, can arise only in the planes of existence where there are sense impressions. Seeing-consciousness and hearing-consciousness arise in the eleven sensuous planes of existence (the four woeful planes, the human being plane and the six heavenly planes which are sensuous planes, the deva planes), and they arise also in fifteen rūpa-brahma planes, thus, they arise in twenty-six planes of existence. They do not arise in the arūpa-brahma planes where there is no rūpa.

Smelling-consciousness, tasting-consciousness and body-consciousness arise only in the eleven sensuous planes of existence. Thus, they do not arise in the rūpa-brahma planes and in the arūpa-brahma planes.

Pañca-dvārāvajjana-citta (five-door-adverting-consciousness), sampaṭicchana-citta (receiving-consciousness) and santīraṇa-citta (investigating-consciousness) arise in all planes where there are sense-impressions, thus, they arise in twenty-six planes: in the eleven sensuous planes and in fifteen rūpa-brahma planes; the asañña-satta plane is excepted.

The mano-dvārāvajjana-citta (mind-door-adverting-consciousness) arises in all planes where there is nāma, thus, it arises in thirty planes.

People are inclined to speculate about the place where they will be reborn. Would we like to be reborn in the human plane? We cling to life in the human plane and we do not always realize the many moments of akusala vipāka we are bound to receive in this world: we are threatened by calamities such as war and hunger; we are subject to old age, sickness and death. Some people would like to be reborn in a heavenly plane; they like to experience pleasant things through the senses. One may wish for rebirth in a heavenly plane, but whether or not this will happen depends on one's kamma. Birth is result, it does not take place without cause. If one performs many good deeds one cultivates the cause which will bring a pleasant result but there is no way to know when the result will take place, this is beyond control.

Are we afraid of death? Most people want to prolong their lives. They fear death because they feel uncertain of the future. If one is not an ariyan (a noble person who has attained enlightenment) there may be rebirth in hell. We do not like to think of rebirth in a woeful plane, but there may be deeds performed in the past which can cause rebirth in hell. Even the Buddha was in one of his former lives born in hell[2]. It is useless to think of hell with aversion and fear, but the thought of hell is beneficial when it reminds us to develop kusala at this moment, instead of akusala.

We read in the Kindred Sayings (V, Mahā-vagga, Kindred Sayings on Streamwinning, chapter VI, paragraph 4, Visiting the sick) that while the Buddha was staying among the Sakyans at Kapilavatthu, in Banyan Park, Mahānāma asked him how a wise lay-follower who is sick should be admonished by another wise lay-follower. The Buddha said:

---

[2] This has been referred to in the "Mūga-Pakkha-Jātaka",VI, no. 538.

A wise lay-disciple, Mahānāma, who is sick. . . should be admonished by another wise lay-disciple with the four comfortable assurances, thus: "Take comfort, dear sir, in your unwavering loyalty to the Buddha, saying: He is the Exalted One, Arahat, fully enlightened One. . . Teacher of devas and mankind, a Buddha, an Exalted One. Take comfort, dear sir, in your unwavering loyalty to the Dhamma, thus: Well proclaimed is the Dhamma. . . Take comfort, dear sir, in your unwavering loyalty to the Sangha. . . Take comfort, dear sir, in your possession of the virtues dear to the Ariyans. . ." A wise lay-disciple, Mahānāma, who is sick. . . should be admonished by another wise lay-disciple with these four comfortable assurances.

Then, supposing he has longing for his parents, he should thus be spoken to:

If he say: "I have longing for my parents", the other should reply: "But, my dear sir, you are subject to death. Whether you feel longing for your parents or not, you will have to die. It were just as well for you to abandon the longing you have for your parents."

If he should say: "That longing for my parents is now abandoned," the other should reply: "Yet, my dear sir, you still have longing for your children. As you must die in any case, it were just as well for you to abandon that longing for your children."

If he should say: "That longing for my children is now abandoned," the other should reply: "Yet, my dear sir, you still have longing for the five human pleasures of sense."

Then, if he say, "That longing for the five human pleasures of sense is now abandoned," the other should reply: "My friend, the heavenly delights are more excellent than the five human pleasures of sense. It were well for you, worthy sir, to remove your thoughts from them and fix them upon the Four Deva Kings."

Suppose the sick man say, "My thoughts are removed from human pleasures of sense and fixed upon the Four Deva Kings," then let the other say: "More excellent than the Four Deva Kings and more choice are the Suite of the Thirty-three. . . the Yama Devas, the Devas of Delight, the Creative Devas. . . the Devas who rejoice in the work of other devas. . . the latter are more excellent and choice than the former. . . so it were better for you to fix your thoughts on the Brahma World."

Then if the sick man's thoughts are so fixed, let the other say: "My friend, even the Brahma World is impermanent, not lasting, prisoned in a person. Well for you, friend, if you raise your mind above the Brahma World and fix it on cessation from the person pack[3].

And if the sick man say he has done so, then, Mahānāma, I declare that there is no difference between the lay-disciple who thus avers and the

[3] The five khandhas of clinging.

> monk whose heart is freed from the āsavas, that is, between the release of the one and the release of the other.

Being subject to birth is dangerous. No rebirth at all in any plane of existence is better than birth even in the highest heavenly plane. If one wants to have no more rebirth right understanding of realities should be developed in order to realize the four ariyan (noble) Truths. Then one is on the way leading to the end of rebirth.

The first ariyan Truth is the truth of dukkha. If we could experience, for instance, that seeing at this moment, hearing, attachment or any other nāma or rūpa which appears now is only an element which arises and falls away, we would have more understanding of the truth of dukkha. What arises and falls away cannot give satisfaction, it is dukkha. The second ariyan Truth is the truth of the origin of dukkha. Craving is the origin of dukkha. Through the development of the eightfold Path there will be less craving, less clinging to nāma and rūpa. When there finally is no more craving, there will be an end to rebirth, and this is the end of dukkha. The third ariyan Truth is the extinction of dukkha, which is nibbāna, and the fourth ariyan Truth is the Path leading to the extinction of dukkha, which is the eightfold Path.

We read in the Mahā-parinibbāna-sutta (Dialogues of the Buddha II, no. 16, chapter II, 1-4):

> ...The Exalted One proceeded with a great company of the monks to Kotigāma; and there he stayed in the village itself.
>
> And at that place the Exalted One addressed the monks, and said: "It is through not understanding and grasping four Ariyan Truths, O monks, that we have had to run so long, to wander so long in this weary path of rebirth, both you and I!"
>
> "And what are these four?"
>
> "The Ariyan truth about dukkha; the Ariyan truth about the cause of dukkha; the Ariyan truth about the cessation of dukkha; and the Ariyan truth about the path that leads to that cessation. But when these Ariyan truths are grasped and known the craving for future life is rooted out, that which leads to renewed becoming is destroyed, and then there is no more birth!"

Questions

1. Why do the Buddha's teachings speak about hell?
2. What is a plane of existence?
3. What is the difference between "plane of citta" and "plane of existence"?
4. The human plane is a sensuous plane of existence. Are there in the human plane only cittas which are kāmāvacara cittas (cittas of the sensuous plane of citta)?
5. The rūpa-brahma planes are not sensuous planes of existence. Can there be kāmāvacara cittas in the rūpa-brahma planes? If so, all types?

21 Samatha

We would like to have more wholesomeness in life, but often we are unable to do wholesome deeds, to speak in a wholesome way or to think wholesome thoughts. Our accumulated defilements hinder us in the performing of kusala. We learn from the Buddhist teachings that there are "hindrances" (nīvaraṇa), which are akusala cetasikas arising with akusala cittas. The hindrances arise time and again in daily life. They are:

- sensuous desire, in Pāli: kāmacchandha
- ill-will, in Pāli: vyāpāda
- torpor and languor, in Pāli: thīna and middha
- restlessness and worry, in Pāli: uddhacca and kukkucca
- doubt, in Pāli: vicikicchā

Kāmacchandha or sensuous desire is the cetasika which is lobha (attachment). It is attachment to the objects we can experience through the sense-doors and the mind-door. We all have kāmacchandha in different forms and intensities. Because of economic progress and technical inventions there is more prosperity in life. One can afford more things which make life pleasant and comfortable. This, however, does not bring contentedness; on the contrary, we are not satisfied with what we have and we are forever looking for more enjoyment and happiness. There is kāmacchandha with our deeds, words and thoughts. Even when we think that we are doing good deeds and helping others, kāmacchandha can arise. Kāmacchandha makes us restless and unhappy.

Vyāpāda or ill-will is the cetasika which is dosa. Vyāpāda can trouble us many times a day; we feel irritated about other people or about things which happen in life. Vyāpāda prevents us from kusala. When there is vyāpāda we cannot have loving kindness and compassion for other people.

Thīna and *middha* are translated as "torpor" and "languor", or as "sloth" and "torpor". Thīna and middha cause us to have lack of energy for kusala. The Visuddhimagga (XIV, 167) states concerning thīna and middha:

> . . . Herein, stiffness (thīna) has the characteristic of lack of driving power. Its function is to remove energy. It is manifested as subsiding. Torpor (middha) has the characteristic of unwieldiness. Its function is to smother. It is manifested as laziness, or it is manifested as nodding and sleep. The proximate cause of both is unwise attention to boredom, sloth, and so on.

Don't we all have moments in a day when there is laziness and lack of energy to perform kusala? When, for example, we are listening to the preaching of Dhamma or reading the scriptures, there are opportunities for kusala cittas. Instead, we may feel bored and we lack energy for kusala. It may happen that we see someone else who needs our help, but we are lazy and do not move. Time and again we are hindered by thīna and middha. Thīna and middha make the mind unwieldy[1].

---

[1] See Visuddhimagga IV, 105, where the hindrances are mentioned as being specifically obstructive to jhāna.

Uddhacca is translated as "agitation" or "excitement" and kukkucca as "worry" or "regret". Uddhacca arises with each and every type of akusala citta. It prevents the citta from wholesomeness. As regards kukkucca, worry or regret, the Visuddhimagga (XIV, 174) states:

> ...It has subsequent regret as its characteristic. Its function is to sorrow about what has and what has not been done. It is manifested as remorse. Its proximate cause is what has and what has not been done. It should be regarded as slavery.

When we have done something wrong or we have not done the good deed we should have done, we might be inclined to think about it again and again. We may ask ourselves why we acted in the way we did, but we cannot change what is past already. While we worry we have akusala cittas; worry makes us enslaved. Uddhacca and kukkucca prevent us from being tranquil.

As regards vicikicchā, doubt, there are many kinds of doubt. One may have doubt about the Buddha, the Dhamma and the Sangha, or doubt about the eightfold Path. Doubt is akusala and a hindrance to the performing of kusala.

All of the hindrances are obstructions to the performing of kusala. Is there a way to eliminate them? Samatha or the development of calm is a way to temporarily eliminate the hindrances. The calm which is developed in samatha has to be wholesome calm, it cannot arise with akusala citta. There is a degree of calm with each kusala citta but it is hard to know the characteristic of calm precisely, because there are bound to be akusala cittas very shortly after the kusala cittas. In order to develop the calm which is temporary freedom from the hindrances right understanding, paññā, is indispensable. If one merely tries to concentrate on a meditation subject without right understanding of kusala and akusala and of the characteristic of calm, calm cannot grow. The paññā of the level of samatha does not eradicate defilements, but it knows the characteristic of calm and it knows how it can be developed by means of a suitable meditation subject. Akusala citta is likely to arise time and again, even when one tries to develop samatha. One may be attached to silence and then there is akusala citta instead of the calm of samatha. Or one may think, when there is no pleasant feeling nor unpleasant feeling but indifferent feeling, that there is calm. However, indifferent feeling can arise with kusala citta as well as with akusala citta; lobha-mūla-citta can be accompanied by indifferent feeling and moha-mūla-citta is invariably accompanied by indifferent feeling. Thus, when there is indifferent feeling it may seem that one is calm, but there is not necessarily the wholesome calm of samatha. The paññā of samatha must be very keen so as to be able to recognize even the more subtle defilements which arise.

We read in the scriptures about people who could attain jhāna if they cultivated the right conditions for it. Before the Buddha's enlightenment, jhāna was the highest form of kusala people could attain. Jhāna, which is sometimes translated as absorption[2], is a high degree of calm. At the moment of jhānacitta one is free from sense-impressions and from the defilements which are bound up with them. The attainment of jhāna is extremely difficult, not everybody who applies himself

---

[2] In the suttas we also come across translations of jhāna as "trance" or "musing". Trance, however, gives a wrong association of meaning.

to samatha can attain jhāna. However, even if one has no intention to cultivate jhāna there can be conditions for moments of calm in daily life; but one must have right understanding of the characteristic of calm and of the way to develop it.

When one applies oneself to samatha one should develop five cetasikas which can eliminate the hindrances; they are the jhāna-factors. The first jhāna-factor is *vitakka*, which is translated into English as "applied thinking". Vitakka is a mental factor, a cetasika, which arises with many kinds of citta; it can arise with kusala citta as well as with akusala citta. The wholesome kind of vitakka which is developed in samatha is one of the jhāna-factors. The Visuddhimagga (IV, 88) states concerning vitakka:

> . . . Herein, applied thinking (vitakkana) is applied thought (vitakka); hitting upon, is what is meant. It has the characteristic of directing the mind onto an object (mounting the mind on its object). Its function is to strike at and thresh – for the meditator is said, in virtue of it, to have the object struck at by applied thought, threshed by applied thought. It is manifested as the leading of the mind onto an object. . .

Vitakka, when it is a jhāna-factor, is opposed to thīna and middha (sloth and torpor). In "thinking" of the meditation subject vitakka helps to inhibit thīna and middha temporarily[3].

Another jhāna-factor is vicāra, which is translated as "sustained thinking". This cetasika arises with different kinds of citta, but when it is developed in samatha, it is a jhāna-factor. The Visuddhimagga (IV, 88) states concerning vicāra:

> . . . Sustained thinking (vicaraṇa) is sustained thought (vicāra); continued sustainment (anusañcaraṇa), is what is meant. It has the characteristic of continued pressure on (occupation with) the object. Its function is to keep conascent (mental) states (occupied) with that. It is manifested as keeping consciousness anchored (on that object).

In samatha, vicāra keeps the citta anchored on the meditation subject. When we continue to think of wholesome subjects such as the Buddha's virtues or his teachings there is no vicikicchā or doubt. Vicāra helps to inhibit doubt.

Another jhāna-factor is *pīti*, translated as "rapture", "enthusiasm" or "happiness". Pīti can also arise with lobha-mūla-citta and then it is akusala. The wholesome kind of pīti, arising with kusala citta, which is developed in samatha is a jhāna-factor. The Visuddhimagga (IV, 94) states concerning pīti:

> . . . It refreshes (pīṇayati), thus it is happiness (pīti). It has the characteristic of endearing (sampiyāna). Its function is to refresh the body and the mind; or its function is to pervade (thrill with rapture). It is manifested as elation. But it is of five kinds as minor happiness, momentary happiness, showering happiness, uplifting happiness, and pervading (rapturous) happiness.

According to the Visuddhimagga (IV, 99) the jhāna-factor pīti is the "pervading happiness" which is the "root of absorption". When pīti is developed in samatha it inhibits the hindrance which is ill-will (vyāpāda). However, keen understanding is

[3] See also the Atthasālinī, "The Expositor ", Part V, chapter I, 165.

needed in order to know whether there is akusala pīti which arises with attachment or kusala pīti. Even when one thinks that one has wholesome enthusiasm about a meditation subject, there may be clinging. The jhāna-factor pīti takes an interest in the meditation subject without clinging. Wholesome pīti which delights in the Buddha, the Dhamma and the Sangha or in another meditation subject refreshes the mind and then there is no aversion, no boredom as to kusala.

Another jhāna-factor is sukha, happy feeling. This jhāna-factor is not pleasant bodily feeling, but it is happy mental feeling or somanassa. Sukha which is developed in samatha is happy feeling about a meditation subject. However, as we know, happy feeling arises also with attachment. Paññā should know precisely when happy feeling is akusala and when it is kusala. The jhāna-factor which is wholesome sukha inhibits the hindrances which are restlessness and regret (uddhacca and kukkucca). When there is wholesome happy feeling about a meditation subject, restlessness and regret do not arise.

Pīti and sukha are not the same. *Sukha*, which is translated as happiness, bliss, ease or joy, is happy feeling. Pīti, which is translated as joy, rapture, zest, and sometimes also as happiness, is not feeling; it is not vedanākkhandha, but saṅkhārakkhandha (the khandha which is all cetasikas, except vedanā and saññā[4]). When reading the English translations, we have to find out from the context which cetasika is referred to, pīti or sukha.

The Visuddhimagga (IV, 100) states concerning the difference between happiness (pīti) and bliss (sukha):

> And whenever the two are associated, happiness (pīti) is the contentedness at getting a desirable object, and bliss (sukha) is the actual experiencing of it when got. Where there is happiness there is bliss (pleasure); but where there is bliss there is not necessarily happiness. Happiness is included in the formations aggregate (saṅkhārakkhandha) ; bliss is included in the feeling aggregate (vedanākkhandha). If a man exhausted in a desert saw or heard about a pond on the edge of a wood, he would have happiness; if he went into the wood's shade and used the water, he would have bliss. . .

The jhāna-factor *samādhi* or concentration is the cetasika which is *ekaggatā* cetasika. This cetasika arises with every citta and its function is to focus on an object. Each citta can experience only one object and ekaggatā cetasika focuses on that one object. Ekaggatā cetasika or samādhi can be kusala as well as akusala. Samādhi when it is developed in samatha is wholesome concentration on a meditation subject. Together with samādhi there must be right understanding which knows precisely when the citta is kusala citta and when akusala citta and which knows how to develop calm, otherwise the right concentration of samatha will not grow. If one tries very hard to concentrate but right understanding is lacking, there may be attachment to one's effort to become concentrated, or, if one cannot become concentrated, aversion may arise. Then calm cannot grow. If there is right understanding there are conditions for samādhi to develop. The Visuddhimagga (XIV, 139) states concerning samādhi:

---

[4] See chapter 2.

> It puts (ādhiyati) consciousness evenly (samaṁ) on the object, or it puts it rightly (sammā) on it, or it is just the mere collecting (samādhāna) of the mind, thus it is concentration (samādhi). Its characteristic is non-wandering, or its characteristic is non-distraction. Its function is to conglomerate conascent states as water does bath powder. It is manifested as peace. Usually its proximate cause is bliss. It should be regarded as steadiness of the mind, like the steadiness of a lamp's flame when there is no draught.

Samādhi inhibits kāmacchandha (sensuous desire). When there is right concentration on a wholesome subject of meditation, one is at that moment not hindered by kāmacchandha.

Summarising the five jhāna-factors, necessary for the attainment of the first stage of jhāna, they are:

- vitakka, applied thinking
- vicāra, sustained thinking
- pīti, enthusiasm, rapture or happiness
- sukha, happy feeling or bliss
- samādhi, concentration

The Atthasālinī (Expositor I, Book I, Part V, chapter I, 165) states concerning the jhāna-factors which inhibit the hindrances:

> . . . For it is said that the Hindrances are opposed to the jhāna-factors, which are hostile to them and dispel and destroy them. Likewise it is said, in the "Peṭakopadesa", that concentration is opposed to sensuous desire, rapture (pīti) to ill-will, initial application of mind (vitakka) to sloth and torpor, bliss (sukha) to flurry and worry (uddhacca and kukkucca), sustained application of mind (vicāra) to perplexity (vicikicchā, doubt). . .

The jhāna-factors have to be developed in order to temporarily eliminate the hindrances. For the person who wants to develop the jhāna-factors and attain jhāna a great deal of preparation is required. We read in the Visuddhimagga (II, 1 and III, 1) that the person who wants to cultivate samatha should be well established in sīla (morality), which is purified by such qualities as fewness of wishes, contentment, effacement, seclusion, energy and modest needs. Sīla will become more perfected by the observation of ascetic practices (as described in Ch II of the Visuddhimagga), which pertain mostly to the monk with regard to the use of his robes, his almsfood and his place of dwelling.

In the Buddha's time laypeople too could attain jhāna, if they had accumulated the inclination and skill to develop it and if they would lead a life which was compatible with its development[5]. One should lead a secluded life and many conditions have to be fulfilled. Jhāna is quite incompatible with sense desires. One has to be "quite secluded from sense desires. . . " in order to attain jhāna, as we read in many suttas[6].

---

[5] An example is Nanda's mother, about whom we read in the Gradual Sayings, Book of the Sevens, chapter V, paragraph 10.

[6] For example, in the "Middle Length Sayings" I, no. 21, Discourse on Fear and Dread.

The Visuddhimagga (IV, 81) explains that sense-desires are incompatible with the attainment of jhāna. The development of jhāna is not for everyone. Jhāna cannot be attained if one leads a "worldly life", full of sense-pleasures, instead of a life of "fewness of wishes, seclusion, modest needs".

The Visuddhimagga (III, 129) states that one should sever anything which can be an impediment to the development of samatha. Impediments are, for example, travelling and sickness, and also the place where one lives can be an impediment. One should avoid living in a monastery which, for various reasons, is unfavourable to the development of samatha. Thus, even before one begins to develop samatha, many conditions have to be fulfilled.

For the development of samatha one has to apply oneself to a suitable subject of meditation. There are forty meditation subjects which can condition calm and these are the following:

- 10 kasina exercises, which are, for example, kasinas (disks) of particular colours, the earth kasina or the kasina of light.
- 10 loathsome subjects (in Pāli: asubha), the "cemetery meditations".
- 10 recollections, comprising the recollection of the Buddha, the Dhamma, the Sangha, virtue, generosty, deities, and also the recollections which are: mindfulness of death, mindfulness of the body, mindfulness of breathing and the recollection of peace (nibbāna).
- 1 The perception of repulsiveness in nutriment.
- 1 The definition of the four elements (earth, water, fire and wind).
- 4 brahma-vihāras (divine abidings), comprising: loving kindness (mettā), compassion (karuṇā), altruistic joy (muditā) and equanimity (upekkhā, which in this case is not upekkhā vedanā or indifferent feeling, but the wholesome cetasika which is tatramajjhattatā).
- 4 meditation subjects for the development of arūpa-jhānas (immaterial jhānas), which will be dealt with later on.

Not all subjects are suitable for everybody, it depends on the individual which subject is a means for him to develop calm. If there is right understanding of the way to become calm by means of a suitable meditation subject, calm can grow, even in our daily life. Loving kindness and compassion, for instance, can and should be developed in our daily life, when we are in the company of other people, and then there are kusala cittas instead of akusala cittas. Recollection of the Dhamma includes also reflection on the teachings and this is beneficial for everybody; it helps one to begin to understand life. While we reflect with kusala citta on the teachings or on one of the other meditation subjects, moments of calm can arise if we do not cling to calm.

In the Visuddhimagga it is explained how one can develop higher degrees of calm by means of a meditation subject. It is explained (Vis. III, 119) that meditation subjects are learned by sight, by touch and by hearsay (words), depending on the nature of the subject. As regards the subjects which are learned by sight (such as coloured kasinas and the cemetery meditations), the Visuddhimagga (IV, 31) states that in the beginning one has to look closely at the meditation subject, and that later on one acquires a mental image ("sign", in Pāli: nimitta) of it; one no longer needs to look at the original object. At first the mental image is still unsteady and unclear, but later on it appears "a hundred times, a thousand times more purified..." The original object, for example a coloured kasina or the earth kasina, could have flaws, but the perfected mental image which is acquired when one is more advanced, does not have the imperfections of the original object one was looking at in the beginning. This perfected image is called the counterpart sign (paṭibhāga nimitta).

At the moment the "counterpart sign" appears there is a higher degree of calm and concentration is more developed. This stage is called "access-concentration" (upacāra samādhi). The citta is not jhānacitta, it is still kāmāvacara citta (of the sense sphere), but the hindrances do not arise at the moment of "access concentration". However, the jhāna-factors are not developed enough yet to attain jhāna, and moreover, there are still other conditions needed to attain it. One has to "guard the sign" (nimitta) in order not to lose the perfected mental image one has developed. "Access concentration" is already very difficult to attain, but "guarding the sign" which is necessary in order to attain jhāna is also very difficult. The conditions for guarding the sign are, among others, the right dwelling place, suitable food, and avoidance of aimless talk. One should "balance" the five "spiritual faculties" (indriyas) which are the following cetasikas:

- saddhā (confidence in wholesomeness)
- viriya (energy)
- sati (mindfulness)
- samādhi (concentration)
- paññā (wisdom)

Confidence should be balanced with wisdom so that one has not confidence uncritically and groundlessly. Concentration should be balanced with energy, because if there is concentration but not enough energy there will be idleness and jhāna cannot be attained. Too much energy and not enough concentration leads to agitation and then one cannot attain jhāna either. All five indriyas should be balanced.

From the foregoing examples we see that samatha cannot be cultivated without a basic understanding and careful consideration of the realities taught in the Abhidhamma which are in fact the realities of daily life. One should know precisely when the citta is kusala citta and when it is akusala citta. One should know which realities the jhāna-factors are and one should realize as regards oneself whether or not the jhāna-factors are developed. One should know whether or not the cetasikas which are the five indriyas (faculties) are developed, whether or not they are balanced. If one does not have right understanding of all these different factors and conditions necessary for the attainment of "access concentration" and of jhāna, one is in danger of taking for "access concentration" what is not "access concentration" and taking for jhāna what is not jhāna. Neither "access concentration" nor jhāna can be attained without having cultivated the right conditions.

Not all meditation subjects lead to jhāna, some have only "access concentration" as their result, such as the recollections of the Buddha, the Dhamma and the Sangha.

Some meditation subjects lead only to the first stage of rūpa-jhāna[7], some to all stages of rūpa-jhāna. The meditation subject which is mindfulness of breathing can lead to all stages of rūpa-jhāna. This meditation subject which is considered by many to be relatively easy, is one of the most difficult. One has to be mindful of one's in-breath and out-breath where they touch the tip of the nose or the upper-lip. This meditation subject is not learnt by sight, but by touch: the in-breath and out-breath are the "sign" (nimitta) one has continuously to give attention to. We read in the Visuddhimagga (VIII, 208):

> For while other meditation subjects become clearer at each higher stage, this one does not: in fact, as he goes on developing it, it becomes more subtle for him at each higher stage, and it even comes to the point at which it is no longer manifest.

Further on (VIII, 211) we read:

> Although any meditation subject, no matter what, is successful only in one who is mindful and fully aware, yet any meditation subject other than this one gets more evident as he goes on giving it his attention. But this mindfulness of breathing is difficult, difficult to develop, a field in which only the minds of Buddhas, Pacceka Buddhas[8], and Buddhas's sons are at home. It is no trivial matter, nor can it be cultivated by trivial persons. In proportion as continued attention is given to it, it becomes more peaceful and more subtle. So strong mindfulness and understanding are necessary here.

> Mindfulness of breathing is most difficult, "it is no trivial matter", as the Visuddhimagga stated. The Buddha and his great disciples were endowed with great wisdom and other excellent qualities and thus, for them it was a "field" in which their minds were at home.

When one continues to be mindful of breathing, the in-breaths and out-breaths become more and more subtle and thus harder to notice. We just read in the quotation that strong mindfulness and understanding are necessary here. Not only in vipassanā, but also in samatha, mindfulness, sati, and understanding, paññā, are necessary, but the object of awareness in samatha is different from the object of awareness in vipassanā. In samatha the object of awareness is one among the forty meditation subjects and the aim is the development of calm. In vipassanā the object of awareness is any nāma or rūpa which appears at the present moment through one of the six doors, and the aim is to eradicate the wrong view of self and eventually all defilements. Through samatha defilements can be temporarily subdued, but the latent tendencies of defilements are not eradicated; when there are conditions for akusala cittas they arise again. We read in the Gradual Sayings

---

[7] Both rūpa-jhāna ("material jhāna") and arūpa-jhāna ("immaterial jhāna", for which the meditation subject is no longer dependent on materiality) are developed in different stages of jhāna. Arūpa-jhāna is more refined than rūpa-jhāna.

[8] A Pacceka Buddha is a "Silent Buddha" who has attained enlightenment without the help of a teacher, but who has not accumulated wisdom and the other excellent qualities, the "perfections", to the extent that he is able to teach others the eightfold Path.

(Book of the Sixes, chapter VI, paragraph 6, Citta Hatthisāriputta) that even the monk who can attain jhāna may "disavow the training" and return to the layman's life. We read that when the Buddha was staying near Vārānasi, in the Deer Park at Isipatana, a number of "elders" were having a conversation on Abhidhamma. Citta Hatthisāriputta interrupted their talk from time to time. Mahā Koṭṭhita said to him:

> "Let not the venerable Citta Hatthisāriputta constantly interrupt the elders' Abhidhamma talk; the venerable Citta should wait until the talk is over!"
>
> And when he had thus spoken, Citta's friends said: "The venerable Mahā Koṭṭhita should not censure the venerable Citta Hatthisāriputta. A wise man is the venerable Citta and able to talk to the elders on Abhidhamma."
>
> "It is a hard thing, sirs, for those who know not another person's ways of thought. Consider, sirs, a person who, so long as he lives near the Master or a fellow-teacher in the holy life, is the most humble of the humble, the meekest of the meek, the quietest of the quiet; and who, when he leaves the Master or his fellow-teachers, keeps company with monks, nuns, lay-disciples, men and women, rajahs, their ministers, course-setters or their disciples. Living in company, untrammelled, rude, given over to gossip, passion corrupts his heart; and with his heart corrupted by passion, he disavows the training and returns to the lower life...
>
> Consider again a person who, aloof from sensuous appetites...enters and abides in the first jhāna. Thinking: 'I have won to the first jhāna', he keeps company...Living in company, untrammelled, rude, given over to gossip, passion corrupts his heart; and with his heart corrupted by passion, he disavows the training and returns to the lower life..."

The same is said about the other stages of jhāna. We then read that Citta Hatthisāriputta disavowed the training and returned to the lower life. But not long after that he "went forth" (became a monk) again. We read:

> And the venerable Citta Hatthisāriputta, living alone, secluded, earnest, ardent, resolved, not long after, entered and abode in that aim above all of the holy life – realizing it here and now by his own knowledge – for the sake of which clansmen rightly go forth from home to the homeless life; and he knew: "Birth is destroyed, the holy life is lived, done is what was to be done, there is no more of this."
>
> And the venerable Citta Hatthisāriputta was numbered among the arahats.

Even if one can attain the highest stage of jhāna, one's heart can still become "corrupted by passion", as we read in the sutta. When Citta Hatthisāriputta had attained arahatship, he had realized the "aim above all of the holy life". The "hindrances" could not arise any more.

Through vipassanā, hindrances are eradicated in the successive stages of enlightenment. The sotāpanna (who has attained the first stage of enlightenment) has eradicated the hindrance which is doubt (vicikicchā); the anāgāmī (who has attained the third stage of enlightenment) has eradicated sensuous desire (kāmacchandha), ill-will (vyāpāda) and regret (kukkucca); the arahat has eradicated sloth and torpor (thīna and middha) and restlessness (uddhacca), he has eradicated all defilements.

Questions

1. Which paramattha dhamma are the jhāna-factors?
2. Which khandha is the jhāna-factor which is pīti (rapture)?
3. Which khandha is the jhāna-factor which is sukha (happy feeling)?
4. When seeing now, is there ekaggatā cetasika? What is ts function?
5. What is the function of ekaggatā cetasika which arises with the jhāna-citta? What is its object?
6. Why is mindfulness of breathing one of the most difficult subjects of meditation?
7. What is the difference between sammā-sati (right mindfulness) in samatha and sammā-sati in vipassanā? What are their respective objects of awareness?
8. If one only develops samatha and not vipassanā, why can the hindrances not be eradicated?

22 Jhānacittas

There are many different cittas arising in our daily life which experience objects through the five sense-doors and through the mind-door. Both in the sense-door process and in the mind-door process of cittas there are javana-cittas which are, in the case of the non-arahat, either kusala cittas or akusala cittas. The javana-cittas are most of the time akusala cittas because we cling to all objects which are experienced through the sense-doors and through the mind-door. We cling to visible object and seeing, to sound and hearing, to all the objects we experience. We cling to life, we want to go on living and receiving sense-impressions. We may not notice when there is clinging after seeing or hearing, especially when we do not feel particularly glad about what was seen or heard. But there may be lobha-mūla-cittas with indifferent feeling. There are likely to be many moments of clinging which pass unnoticed, both in the sense-door processes and in the mind-door processes. Time and again an object is experienced through one of the sense-doors and then through the mind-door and there are also mind-door processes of cittas which think of concepts such as people, animals or things. Clinging to concepts is likely to arise very often and thus we think most of the time with akusala citta. When we do not apply ourselves to dāna, sīla or bhāvanā, thinking is done with akusala citta. Even when we perform good deeds there are bound to be akusala cittas shortly after the kusala cittas. Seeing and hearing arise time and again, and after seeing or hearing attachment or aversion on account of what we experience may arise. The cittas which experience sense-objects, the kusala cittas and akusala cittas, all the cittas which arise in our daily life are of the "sensuous plane of consciousness", or kāmāvacara cittas.

On account of the experience of sense-objects defilements tend to arise. Therefore wise people, even those who lived before the Buddha's time, who saw the disadvantages of sense-impressions, developed jhāna in order to be temporarily freed from sense-impressions. Jhāna-cittas are not kāmāvacara cittas, they are of another plane of consciousness; these cittas experience with absorption a meditation subject through the mind-door. At the moment of jhāna one is freed from sense-impressions and from the defilements which are bound up with them. Jhānacittas comprise rūpāvacara cittas (rūpa-jhānacittas) and arūpāvacara cittas (arūpa-jhānacittas). Arūpa-jhāna (immaterial jhāna) is more refined than rūpa-jhāna (fine-material jhāna), since the meditation subjects of arūpa-jhāna are no longer dependent on materiality. Later on I will deal with their difference.

Apart from the planes of citta which are kāmāvacara cittas, rūpāvacara cittas and arūpāvacara cittas, there is still another plane of citta: the lokuttara cittas (translated as "supramundane cittas") which have nibbāna as their object. Those who attain enlightenment have lokuttara cittas, experiencing nibbāna.

Now I shall deal first with *jhānacitta*. Jhānacittas do not have as their object visible object, sound, or any other sense-object. Jhānacittas arise in a process of cittas experiencing a meditation subject through the mind-door. In this process there are first kāmāvacara cittas which experience the meditation subject and then, in that same process, the jhānacitta arises.

The process is as follows:

1. mano-dvārāvajjana-citta or mind-door adverting-consciousness
2. parikamma or preparatory consciousness
3. upacāra, which means: proximity or access
4. anuloma or adaptation cittas
5. gotrabhū, which means: that which overcomes the sense-sphere, or "change of lineage"
6. jhānacitta, appanā or absorption (the moment of citta which attains jhāna)

For some, "parikamma" (preparatory consciousness) is not necessary, and in this case there are, after the mind-door-adverting-consciousness, only three kāmāvacara cittas arising, instead of four, before the jhānacitta arises. Gotrabhū (which "overcomes" the sense-sphere) is the last citta in that process which is kāmāvacara citta.

In the Visuddhimagga (IV, 74) we can read about the process of cittas in which jhāna occurs for the first time. The Visuddhimagga (IV, 78) states that in that case only one single moment of jhānacitta arises, which is then succeeded by the bhavanga-citta (life-continuum). After that there is a process of kāmāvacara cittas, reviewing through the mind-door the jhāna which has just occurred. For that person the ability to attain jhāna is still weak, he has to continue to purify himself of the hindrances in developing the jhāna-factors until these have become stronger. Further on (Vis. IV, 123 and following) we read that absorption can "last" only when it is absolutely purified of states which obstruct concentration. One must first completely suppress lust by reviewing the dangers of sense-desires and also suppress the other "hindrances". When someone has become more accomplished there can be jhānacittas succeeding one another, even for a long time. We read (Vis. IV, 125):

> But when he enters upon a jhāna after (first) completely purifying his mind of states that obstruct concentration, then he remains in the attainment even for a whole day, like a bee that has gone into a completely purified hive...

Jhānacittas are kusala kamma of a high degree. When jhāna has been attained the hindrances of sensuous desire, ill-will, sloth, torpor, restlessness, regret and doubt are temporarily eliminated. Thus one is truly calm, at least at that moment.

As we have seen in the preceding chapter, the person who wants to develop samatha so as to be able to attain jhāna, has to develop the five jhāna-factors which can inhibit the hindrances, namely:

- applied thinking (vitakka)
- sustained thinking (vicāra)
- rapture (pīti)
- happy feeling (sukha)
- concentration (samādhi)

Jhāna is developed in stages, with each succeeding stage being more refined than the preceding one. There are five stages of rūpa-jhāna (fine-material jhāna) in all. For the first stage of rūpa-jhāna it is still necessary that all five jhāna-factors arise with the jhānacitta, but at each higher stage, when one has become more advanced, jhāna-factors are successively abandoned. When one attains to the rūpa-jhāna of the second stage, one does not need the jhāna-factor which is vitakka, applied thinking. At this point the jhānacitta can experience the meditation subject without vitakka, which has the characteristic of directing the mind unto an object and the function of "touching" the object. The other four jhāna-factors still arise with the jhānacitta of the second stage.

At the third stage of rūpa-jhāna vicāra, sustained thinking, is abandoned. At this stage one does not need vitakka nor vicāra any longer in order to become absorbed in the meditation subject. Now three factors remain: pīti, rapture, sukha, happy feeling, and samādhi, concentration. At the fourth stage pīti is abandoned. There is still sukha, happy feeling, accompanying the jhāna-citta, but pīti does not arise. Without pīti the jhānacitta is more quiet, more refined. At the fifth stage sukha, happy feeling, too is abandoned and indifferent feeling (upekkhā vedanā) accompanies the jhānacitta instead. At this stage one is no longer attached to happy feeling. The jhāna-factor which is samādhi, concentration, remains.

Some people can, at the second stage of jhāna, abandon both vitakka, applied thinking, and vicāra, sustained thinking. Consequently, they can, in the third stage, abandon pīti, rapture, and in the fourth stage sukha, happy feeling. Thus for them there are only four stages of jhāna instead of five. That is the reason why rūpa-jhānas can be counted as four stages or as five stages (as the fourfold system or the five-fold system). When we read in the suttas about four stages of jhāna, it is the fourfold system which is referred to.

There can be up to five stages of rūpa-jhāna in all and thus there are five types of rūpāvacara kusala cittas (rūpa-jhāna kusala cittas). Jhānacitta is kusala kamma of a high degree and thus its result is kusala vipāka of a high degree. Jhānacittas do not produce vipāka in the same lifespan: their result is rebirth in higher planes of existence. The result of rūpāvacara kusala cittas is rebirth in rūpa-brahma planes. Rūpāvacara kusala citta can produce result only if one's ability to attain jhāna does not decline and jhānacittas arise shortly before dying. If rūpāvacara kusala citta is to produce the next rebirth, rūpāvacara kusala cittas arise shortly before the cuti-citta, dying-consciousness. The paṭisandhi-citta of the next life is rūpāvacara vipākacitta and this arises in the appropriate rūpa-brahma plane. It experiences the same meditation subject as the rūpāvacara kusala cittas arising shortly before the cuti-citta of the preceding life. The five types of rūpāvacara kusala cittas are able to produce five types of rūpāvacara vipākacittas.

When one is born with a paṭisandhi-citta which is rūpāvacara vipākacitta, all bhavanga-cittas and the cuti-citta of that life are of the same type of citta as the paṭisandhi-citta. Rūpāvacara vipākacitta can only perform the functions of paṭisandhi, bhavanga and cuti.

There are five types of rūpāvacara kiriyacittas which are the cittas of the arahat who attains rūpa-jhāna. He does not have kusala cittas but he has kiriyacittas instead. Thus, there are fifteen rūpāvacara cittas in all. Summarising them, they are:

- 5 rūpāvacara kusala cittas
- 5 rūpāvacara vipākacittas

- 5 rūpāvacara kiriyacittas

Those who have attained the highest stage of rūpa-jhāna and see the disadvantages of rūpa-jhāna which is still dependent on materiality[1], might want to cultivate arūpa-jhāna or "immaterial jhāna". The meditation subjects of arūpa-jhāna are not connected with materiality. There are four stages of arūpa-jhāna. The first stage of arūpa-jhāna is the "Sphere of Boundless Space"[2] (ākāsānañcāyatana). In order to attain this stage of arūpa-jhāna one has to attain first the highest stage of rūpa-jhāna in any one of the kasina meditations (excepting the "kasina of limited space") and achieve mastery in it. We read in the Visuddhimagga (X, 6):

> When he has seen the danger in that (fine-material fourth jhāna[3]) in this way and has ended his attachment to it, he gives attention to the "Base consisting of Boundless Space" as peaceful. Then, when he has spread out the kasina to the limit of the world-sphere, or as far as he likes, he removes the kasina (materiality) by giving his attention to the space touched by it, (regarding that) as "space" or "boundless space".

As regards the "Sphere of Boundless Space", the Visuddhimagga (X, 8) explains about the "removing" of the kasina:

> And when the kasina is being removed, it does not roll up or roll away. It is simply that it is called "removed" on account of his non-attention to it, his attention being given to "space, space". This is conceptualized as the mere space left by the removal of the kasina (materiality)...

In this way he can surmount the materiality of the kasina and attain the first arūpa-jhāna, the "Sphere of Boundless Space". There are three more stages of arūpa-jhāna, and each one of these is more subtle and more peaceful than the preceding one. The second stage of arūpa-jhāna is: the "Sphere of Boundless Consciousness" (viññāṇañcāyatana). The meditation subject of this stage of arūpa-jhāna is the consciousness which is the first arūpa-jhānacitta. This citta had as its object "Boundless Space". The person who wants to attain the second stage of arūpa-jhāna should first achieve "mastery" in the "Sphere of Boundless Space"; he should see the disadvantages of this stage and end his attachment to it. We read in the Visuddhimagga (X, 25):

> ...So having ended his attachment to that, he should give his attention to the base consisting of boundless consciousness as peaceful, adverting again and again as "Consciousness, consciousness", to the consciousness that occurred pervading that space (as its object)...

The third stage of arūpa-jhāna is the "Sphere of Nothingness" (ākiñcaññāyatana). We read in the Visuddhimagga (X, 32) that the person who wants to attain this stage should give his attention to the present non-existence of the past consciousness which pervaded the "boundless space" and

---

[1] The meditation subjects of rūpa-jhāna are connected with materiality, they are learnt by sight, touch or hearsay.

[2] The fourth rūpa-jhāna. Here the counting is according to the "fourfold system".

[3] The Sphere of Boundless Space, ākāsānañcāyatana.

which was the object of the second stage of arūpa-jhāna, the "Sphere of Boundless Consciousness". We read (X, 33):

> Without giving (further) attention to that consciousness, he should (now) advert again and again in this way, "There is not, there is not", or "Void, void", or "Secluded, secluded", and give his attention to it, review it, and strike at it with thought and applied thought.

Further on (X, 35) we read:

> . . . he dwells seeing only its non-existence, in other words its departedness when this consciousness has arisen in absorption.

The fourth arūpa-jhāna is the "Sphere of Neither Perception Nor Non-Perception" (n'eva-saññā-n'āsaññāyatana). The object of this jhāna is the four nāmakkhandhas (citta and the accompanying cetasikas) which attained the Sphere of Nothingness,(at the third stage of arūpa-jhāna.) We read in the Visuddhimagga (X, 49):

> The word meaning here is this: that jhāna with its associated states neither has perception nor has no perception because of the absence of gross perception and presence of subtle perception, thus it is "neither perception nor non-perception" (n'eva-saññā-n'āsaññaṃ).

Further on (X, 50) we read:

> . . . Or alternatively: the perception here is neither perception, since it is incapable of performing the decisive function of perception, nor yet non-perception, since it is present in a subtle state as a residual formation, thus it is "neither-perception-nor-non-perception". . .

It is also explained that the feeling arising with this jhānacitta is "neither-feeling-nor-non-feeling" (since it is present in a subtle state as a residual formation); the same applies to consciousness, contact (phassa) and the other cetasikas arising with the jhānacitta.

Since there are four stages of arūpa-jhāna, there are four types of arūpāvacara kusala cittas. They can produce vipāka in the form of rebirth in the happy planes of existence which are the arūpa-brahma planes. The four types of arūpāvacara kusala cittas produce four types of arūpāvacara vipākacittas. When the paṭisandhi-citta is arūpāvacara vipākacitta, all bhavanga-cittas and the cuti-citta of that life are of the same type of arūpāvacara vipākacitta. Arūpāvacara vipākacitta can only perform the functions of paṭisandhi, bhavanga and cuti[4].

There are four types of arūpāvacara kiriyacittas which are the cittas of the arahat who attains arūpa-jhāna. Thus, there are twelve arūpāvacara cittas in all. Summarising them, they are:

- 4 arūpāvacara kusala cittas
- 4 arūpāvacara vipākacittas
- 4 arūpāvacara kiriyacittas

---

[4] Just as in the case of rūpāvacara kusala citta, arūpāvacara kusala citta cannot produce vipāka in the same lifespan. Therefore it performs only the functions of paṭisandhi, bhavanga and cuti.

Those who have cultivated jhāna can develop the various types of "direct knowledge" (abhiññā)[5]. They should attain the highest stage of rūpa-jhāna (the fourth according to the fourfold system and the fifth according to the fivefold system) in the kasina meditations, and they should exercise "complete mind-control in fourteen ways" (described in the Visuddhimagga, chapter XII). For example, they should, with the different kasina meditations, be able to attain the subsequent stages of rūpa-jhāna in order and in reverse order. In developing the kinds of "direct knowledge" or "supernormal powers", one's concentration will become more advanced. The "supernormal powers" (abhiññā) are the following:

1. Magical powers such as passing through walls, walking on water, travelling through the air.
2. Divine ear, by which one hears sounds both heavenly and human, far and near.
3. Knowledge of the minds of other people.
4. Divine Eye, by which one sees the deceasing and rebirth of beings.
5. Remembrance of one's former lives.

These are the five "mundane supernormal powers". However, there is a sixth power, which is realized by lokuttara citta, namely, the eradication of all defilements, when arahatship is attained. The sixth power is the greatest and in order to realize it insight has to be fully developed.

Those who have cultivated the right conditions can achieve "marvels". In the Gradual Sayings (Book of the Threes, chapter VI, paragraph 60, III, Sangārava) we read about the greatest "marvel". The Buddha asked the brāhmin Sangārava about the topic of conversation of the royal party, when they were together in the palace. The brāhmin Sangārava answered that they were talking about the fact that in former times the monks were fewer in number, but those possessed of supernormal powers were more numerous, and that now it was just the opposite. The Buddha said to him:

> "Now as to that, brāhmin, there are these three marvels. What three?
>
> The marvel of more-power, the marvel of thought-reading, the marvel of teaching. And what, brāhmin, is the marvel of more-power?
>
> In this case a certain one enjoys sorts of more-power in various ways. From being one he becomes many, from being many he becomes one; manifest or invisible he goes unhindered through a wall, through a rampart, through a mountain, as if through the air; he plunges into the earth and shoots up again as if in water; he walks upon the water without parting it as if on solid ground; he travels through the air sitting cross-legged, like a bird upon the wing; even this moon and sun, though of such mighty power and majesty, – he handles them and strokes them with his hand; even as far as the Brahma world he has power with his body. This, brāhmin, is called 'the marvel of more-power'.
>
> And what, brāhmin, is the marvel of thought-reading? In this case a certain one can declare by means of a sign 'Thus is your mind. Such and such is your mind. Thus is your consciousness'. . . "

---

[5] Also translated as "supernormal powers" or "higher intellectual powers".

The Buddha explained more about mind-reading, and then he said:

> "And what, brāhmin, is the marvel of teaching? In this case a certain one teaches thus: 'Reason thus, not thus. Apply your mind thus, not thus. Abandon this state, acquire that state and abide therein.' This, brāhmin, is called 'the marvel of teaching'. So these are the three marvels. Now of these three marvels, which appeals to you as the more wonderful and excellent?"
>
> "Of these marvels, Master Gotama, the marvel of more-power. . . seems to me to be of the nature of an illusion. Then again as to the marvel of thought-reading. . . this also, master Gotama, seems to me of the nature of an illusion. But as to the marvel of teaching. . . of these three marvels this one appeals to me as the more wonderful and excellent."

Sangārava then asked the Buddha whether he possessed all three marvels and the Buddha told him that he did. Sangārava also asked whether any other monk possessed them and the Buddha answered:

> "Yes, indeed, brāhmin. The monks possessed of these three marvellous powers are not just one or two or three, four, or five hundred, but much more than that in number."

Sangārava then expressed his confidence in taking refuge in the Buddha, the Dhamma and the Sangha, and he asked to be accepted as a lay-follower.

In the Buddha's time many monks had cultivated conditions for "marvellous powers". The greatest "marvel" of these, however, is the "marvel of teaching" since it can lead to the eradication of all defilements, to the end of all sorrow.

For those who have accumulations for jhāna there are many benefits since jhāna is kusala kamma of a high degree. One of the benefits is a happy rebirth, even for those who can attain only "access-concentration" or upacāra samādhi (Vis. XI, 123). However, even rebirth in a happy plane of existence is dukkha, because life in a happy plane may be followed by rebirth in an unhappy plane. Therefore, no birth at all is to be preferred to any kind of rebirth. This can be realized only by developing the wisdom which eradicates defilements.

Jhāna is called in the teachings an "abiding in ease, here, now" (for example, in the "Discourse on Expunging", Middle Length Sayings I, no. 8). Those who have become advanced in the development of calm can have many jhānacittas in succession, since they have cultivated conditions for this. They truly are "abiding in ease, here, now". However, the Buddha would point out that "abiding in ease" is not the same as "expunging" (eradication). We read in the Discourse on Expunging that the Buddha said to Cunda with regard to the monk who could attain rūpa-jhāna:

> The situation occurs, Cunda, when a monk here, aloof from pleasures of the senses, aloof from unskilled states of mind, may enter on and abide in the first jhāna which is accompanied by initial thought (vitakka) and discursive thought (vicāra), is born of aloofness, and is rapturous and joyful. It may occur to him: "I fare along by expunging". But these, Cunda, are not called expungings in the discipline for an ariyan. These are called "abidings in ease, here, now" in the discipline for an ariyan.

The Buddha said the same with regard to the attainment of the other stages of rūpa-jhāna. With regard to the monk who could attain arūpa-jhāna, he said:

> . . . It may occur to him: "I fare along by expunging". But these, Cunda, are not called "expungings" in the discipline for an ariyan; these are called "abidings that are peaceful" in the discipline for an ariyan. . .

Those who have accumulated great skill for jhāna and have developed vipassanā can attain enlightenment with lokuttara jhānacittas, that is, lokuttara cittas accompanied by jhāna-factors of the different stages of jhāna, according to their accumulations[6]. Instead of a meditation subject of samatha, nibbāna is the object which is experienced with absorption by the lokuttara jhānacitta. In the process during which enlightenment is attained the magga-citta (path-consciousness, lokuttara kusala citta) is immediately followed by the phala-citta (fruition-consciousness, the result of the magga-citta). When the phala-cittas have fallen away that process of cittas is over. The magga-citta of that stage of enlightenment cannot arise again, but for those who have developed jhāna and attained enlightenment with lokuttara jhānacitta, the phala-citta can arise again, having nibbāna as object, even many times in life.

Those who have attained the fourth stage of arūpa-jhāna, the "Sphere of Neither Perception Nor Non-Perception", and have also realized the third stage of enlightenment, the stage of the anāgāmī or who have realized the stage of the arahat, can attain "cessation" (nirodha-samāpatti) which is the temporary ceasing of bodily and mental activities.

The person who has attained "cessation" ("the stopping of perception and feeling") is different from a corpse. We read in the Greater Discourse of the Miscellany (Middle Length Sayings I, no. 43) that Mahā-Koṭṭhita asked Sāriputta a number of questions. He also asked questions about the dead body and about the difference between the dead body and the monk who has attained cessation. We read that Mahā-Koṭṭhita asked:

> "In regard to this body, your reverence, when how many things are got rid of, does this body lie cast away, flung aside like unto a senseless log of wood?"
>
> "In regard to this body, your reverence, when three things are got rid of: vitality, heat and consciousness, then does this body lie cast away, flung aside like unto a senseless log of wood."
>
> "What is the difference, your reverence, between that dead thing, passed away, and that monk who has attained to the stopping of perception and feeling?"
>
> "Your reverence, the bodily activities of that dead thing, passed away, have been stopped, have subsided, the vocal activities have been stopped, have subsided, the mental activities have been stopped, have subsided, the vitality is entirely destroyed, the heat allayed, the sense-organs are entirely broken asunder. But that monk who has attained to the stopping of perception and feeling, although his bodily activities have been

[6] This will be further explained in chapter 23.

> stopped, have subsided, although his vocal activities have been stopped, have subsided, although his mental activities have been stopped, have subsided, his vitality is not entirely destroyed, his heat is not allayed, his sense-organs are purified. This, your reverence, is the difference between a dead thing, passed away, and that monk who has attained to the stopping of perception and feeling."

For those who emerge from cessation, the first citta which arises is a phala-citta (lokuttara vipākacitta), having nibbāna as its object. In the case of the anāgāmī it is the phala-citta of the stage of the anāgāmī and in the case of the arahat it is the phala-citta of the arahat. The Visuddhimagga (XXIII, 50) states that their minds tend towards nibbāna. We read:

> Towards what does the mind of one who has emerged tend? It tends towards nibbāna. For this is said: "When a bhikkhu has emerged from the attainment of the cessation of perception and feeling, friend Visākha, his consciousness inclines to seclusion, leans to seclusion, tends to seclusion" (Middle Length Sayings I, no. 44, 302).

In the Lesser Discourse in Gosiṅga (Middle Length Sayings I, no. 31) we read that the Buddha came to see Anuruddha, Nandiya and Kimbila when they were staying in the Gosiṅga sāl-wood. The Buddha asked them about their life in the forest. They could attain all stages of rūpa-jhāna and arūpa-jhāna and they could "abide" in them for as long as they liked. The Buddha said:

> "It is good, Anuruddhas, it is good. But did you, Anuruddhas, by passing quite beyond this abiding, by allaying this abiding, reach another state of further-men, an excellent knowledge and vision befitting the ariyans, an abiding in comfort?"
>
> "How could this not be, Lord? Here we, Lord, for as long as we like, by passing quite beyond the plane of neither perception-nor-non-perception, entering on the stopping of perception and feeling, abide in it, and having seen through intuitive wisdom, our cankers come to be utterly destroyed. By passing quite beyond that abiding, Lord, by allaying that abiding, another state of further-men, an excellent knowledge and vision befitting the ariyans, an abiding in comfort is reached. But we, Lord, do not behold another abiding in comfort that is higher or more excellent than this abiding in comfort."
>
> "It is good, Anuruddhas, it is good. There is no other abiding in comfort that is higher or more excellent than this abiding in comfort."

Questions

1. What is the advantage of arūpa-jhāna, compared to rūpa-jhāna?
2. What is the difference between the fourth stage of arūpa-jhāna, the "Sphere of neither perception nor non-perception", and "cessation"?
3. Can anybody who has developed the fourth stage of arūpa-jhāna attain cessation?
4. What is the purpose of the "supernormal powers" (abhiññās)?

5. When six abhiññās are mentioned, which of those is the greatest?
6. What benefit is there for those who develop both jhāna and vipassanā and attain enlightenment?
7. What is the object of citta at the moment of jhāna?
8. Through which door can the jhānacitta experience an object?
9. What is the object of lokuttara jhānacitta?

23 Lokuttara Cittas

The Abhidhamma teaches us about different kinds of wholesome cittas. There are kāmāvacara kusala cittas (kusala cittas of the sensuous plane of consciousness, mahā-kusala cittas), rūpāvacara kusala cittas (rūpa-jhānacittas) and arūpāvacara kusala cittas (arūpa-jhānacittas). All these types of citta are kusala, but they do not eradicate the latent tendencies of defilements. Only lokuttara kusala cittas, magga-cittas[1], eradicate the latent tendencies of defilements. When all defilements are eradicated completely there will be an end to the cycle of birth and death. We may wonder whether lokuttara kusala cittas really eradicate defilements so that they never arise again. There are many defilements. We are full of lobha, dosa and moha. We have avarice, jealousy, worry, doubt, conceit and many other defilements. The clinging to the self is deeply rooted: we take our mind and our body for self. It is hard to understand how all these defilements can be eradicated. Defilements can be eradicated and there is a Path leading to it, but we have accumulated defilements to such an extent that they cannot be eradicated all at once. Diṭṭhi, wrong view, has to be eradicated first; so long as we take realities for self there cannot be eradication of any defilement. There are four stages of enlightenment: the stages of the sotāpanna (streamwinner), the sakadāgāmī (once-returner), the anāgāmī (no-returner) and the arahat. At each of these stages the lokuttara kusala citta, the magga-citta, arises which experiences nibbāna and eradicates defilements. The sotāpanna, the ariyan who has attained the first stage of enlightenment, has eradicated diṭṭhi completely, so that it can never arise again, but he has not eradicated all defilements. Defilements are eradicated stage by stage and only when arahatship has been attained all defilements have been eradicated.

People may wonder how one can know that one has attained enlightenment. The lokuttara citta is accompanied by paññā (wisdom) which has been developed in vipassanā. One does not attain enlightenment without having developed insight-wisdom, vipassanā. There are several stages of insight-wisdom. First, doubt about the difference between nāma and rūpa is eliminated. It may be understood in theory that nāma is the reality which experiences an object and rūpa is the reality which does not know anything. However, theoretical understanding, understanding of the level of thinking, is not the same as direct understanding which realizes nāma as nāma and rūpa as rūpa. When there is, for example, sound, which is rūpa, there is also hearing, which is nāma, and these realities have different characteristics. There can be mindfulness of only one characteristic at a time and at such a moment right understanding of the reality which presents itself can develop. So long as there is not right mindfulness of one reality at the time there will be doubt as to the difference between nāma and rūpa. There has to be mindfulness of the different kinds of nāma and rūpa which appear in daily life in order to eliminate doubt. When the first stage of insight, which is only a beginning stage, is attained, there is no doubt as to the difference between the characteristics of nāma and rūpa. The characteristics of nāma and rūpa have to be investigated over and over again until

[1] Magga means path. The lokuttara kusala citta is called magga-citta or path-consciousness.

they are clearly understood as they are and there is no more wrong view about them. The realization of the arising and falling away of nāma and rūpa is a higher stage of insight which cannot be attained so long as the characteristic of nāma cannot be distinguished from the characteristic of rūpa. All the different stages of insight have to be attained in the right order[2]. Paññā should continue to investigate the characteristics of realities as they appear through the six doors so that the three characteristics of conditioned realities, namely: impermanence (anicca), dukkha and non-self (anattā), can be penetrated more and more. When paññā has clearly understood these three characteristics enlightenment can be attained; paññā can then experience nibbāna, the unconditioned reality. When paññā has been developed to that degree there cannot be any doubt as to whether one has attained enlightenment or not.

The English word enlightenment can have different meanings and therefore it may create confusion. The Pāli term for enlightenment is "*bodhi*". Bodhi literally means knowledge or understanding. The attainment of enlightenment in the context of the Buddhist teachings refers to paññā which has been developed to the degree that it has become *lokuttara* paññā, "supramundane paññā", which accompanies lokuttara cittas experiencing nibbāna. Enlightenment is actually a few moments of lokuttara cittas which do not last. Nibbāna does not arise and fall away, but the lokuttara cittas which experience nibbāna fall away and are followed by cittas of the sense-sphere; in the case of the ariyans who have not yet attained the fourth stage of enlightenment, also akusala cittas are bound to arise again. However, the defilements which have been eradicated at the attainment of enlightenment do not arise anymore.

Only the right Path, the eightfold Path, can lead to enlightenment. If one develops the wrong path the goal cannot be attained. When the wrong path is developed one has diṭṭhi, wrong view. In the Abhidhamma defilements are classified in different ways and also different kinds of wrong view are classified in various ways. For example, different kinds of wrong view are classified under the group of defilements which is clinging (upādāna). Three of the four kinds of clinging mentioned in this group are clinging to various forms of diṭṭhi; these three kinds of clinging have been completely eradicated by the sotāpanna. One of them is: "clinging to rules and ritual" (sīlabbatupādāna), which includes the wrong practice of vipassanā. Some people think that they can attain enlightenment by following some path other than the eightfold Path but this is an illusion. There are no other ways leading to enlightenment.

The eightfold Path is developed by being mindful of the nāma and rūpa which appear in daily life, such as seeing, visible object, hearing, sound, thinking, feeling, attachment, anger or the other defilements which arise. If the eightfold Path is not developed by being mindful of all realities which appear in one's daily life, wrong view cannot be eradicated and thus not even the first stage of enlightenment, the stage of the *sotāpanna*, can be attained. Therefore, there is no way leading to

[2] See Visuddhimagga chapter XX and XXI and "Path of Discrimination" I, Treatise on Knowledge, chapters V-X.

enlightenment other than the development of right understanding of realities, which is the wisdom (paññā) of the eightfold Path.

What is right understanding? The answer is: seeing nāma and rūpa as they are: impermanent, dukkha and non-self. Right understanding can be developed. When we still have wrong view, we take realities for self: we take seeing for self, we take visible object for self, we take feeling for self, we take saññā (remembrance or "perception") for self, we take thinking for self, we take defilements for self, we also take good qualities such as mindfulness and wisdom for self. In being mindful of the characteristics of nāma and rūpa which appear, right understanding can develop and the wrong view of self can be eliminated.

So long as one has not become a sotāpanna one may deviate from the right Path, there can be wrong practice. There is wrong practice, for example, when one thinks that there should be awareness only of particular kinds of nāma and rūpa, instead of being aware of whatever kind of nāma or rūpa appears. People may for example believe that lobha, dosa and moha should not or cannot be objects of mindfulness. However, akusala cittas are realities which arise because of their appropriate conditions, they are part of one's daily life. If one selects the objects of awareness, one will continue to cling to a concept of self who could exert control over one's life. Some people believe that vipassanā can only be developed when sitting in a quiet place, but then they set rules for the practice, and thus, they will not be able to see that mindfulness too is anattā.

The sotāpanna has, apart from diṭṭhi, also eradicated other defilements. He has eradicated doubt or vicikicchā. Doubt is classified as one of the "hindrances"; it prevents us from performing kusala. We may doubt about the Buddha, the Dhamma, the Sangha, about the right practice. The sotāpanna has no more doubt.

Another akusala cetasika, eradicated by the sotāpanna, is stinginess, macchariya. The Visuddhimagga (XXII, 52) mentions five kinds of avarice:

The kinds of avarice are the five, namely, avarice about dwellings, families, gain, Dhamma and praise, which occur as inability to bear sharing with others any of these things beginning with dwellings.

The Atthasālinī (Expositor, Book II, part II, chapter II, 374, 375) gives an explanation of these five kinds of avarice concerning the monk's dwelling-place, the family he is used to visiting in order to receive the four requisites (robes, food, shelter and medicines), the four requisites themselves (mentioned as "gain"), knowledge of the Dhamma and praise (concerning personal beauty or virtues).

It is explained that there is stinginess if one does not want to share any of these things with others. However, there is no stinginess if one does not want to share these things with someone who is a bad person or someone who would abuse these things. For instance, if one does not teach Dhamma to someone who will abuse Dhamma, there is no stinginess as to Dhamma. Thus we see that the eradication of stinginess does not mean sharing everything one has with anybody. The sotāpanna has eradicated stinginess; the five kinds of stinginess just mentioned do not arise anymore.

Furthermore, the sotāpanna has eradicated envy, issā. Envy can arise with dosa-mūla-citta (citta rooted in aversion). The Visuddhimagga (XIV, 172) states concerning envy:

> Envying is envy. It has the characteristic of being jealous of others' success. Its function is to be dissatisfied with that. It is manifested as averseness from that. Its proximate cause is another's success...

The sotāpanna is an ariyan, a "noble person", although not all defilements are eradicated by him. He is an ariyan, because at the moment of enlightenment, when the magga-citta arose, he became a different person; he is no longer a "worldling", puthujjana. There are no more latent tendencies of wrong view, diṭṭhi, and doubt, vicikicchā, accumulated in the citta, and there are no more inclinations to stinginess, macchariya, or envy, issā.

What is a latent tendency? When we desire something we have lobha. When the lobha-mūla-cittas have fallen away, there are other kinds of citta which are not accompanied by lobha. However, the lobha which arose before has been accumulated, it remains latent. When there are conditions for its arising, it can arise again with the akusala citta. Latent tendencies lie dormant in every citta, even in the bhavanga-citta (life-continuum) which does not experience an object through one of the sense-doors or the mind-door.

The question may occur whether the latent tendency of diṭṭhi is eradicated gradually or all at once. The answer is that in the course of the development of right understanding diṭṭhi is gradually eliminated until the latent tendency of diṭṭhi is completely eradicated at the attainment of enlightenment. One cannot attain enlightenment without having cultivated the right conditions. We see that in the Buddha's time some people could attain enlightenment quickly, even during a discourse; some could attain enlightenment after a more detailed explanation of the truth, whereas others had to develop the eightfold Path for a longer time before they could attain enlightenment. It all depends on how much wisdom has already been accumulated, also during previous lives. As to the attainment of enlightenment in the present time, the right conditions have to be cultivated; enlightenment cannot occur all of a sudden. If there is awareness of all kinds of nāma and rūpa appearing in daily life, paññā can investigate their characteristics and in this way it can gradually develop. We cannot expect a great deal of sati and paññā in the beginning. However, each moment of right awareness is fruitful, because it can condition further moments of awareness and thus it can be accumulated. Through the development of right understanding of nāma and rūpa, wrong view will gradually become less, until finally the latent tendency of diṭṭhi is completely eradicated by the magga-citta (lokuttara kusala citta) of the sotāpanna. Then diṭṭhi will never arise again.

The sotāpanna has not eradicated all defilements. One may wonder whether he can still talk in an unpleasant way to others. Of the ten kinds of akusala kamma-patha (unwholesome courses of action) there are four akusala kamma-patha through speech which are: lying, slandering, rude speech and idle, useless talk. The sotāpanna has eradicated lying. He can still speak in an unfriendly way to others or use harsh speech, but not to the extent that it would lead to rebirth in a woeful plane. The sotāpanna cannot be reborn in a woeful plane anymore.

Useless talk is speech which has not as objective dāna, sīla or bhāvanā. This is not eradicated by the sotāpanna, it can only be eradicated by the arahat.

The question may arise whether it is necessary to classify defilements in such a detailed way. The purpose of the study of the Abhidhamma is right understanding of realities. If one does not study at all one will not be able to judge what is the right Path and what the wrong Path. We do not live in the Buddha's time; since we cannot hear the teachings directly from him, we are dependent on the teachings as they come to us through the scriptures. Therefore, it is beneficial to study the scriptures and also the Abhidhamma. It depends on one's personal inclination to what extent one will study the details about realities. Learning about the different ways of classifying defilements helps us to see their different aspects. For instance, diṭṭhi is classified under the group of defilements known as the latent tendencies or proclivities (anusayas) and it is also classified as one of the āsavas, "cankers" or "influxes", which is another group of defilements. Furthermore, defilements are classified as ways of clinging (upādānas); as we have seen, three classes of diṭṭhi are classified under this group of defilements. Defilements are also classified as "bonds" (ganthas), as "hindrances" (nīvaraṇas), and in several other ways. Each way of classifying shows us a different aspect of defilements and thus we understand better how deeply accumulated defilements are and how difficult it is to eradicate them. Only magga-cittas (lokuttara kusala cittas) can eradicate them. Not all defilements can be eradicated by the magga-citta of the first stage of enlightenment. As we have seen, there are four stages of enlightenment (the stages of the sotāpanna, the sakadāgāmī, the anāgāmī and the arahat), and for each of these stages there is a magga-citta which experiences nibbāna and eradicates defilements. Defilements are progressively eradicated by the magga-citta at each of the four stages of enlightenment. Thus, there are four types of magga-citta. There are four types of phala-citta (lokuttara vipākacitta or "fruition-consciousness") which are the results of the four magga-cittas. Only the magga-citta eradicates defilements; the phala-citta, which also experiences nibbāna, is vipāka, result of the magga-citta.

At the moment of enlightenment nibbāna is the object which is experienced by the lokuttara citta. Some people think that nibbāna is a place which one can reach, a plane of life. In order to have more understanding of what nibbāna is, we have to consider what our life now is: nāma and rūpa arising and falling away. Our life is dukkha, because what arises and falls away is unsatisfactory. If nibbāna would be a plane where we would continue to live, there would be no end to the arising and falling away of nāma and rūpa, no end to dukkha. Nibbāna, however, is the unconditioned dhamma, it does not arise and fall away. Nibbāna is therefore the end of the arising and falling away of nāma and rūpa, the end of birth, old age, sickness and death. Nibbāna is the end to dukkha. When one has attained the first stage of enlightenment, the stage of the sotāpanna, it is certain that there will eventually be an end to the cycle of birth and death, an end to dukkha.

When the person who is not an arahat dies, the last citta of his life, the cuti-citta (dying-consciousness) is succeeded by the paṭisandhi-citta (rebirth-consciousness) of the next life and thus life goes on. So long as there are defilements life has to continue. The fact that we are here in the human plane is conditioned by defilements. Even if there is birth in a heavenly plane, in a rūpa-brahma plane or in an arūpa-brahma plane, it is conditioned by defilements.

The arahat has no more defilements, he does not have to be reborn in any plane. The arahat has to die, because he was born and birth has to be followed by death. However, for him the cuti-citta will not be succeeded by a paṭisandhi-citta. Thus, for him there will not be the arising of nāma and rūpa in a new life any more, and this means the end to the cycle of birth and death.

For some people this would seem to be the annihilation of life, something which is frightening. We can make ourselves believe that life is good and that it should continue forever, but if we develop insight we will see more and more that life is nāma-elements and rūpa-elements which arise because of their own conditions and then have to fall away; they are beyond control, nobody can cause them to remain. We cannot cause the arising of happy feeling, if it arises it does so because of its own conditions. It is only present for an extremely short while and then there may be unhappy feeling. The ideas we used to have about life and happiness will gradually be changed. If one still clings to the "self" one is anxious about what will happen to the "self" after one's death. For the arahat the question of what will happen after his death does not occur; he has no more defilements and thus no more clinging to life. The ariyan knows that what the non-ariyan takes for happiness is dukkha; the non-ariyan takes for misery what the ariyan knows as happiness. The development of wisdom brings a kind of happiness which is different from what one used to take for happiness. Our defilements are the real cause of disturbance, worry and restlessness, they are the cause of all sorrow. Nibbāna is the end of lobha, dosa and moha, and thus the end of all sorrow.

When one is not an ariyan one cannot really understand what nibbāna is. If we cannot experience yet the true nature of the conditioned dhammas which arise and fall away, we cannot experience the unconditioned dhamma, the dhamma which does not arise and fall away.

As we have seen, there are four paramattha dhammas: citta, cetasika, rūpa and nibbāna. Citta, cetasika and rūpa are realities which arise and fall away, they are conditioned dhammas and thus dukkha. *Nibbāna* does not arise and fall away; it has no conditions through which it arises, it is an unconditioned dhamma. Nibbāna is the end to dukkha. If there were no cessation of dukkha the Buddha would not have taught the Path leading to the cessation of dukkha. However, since there is the cessation of dukkha, the Buddha taught the Path leading to it. We read in the Verses of Uplift (Udāna, chapter VIII, 3, Khuddaka Nikāya) that the Buddha, while he was staying in Anāthapiṇḍika's Park, said to the monks:

> Monks, there is a not-born, a not-become, a not-made, a not-compounded[3]. Monks, if that unborn, not-become, not-made, not-compounded were not, there would be apparent no escape from this here that is born, become, made, compounded[4].

---

[3] asaṅkhata, unconditioned, not proceeding from conditions.

[4] saṅkhata, conditioned. This is translated into English as "compounded" or "constructed". It is that which has been "put together " (sankharoti), produced, by the association of different conditions.

> But since, monks, there is an unborn. . . therefore the escape from this here that is born, become. . . is apparent.

Nibbāna can be experienced at the attainment of enlightenment, but enlightenment cannot be attained unless paññā has been developed to the degree that it can experience the conditioned dhammas as they are: impermanent, dukkha and non-self (anattā).

At the attainment of enlightenment the magga-citta (lokuttara kusala citta) directly experiences nibbāna. When the magga-citta has fallen away, it is succeeded immediately by the phala-citta (lokuttara vipākacitta) which experiences the same object. Kāmāvacara kusala kamma may produce vipāka in the same lifespan but never in the same process. Rūpāvacara kusala citta and arūpāvacara kusala citta produce vipāka only in a next life as rebirth-consciousness and bhavangacitta. It is different in the case of the magga-citta which is followed immediately, in the same process, by the phala-cittas, which are two or three moments of vipākacitta, depending on the individual.

When someone attains enlightenment of the stage of the sotāpanna, the magga-citta and the phala-cittas of the sotāpanna arise. The magga-citta of the sotāpanna eradicates the defilements which are to be eradicated at that stage, and this is once and for all. Thus, the magga-citta of the sotāpanna can arise only once in the cycle of birth and death.

The phala-citta can arise again in other processes of citta if enlightenment has been attained with lokuttara jhānacitta. Someone who has developed jhāna and acquired "mastery" in jhāna (Vis. IV, 131) and also develops insight can attain enlightenment with lokuttara jhānacitta, lokuttara citta accompanied by jhānafactors of one of the stages of jhāna. It is extremely difficult to acquire "mastery" in jhāna; one should be able, for example, to determine when one enters jhāna and when one emerges from jhāna. Only if mastery has been acquired, jhāna can be a "base" for insight, that is, an object of mindfulness in vipassanā. In that way the clinging to a self who attains jhāna can be eliminated. Those who attain enlightenment have different accumulations and according to one's accumulations the lokuttara jhānacittas are accompanied by jhāna-factors of different stages of jhāna. The phala-citta which is accompanied by jhāna-factors can arise many times again, experiencing nibbāna[5].

Cittas can be counted as eighty-nine or as hundred and twenty-one. When cittas are counted as hundred and twenty-one, there are, instead of eight lokuttara cittas[6], forty lokuttara cittas, and these are lokuttara cittas accompanied by the jhāna-factors of the different stages of jhāna. As we have seen, there are five stages of rūpa-jhāna and at each stage jhāna-factors are successively abandoned[7], until at the fifth stage (or at the fourth stage of the fourfold system) there are the remaining factors of samādhi (concentration) and upekkhā (indifferent feeling) which arises instead of sukha (pleasant feeling). Lokuttara cittas can be accompanied by jhāna-

---

[5] This attainment is called phala samāpatti, attainment of fruition.

[6] A magga-citta, lokuttara kusala citta, and a phala-citta, lokuttara vipākacitta, at each of the four stages of enlightenment.

[7] See chapter 22.

factors of each of the five stages of jhāna. For example, when lokuttara cittas are accompanied by jhāna-factors of the fifth stage of rūpa-jhāna, it means that they are accompanied by samādhi and upekkhā.

As regards arūpa-jhānacittas, they have meditation subjects which are different from the meditation subjects for rūpa-jhāna, but the jhāna-factors which accompany them are the same as the jhāna-factors of the fifth stage of rūpa-jhāna, namely samādhi and upekkhā. Thus, the jhāna-factors of the five types of rūpa-jhāna have to be taken into account when we classify lokuttara jhānacittas, lokuttara cittas accompanied by jhāna-factors of the different stages of rūpa-jhāna and arūpa-jhāna. Consequently, each one of the eight lokuttara cittas can be reckoned as fivefold and then there are forty lokuttara cittas.

When cittas are counted as eighty-nine, they can be summarised as follows:

- 12 akusala cittas
- 18 ahetuka cittas
- 8 mahā-kusala cittas
- 8 mahā-vipākacittas
- 8 mahā-kiriyacittas

Above are 54 kāmāvacara cittas (cittas of the sensuous plane of consciousness)

- 15 rūpāvacara cittas
- 12 arūpāvacara cittas
- 8 lokuttara cittas

When cittas are counted as 121, there are, instead of 8 lokuttara cittas, 40 lokuttara cittas.

The way to nibbāna seems to be extremely long and we may wonder how we could ever reach the goal. We should not be impatient and wish for a result that is far off. Instead, we should consider what has to be done at the present moment: the development of right understanding of the nāma and rūpa appearing right now. In this way there will be conditions eventually to attain nibbāna.

24 Enlightenment

One cannot attain enlightenment without having cultivated the right conditions. We read in the Kindred Sayings (V, Mahā-vagga, Book XI, Kindred Sayings on Streamwinning, chapter I, paragraph 5, Sāriputta) about four conditions for becoming a sotāpanna (streamwinner). The sutta states:

> Now the venerable Sāriputta went to see the Exalted One, and on coming to him saluted him and sat down at one side. To the venerable Sāriputta so seated the Exalted One said this:
>
> " 'A limb of stream-winning! A limb of stream-winning!' is the saying, Sāriputta. Tell me, Sāriputta, of what sort is a limb of stream-winning."
>
> "Lord, association with the upright is a limb of stream-winning. Hearing the good Dhamma is a limb of stream-winning. Applying the mind is a limb of stream-winning. Conforming to the Dhamma is a limb of stream-winning."
>
> "Well said, Sāriputta! Well said, Sāriputta! Indeed these are limbs of stream-winning.
>
> Now again, Sāriputta, they say: 'The stream! The stream!' Of what sort is the stream, Sāriputta?"
>
> "The stream, lord, is just this ariyan eightfold way, to wit: Right view, right thought, right speech, right action, right livelihood, right effort, right mindfulness, right concentration."
>
> "Well said, Sāriputta! Well said, Sāriputta! The stream is just this ariyan eightfold way.
>
> Now again, Sāriputta, they say, 'Streamwinner! Streamwinner!' Of what sort is a streamwinner, Sāriputta?"
>
> "Whosoever, lord, is blessed with this ariyan eightfold way – such an one of such a name, of such and such a clan, is called
>
> 'Streamwinner'."

The first condition, association with the righteous person, is most important. It would not be possible to find the right path by oneself. Only Buddhas have accumulated such wisdom that they can find the Path by themselves, without the help of a teacher. Other people, however, need the teachings of a Buddha in order to find the right path, because ignorance has been accumulated for an endlessly long time. We need association with the right person, the good friend in Dhamma, who can point out to us the right path, because our defilements prevent us from finding the right path. Our friend in Dhamma can encourage us to develop right understanding of nāma and rūpa.

The question may arise what one should do if one is not able to find the right friend in Dhamma. Is reading the scriptures not a condition to find the path leading to enlightenment? It is true that reading the scriptures is also very helpful since they can encourage us to be mindful of nāma and rūpa in daily life. We might, however, interpret the teachings in the wrong way. It depends on conditions whether we come into contact with the right person who can help us to understand the teachings as well as the practice in accordance with the teachings. Accumulated kusala kamma can be the condition for us to meet the right person.

When we have heard the Dhamma from the right person, we should "apply the mind"; this is the third condition. We should not blindly follow the person who teaches us Dhamma, but we should investigate the scriptures ourselves, ponder over the Dhamma, and consider it carefully, in order to test the truth.

The real test of the truth is the practice itself. Therefore, the fourth condition is "conforming to the Dhamma", which is the development of the eightfold Path. By being mindful of the phenomena appearing through the six doors we can find out ourselves whether it is true that these phenomena are only nāma and rūpa, arising because of conditions. We can investigate ourselves whether they are impermanent or permanent, whether they are dukkha or happiness, whether they are non-self, anattā, or "self". We can find out through the practice itself whether we really understand the teachings. If we practise in the wrong way we may eventually find out that this does not lead to right understanding of the realities of our daily life. Through the development of the eightfold Path we will have more confidence (saddhā) in the Buddha's teachings. We will have more confidence when we experience that through right understanding of nāma and rūpa in daily life there will be less clinging to "self".

Lokuttara cittas cannot arise without the cultivation of the right conditions. Some people wish for an end to dukkha but they do not develop understanding in daily life. They hope that one day lokuttara cittas will arise. The Buddha pointed out that the realization of the four noble Truths is difficult, and he said this, not in order to discourage people, but in order to remind them not to be heedless.

We read in the Kindred Sayings (V, Mahā-vagga, Book XII, Kindred Sayings about the Truths, chapter V, paragraph 5, The keyhole) that, when the Buddha was staying at Vesālī in Great Grove, Ānanda went into Vesālī on his rounds for almsfood. In Vesālī he saw the Licchavi youths practising archery. He then went to see the Buddha and said:

> "Here, lord, robing myself in the forenoon and taking bowl and outer robe I set out for Vesālī on my begging rounds. Then, lord, I saw a number of Licchavi youths in the gymnasium making practice at archery, shooting even from a distance through a very small keyhole, and splitting an arrow, shot after shot, with never a miss. And I said to myself, lord: 'Practised shots are these Licchavi youths! Well practised shots indeed are these Licchavi youths, to be able even at a distance to splinter an arrow through a very small keyhole, shot after shot, with never a miss!' "
>
> "Now what think you, Ānanda? Which is the harder, which is the harder task to compass: To shoot like that or to pierce one strand of hair, seven times divided, with another strand?"
>
> "Why, lord, of course to split a hair in such a way is the harder, much the harder task."
>
> "Just so, Ānanda, they who penetrate the meaning of: This is dukkha, this is the arising of dukkha, this is the ceasing of dukkha, this is the

> practice that leads to the ceasing of dukkha, pierce through something much harder to pierce.
>
> Wherefore, Ānanda, you must make an effort to realize: This is dukkha. This is the arising of dukkha. This is the ceasing of dukkha. This is the practice that leads to the ceasing of dukkha."

One might feel discouraged when reading this sutta; it would seem that it is impossible to attain enlightenment. However, if one develops the right Path, not the wrong Path, one will realize the four noble Truths; one will attain enlightenment. The way to realize the four noble Truths is to be mindful of the realities which appear now: seeing, visible object, lobha, dosa or any other reality. We should not be discouraged when we do not seem to make rapid progress. Most people cling to a result and they become impatient when they do not notice an immediate result; clinging to a result, however, is not helpful for the development of wisdom, it is akusala.

Some people feel that the development of samatha can give a more immediate result. Samatha, when it has been developed in the right way, has tranquillity as its result. When jhāna is attained, lobha, dosa and moha are temporarily eliminated. However, the attainment of jhāna is extremely difficult and many conditions have to be cultivated. When one is developing samatha, the hindrances may still arise: there will be sensuous desire, ill-will, sloth and torpor, restlessness, worry and doubt, until "access-concentration" or jhāna has been attained.

The aim of vipassanā is not tranquillity, but the eradication of wrong view and eventually of all defilements. This goal may seem far off, but each short moment of right awareness of nāma and rūpa is very fruitful; it will help to eliminate clinging to the concept of self. While one is mindful, there are no lobha, dosa or moha. Although tranquillity is not the aim of vipassanā, at the moment of right mindfulness there is kusala citta, and kusala citta is accompanied by calm.

Vipassanā or insight is the development of right understanding of all nāmas and rūpas which present themselves in daily life. Insight is developed in different stages and in the course of its development the characteristics of nāma and rūpa will be understood more clearly, and their arising and falling away will be known through direct experience. When insight has been developed stage by stage, the nāma and rūpa which present themselves through the six doors can be clearly seen as impermanent, dukkha and non-self, anattā. When paññā has been developed to the degree that enlightenment can be attained, the unconditioned reality, nibbāna, is directly experienced. The direct experience of nibbāna is different from thinking about nibbāna. Nibbāna is directly experienced during a mind-door process of cittas. Nibbāna cannot be experienced through any of the five senses, it can be experienced only through the mind-door.

In the process during which enlightenment is attained, the manodvārāvajjana-citta (the mind-door-adverting-consciousness) takes as its object one of the three characteristics of reality: impermanence, dukkha or anattā. This means that the reality presenting itself at that moment is seen either as impermanent, or as dukkha or as anattā. Anicca, dukkha and anattā are three aspects of the truth of conditioned realities. Thus, if one sees one aspect, one also sees the other aspects.

However, the three characteristics cannot be experienced at the same time, since citta can experience only one object at a time. It depends on one's accumulations which of the three characteristics is realized in the process of cittas during which enlightenment is attained: one person views the reality appearing at that moment as impermanent, another as dukkha, and another again as non-self, anattā. The mano-dvārāvajjana-citta, mind-door-adverting-consciousness, of that process adverts to one of these three characteristics and is then succeeded by three or four cittas which are not yet lokuttara cittas, but mahā-kusala cittas (kusala cittas of the sense-sphere) accompanied by paññā[1]. The first mahā-kusala citta, which is called parikamma or preparatory consciousness, still has the same object as the mano-dvārāvajjana-citta. Whichever of the three characteristics of conditioned realities the mano-dvārāvajjana-citta adverted to, the parikamma realizes that characteristic. The parikamma is succeeded by the upacāra or proximity consciousness which still has the same object as the mano-dvārāvajjana citta. This citta, the second mahā-kusala citta in that process, is nearer to the moment the lokuttara cittas will arise. The upacāra is succeeded by the anuloma, which means conformity or adaptation. This citta still has the same object as the mano-dvārāvajjana-citta. Anuloma is succeeded by gotrabhū which is sometimes translated as change of lineage. This citta is the last kāmāvacara citta in that process. Gotrabhū is the last kāmāvacara citta in a process before a citta of another plane of consciousness arises. The other plane of consciousness may be rūpāvacara, arūpāvacara or lokuttara. In samatha, gotrabhū is the last kāmāvacara citta before the rūpa-jhānacitta or the arūpa-jhānacitta arises. In vipassanā, gotrabhū is the last kāmāvacara citta of the non-ariyan before the lokuttara citta arises and he becomes an ariyan. The object of the gotrabhū arising before the lokuttara cittas is different from the object of gotrabhū in samatha; the gotrabhū preceding the lokuttara cittas experiences nibbāna. It is the first citta in that process which experiences nibbāna, but it is not lokuttara citta. At the moment of gotrabhū the person who is about to attain enlightenment is still a non-ariyan. Gotrabhū does not eradicate defilements. Gotrabhū is succeeded by the magga-citta which eradicates the defilements that are to be eradicated at the stage of the sotāpanna. The magga-citta is the first lokuttara citta in that process of cittas. When it has fallen away it is succeeded by two (or three) phala-cittas (fruition-consciousness) which are the result of the magga-citta and which still have nibbāna as the object. As we have seen, the magga-citta is succeeded immediately by its result, in the same process of citta[2]. The magga-citta cannot produce vipāka in the form of rebirth, such as the kusala citta of the other planes of consciousness. The phala-cittas are succeeded by bhavanga-cittas[3].

---

[1] See Visuddhimagga, chapter XXI, 129-136, and also "The Path of Discrimination" (Paṭisambhidāmagga) I, Treatise on Knowledge, chapter VI-chapter X.

[2] See chapter 23

[3] The names of the cittas arising in the process during which enlightenment occurs are not only in the commentaries but also in the scriptures, in the Path of Discrimination and in the Book of Conditional Relations, the Paṭṭhāna. In the Paṭṭhāna, the "Feeling Triplet", under Proximity Condition, are mentioned: anuloma, gotrabhū, magga-citta and two phala-cittas. Since different names are given to these javana-cittas we can know their number. The names parikamma and upacāra do not occur, but the Visud-

Some people do not need the moment of parikamma (preparatory consciousness) and in that case three moments of phala-citta arise instead of two moments.

Summarising the cittas in the process during which enlightenment is attained, they are the following:

- mano-dvārāvajjana-citta
- parikamma (preparatory consciousness; for some people not necessary)
- upacāra (proximity consciousness)
- anuloma (conformity or adaptation)
- gotrabhū (change of lineage)
- magga-citta
- phala-citta (two or three moments, depending on the individual)

Nibbāna can be the object of kāmāvacara cittas which arise after the lokuttara cittas have fallen away. Before someone becomes an ariyan there can only be speculation about nibbāna. For the ariyan, however, it is different. Since he has directly experienced nibbāna, he can review his experience afterwards. We read in the Visuddhimagga (XXII, 19) that the person who attained enlightenment reviews, after the lokuttara cittas have fallen away, the path, the fruition, the defilements which have been abandoned, the defilements which are still remaining and nibbāna. He reviews these things in different mind-door processes of citta.

Some people think that enlightenment could not occur in daily life, they believe that it is necessary to be in a solitary place in order to attain nibbāna. The development of vipassanā is the development of right understanding of all realities occurring in daily life. When paññā has been developed to the degree that enlightenment can be attained, enlightenment can occur in the middle of one's daily activities. As we have seen, the attainment of enlightenment is only a few moments of citta which arise and fall away within split seconds.

We read in the Discourse to Dīghanakha (Middle Length Sayings II, no. 74) that the Buddha taught Dhamma to the wanderer Dīghanaka on Vulture's Peak near Rājagaha. He taught him about the getting rid of wrong views and about the impermanence of conditioned realities. Sāriputta, who was an ariyan but had not yet attained arahatship, was also present at the time of that discourse. We read:

> Now at that time the venerable Sāriputta was standing behind the Lord, fanning the Lord. Then it occurred to the venerable Sāriputta:
> "The Lord speaks to us of getting rid of these things and those by means of super-knowledge, the Well-farer speaks to us of casting out these things and those by means of superknowledge". While the venerable Sāriputta

---

dhimagga (XXI, 130) states that the three first mahā-kusala cittas in that process can be called by one name: they can be called repetition or preliminary work (parikamma), access (upacāra), or conformity (anuloma). The process where enlightenment occurs is not an ordinary process; it is a process with different types of citta performing the function of javana. Still, this example makes it clearer that the commentaries, when they stated that there are usually 7 javana-cittas in a process, based this on the canonical tradition (see chapter 14).

> was reflecting on this, his mind was freed from the cankers without clinging. But to the wanderer Dīghanakha there arose the stainless, spotless vision of dhamma, that whatever is of the nature to arise all that is of the nature to stop. . .

Sāriputta attained arahatship, but he did not go into solitude in order to attain it; he was fanning the Buddha. Dīghanakha listened to the Buddha and then became a sotāpanna.

We read in the Kindred Sayings (III, Khandhā-vagga, Middle Fifty, chapter 4, paragraph 89, Khema) that Khemaka, who was an anāgāmī, attained arahatship while he was preaching and monks who were listening attained arahatship as well. We read:

> Now when this teaching was thus expounded the hearts of as many as sixty monks were utterly set free from the āsavas, and so was it also with the heart of the venerable Khemaka. . .

If one is on the right Path, paññā can be developed, no matter what the circumstances are, even to the degree of enlightenment. People may wonder whether it would be possible to notice it when a person attains nibbāna. But can one see whether someone else is mindful or not mindful? Who knows the cittas of other people? We cannot know when someone else is mindful of nāma and rūpa or when he attains nibbāna.

The question may arise whether all four stages of enlightenment (the stages of the sotāpanna, the sakadāgāmī, the anāgāmī and the arahat) can be attained in the course of one life. We read in the suttas about disciples of the Buddha who attained the ariyan state but not yet arahatship and realized arahatship later on in life. Ānanda, for example, did not attain arahatship during the Buddha's life, but he became an arahat after the Buddha had passed away, the evening before the first great council was to start (the "Illustrator of Ultimate meaning", commentary to the "Mangala-sutta" or "Good Omen Discourse", Minor Readings, Khuddaka Nikāya).

The arahat has eradicated all defilements and thus he has reached the end of the cycle of birth, old age, sickness and death; he has realized the end of dukkha. The arahat will not be reborn, but he still has to die and therefore one may ask whether he really has attained the end of dukkha at the moment he realizes arahatship. Even the arahat is subject to death, since he was born. He can also experience unpleasant results of akusala kamma committed before he became an arahat. However, he has no more defilements and cannot accumulate any more kamma which might produce vipāka, he is really free from dukkha.

In As it was said (Itivuttaka, The Twos, chapter II, paragraph 7, Khuddaka Nikāya) two "conditions[4] of nibbāna" are explained. In this sutta Sa-upādi-sesa-nibbāna[5], one "condition" of nibbāna, pertains to the arahat who has eradicated all defilements but for whom the five khandhas are still remaining. For the arahat who has not finally passed away yet, there are still citta, cetasika and rūpa arising and

---

[4] dhātu, which literally means element.

[5] Upādi: substratum of life, the five khandhas. Sa: with, sesa: remaining.

falling away. An-upādi-sesa-nibbāna[6], the other "condition" of nibbāna, pertains to the arahat who has finally passed away; for him there are no khandhas remaining, there are no longer citta, cetasika and rūpa arising and falling away.

We read in the verse of this sutta, after the explanation:

```
These two nibbāna-states are shown by him
Who sees, who is such and unattached.
One state is that in this same life possessed
With base remaining, though becoming's stream
Be cut off. While the state without a base
Belongs to the future, wherein all
Becomings utterly do come to cease.
They who, by knowing this state uncompounded[7]
Have heart's release, by cutting off the stream,
They who have reached the core of dhamma, glad
To end, such have abandoned all becomings.
```

When someone has become an arahat there will be no more rebirth for him. When someone has attained enlightenment to the stage of the sotāpanna, he has become an ariyan, but he has not reached the end of rebirth. The sotāpanna will be reborn, but not more than seven times; thus, eventually there will be an end to rebirth for him. If we do not develop vipassanā, the number of rebirths will be endless. It was out of compassion that the Buddha spoke about the dangers of rebirth; he wanted to encourage people to develop right understanding. We read in the Kindred Sayings (V, Mahā-vagga, Book XII, Kindred Sayings about the Truths, chapter V, paragraph 6, Gross darkness) that the Buddha said to the monks:

> "Monks, there is a darkness of interstellar space, impenetrable gloom, such a murk of darkness as cannot enjoy the splendour of this moon and sun, though they be of such mighty magic power and majesty."
>
> At these words a certain monk said to the Exalted One:
>
> "Lord, that must be a mighty darkness, a mighty darkness indeed! Pray, lord, is there any other darkness greater and more fearsome than that?"
>
> "There is indeed, monk, another darkness, greater and more fearsome. And what is that other darkness?
>
> Monk, whatsoever recluses or brahmins understand not, as it really is, the meaning of: This is dukkha, this is the arising of dukkha, this is the ceasing of dukkha, this is the practice that leads to the ceasing of dukkha, such take delight in the activities which conduce to rebirth. Thus taking delight they compose a compound of activities which conduce to rebirth. Thus composing a compound of activities they fall down into the darkness of rebirth, into the darkness of old age and death, of sorrow, grief, woe, lamentation and despair. They are not released from birth, old age and

[6] An-upādi-sesa: without the khandhas remaining.

[7] asaṅkhata, the unconditioned reality.

death, from sorrow, grief, woe, lamentation and despair. They are not released from dukkha, I declare.

But, monk, those recluses or brahmins who do understand as it really is, the meaning of: This is dukkha, this is the arising of dukkha, this is the ceasing of dukkha, this is the practice that leads to the ceasing of dukkha, such take not delight in the activities which conduce to rebirth. . . They are released from dukkha, I declare.

Wherefore, monk, an effort must be made to realize: This is dukkha. This is the arising of dukkha. This is the ceasing of dukkha. This is the practice that leads to the ceasing of dukkha."

Glossary

abhidhamma
: the higher teachings of Buddhism, teachings on ultimate realities.

Abhidhammattha Sangaha
: an Encyclopedia of the Abhidhamma, written by Anuruddha between the 8th and the 12th century A.D.

abhiññā
: supernormal powers.

adosa
: non aversion.

ahetuka cittas
: not accompanied by "beautiful roots" or unwholesome roots.

ākāsānañcāyatana
: sphere of boundless space, the meditation subject of the first immaterial jhānacitta.

akiñcaññāyatana
: sphere of nothingness, the meditation subject of the third immaterial jhānacitta.

akusala
: unwholesome, unskilful.

alobha
: non attachment, generosity.

amoha
: wisdom or understanding.

anāgāmī
: non-returner, person who has reached the third stage of enlightenment, he has no aversion (dosa).

anattā
: not self.

anicca
: impermanence.

anuloma
: conformity or adaptation.

anusaya
: latent tendency or proclivity.

anupādisesa nibbāna
: final nibbāna, without the khandhas (aggregates or groups of existence) remaining, at the death of an arahat.

apo-dhātu
: element of water or cohesion.

appanā
: absorption.

arahat
: noble person who has attained the fourth and last stage of enlightenment.

ārammaṇa
: object which is known by consciousness.

ariyan
: noble person who has attained enlightenment.

arūpa-bhūmi
plane of arūpa jhānacitta.

arūpa-brahma
plane plane of existence attained as a result of arūpa-jhāna. There are no sense impressions, no rūpa experienced in this realm.

arūpa-jhāna
immaterial absorption.

asan̲khārika
unprompted, not induced, either by oneself or by someone else.

asan̲khata dhamma
unconditioned reality, nibbāna.

āsavas influxes or intoxicants, group of defilements .

asobhana not beautiful, not accompanied by beautiful roots.

asubha foul.

asura demon, being of one of the unhappy planes of existence.

atīta-bhavanga
past life-continuum, arising and falling away shortly before the start of a process of cittas experiencing an object through one of the sense-doors.

Atthasālinī
The Expositor, a commentary to the first book of the Abhidhamma Piṭaka.

āvajjana adverting of consciousness to the object which has impinged on one of the six doors.

avijjā ignorance.

ayoniso manasikāra
unwise attention to an object.

bhāvanā mental development, comprising the development of calm and the development of insight.

bhavanga life-continuum.

bhavanga calana
vibrating bhavanga arising shortly before a process of cittas experiencing an object through one of the six doors.

bhavangupaccheda
arrest bhavanga, last bhavanga-citta before a process of cittas starts.

bhikkhu monk.

bhikkhunī nun.

bhūmi plane of existence or plane of citta.

brahma-vihāras the four divine abidings, meditation subjects which are: loving kindness, compassion, sympathetic joy, equanimity.

Buddha a fully enlightened person who has discovered the truth all by himself, without the aid of a teacher and can proclaim Dhamma to the world.

Buddhaghosa commentator on the Tipiṭaka, author of the Visuddhimagga in 5 A.D.

cakkhu eye.

cakkhu-dhātu eye element.

cakkhu-dvāra eyedoor.

cakkhu-dvārāvajjana-citta eye-door-adverting-consciousness.

cakkhuppasāda rūpa rūpa which is the organ of eyesense, capable of receiving visible object.

cakkhu-viññāṇa seeing-consciousness.

cetanā volition or intention.

cetasika mental factor arising with consciousness.

citta consciousness, the reality which knows or cognizes an object.

cuti-citta dying-consciousness.

dāna generosity, giving.

dassana-kicca function of seeing.

dhamma reality, truth, the teachings.

dhamma-dhātu element of dhammas, realities, comprising cetasikas, subtle rūpas, nibbāna.

dhammārammaṇa all objects other than the sense objects which can be experienced through the five sense-doors, thus, objects which can be experienced only through the mind-door.

Dhammasangaṇi the first book of the Abhidhamma Piṭaka.

Dhātukathā
Discussion on the Elements, the third book of the Abhidhamma.

diṭṭhi wrong view, distorted view of realities.

diṭṭhigata sampayutta
accompanied by wrong view.

domanassa unpleasant feeling.

dosa aversion or ill will.

dosa-mūla-citta
citta (consciousness) rooted in aversion.

dukkha suffering, unsatisfactoriness of conditioned realities.

dukkha vedanā
painful feeling or unpleasant feeling.

dvāra doorway through which an object is experienced, the five sense-doors or the mind door.

dvi-pañca-viññāṇa
the five pairs of sense-cognitions, which are seeing, hearing, smelling, tasting and body-consciousness. Of each pair one is kusala vipāka and one akusala vipāka.

ekaggatā concentration, one-pointedness, a cetasika which has the function to focus on one object.

ganthas bonds, a group of defilements.

ghāna-dhātu
nose element.

ghānappasāda rūpa
rūpa which is the organ of smelling sense, capable of receiving odour.

ghāna-viññāṇa
smelling-consciousness.

ghāyana-kicca
function of smelling.

gotrabhū change of lineage, the last citta of the sense-sphere before jhāna, absorption, is attained, or enlightenment is attained.

hadaya-vatthu
heart-base, rūpa which is the plane of origin of the cittas other than the sense-cognitions.

hasituppāda-citta
smile producing consciousness of an arahat.

hetu root, which conditions citta to be "beautiful" or unwholesome.

indriya faculty. Some are rūpas such as the sense organs, some are nāmas such as feeling. Five 'spiritual faculties' are wholesome faculties which should be cultivated, namely: confidence, energy, awareness, concentration and wisdom.

issā envy.

jāti birth, nature, class (of cittas).

javana-citta cittas which 'run through the object', kusala citta or akusala citta in the case of non-arahats.

jhāna absorption which can be attained through the development of calm.

jhāna-factors cetasikas which have to be cultivated for the attainment of jhāna: vitakka, vicāra, pīti, sukha, samādhi.

jivhā-dhātu tongue element.

jivhāppasāda rūpa rūpa which is the organ of tasting sense, capable of receiving flavour.

jivhā-viññāṇa tasting-consciousness.

kāma sensual enjoyment or the five sense objects.

kāma-bhūmi sensuous plane of existence.

kāmacchandha sensuous desire.

kāma-sobhana cittas beautiful cittas of the sense sphere.

kāmāvacara cittas cittas of the sense sphere.

kamma intention or volition; deed motivated by volition.

kammapatha course of action performed through body, speech or mind which can be wholesome or unwholesome.

karuṇā compassion.

kasiṇa disk, used as an object for the development of calm.

kāya body. It can also stand for the "mental body", the cetasikas.

kāya dhātu the element of bodysense.

kāyappasāda rūpa
: bodysense, the rūpa which is capable of receiving tangible object. It is all over the body, inside or outside.

kāya-viññatti
: bodily intimation, such as gestures, facial expression, etc.

kāya-viññāṇa
: body-consciousness.

khandhas
: aggregates of conditioned realities classified as five groups: physical phenomena, feelings, perception or remembrance, activities or formations (cetasikas other than feeling or perception), consciousness.

kicca
: function.

kilesa
: defilements.

kiriya citta
: inoperative citta, neither cause nor result.

kukkucca
: regret or worry.

kusala citta
: wholesome consciousness.

kusala kamma
: a good deed.

kusala
: wholesome, skillful.

lobha
: attachment, greed.

lobha-mūla-citta
: consciousness rooted in attachment.

lokiya citta
: citta which is mundane, not experiencing nibbāna.

lokuttara citta
: supramundane citta which experiences nibbāna.

lokuttara dhammas
: the unconditioned dhamma which is nibbāna and the cittas which experience nibbāna.

macchariya
: stinginess.

magga
: path (eightfold Path).

magga-citta
: path consciousness, supramundane citta which experiences nibbāna and eradicates defilements.

mahā-bhūta-rūpas
the rūpas which are the four great elements of "earth" or solidity, "water " or cohesion, "fire" or temperature, and "wind" or motion.

mahā-kiriyacitta
inoperative sense-sphere citta of the arahat, accompanied by "beautiful" roots.

mahā-kusala citta
wholesome citta of the sense sphere.

mahā-vipākacitta
citta of the sense sphere which is result, accompanied by "beautiful" roots.

manāyatana
mind-base, including all cittas.

mano mind, citta, consciousness.

mano-dhātu
mind-element, comprising the five-sense-door adverting- consciousness, and the two types of receiving-consciousness.

mano-dvārāvajjana-citta
mind-door-adverting-consciousness.

mano-dvāra-vīthi-cittas
cittas arising in a mind-door process.

mano-viññāṇa-dhātu
mind-consciousness element, comprising all cittas other than the sense-cognitions (seeing, etc.) and mind-element.

māra "the evil one"—all that leads to dukkha

mettā loving kindness.

middha torpor or languor.

moha ignorance. moha-mūla-citta citta rooted in ignorance.

muditā sympathetic joy.

nāma mental phenomena, including those which are conditioned and also the unconditioned nāma which is nibbāna.

natthika diṭṭhi
wrong view of annihilation, assumption that there is no result of kamma.

n'eva-saññā-n'āsaññāyatana
sphere of neither perception nor non-perception, the meditation subject of the fourth immaterial jhāna.

nibbāna the unconditioned reality, the reality which does not arise and fall away.The destruction of lust, hatred and delusion. The deathless. The end of suffering.

nimitta mental image one can acquire of a meditation subject in tranquil meditation.

nirodha-samāpatti attainment of cessation of consciousness.

nīvaraṇa hindrances, a group of defilements.

ñāṇa wisdom, insight.

ojā the rūpa which is nutrition.

oḷārika rūpas gross rūpas (sense objects and sense organs).

Pacceka Buddha Silent Buddha, an enlightened one who has found the truth by himself but does not proclaim Dhamma to the world.

paṭibhāga nimitta counterpart image, more perfected mental image of a meditation subject, acquired in tranquil meditation.

paṭigha aversion or ill will.

Paṭṭhāna Conditional Relations, the seventh book of the Abhidhamma.

paṭisandhi citta rebirth consciousness.

Pāli the language of the Buddhist teachings.

pañcadvārāvajjana-citta five-sense-door-adverting-consciousness.

pañcaviññāṇa (or dvi-pañcaviññāṇa), the sense cognitions (seeing etc.) of which there are five pairs.

paññā wisdom or understanding.

paññatti concepts, conventional terms.

paramattha dhamma truth in the absolute sense: mental and physical phenomena, each with their own characteristic.

parikamma preparatory consciousness, the first javana citta arising in the process during which absorption or enlightenment is attained.

pasāda-rūpas rūpas which are capable of receiving sense-objects such as visible object, sound, taste, etc. peta ghost.

phala-citta
: fruition consciousness experiencing nibbāna. It is result of magga-citta, path-consciousness.

phassa
: contact.

phoṭṭhabbārammaṇa
: tangible object, experienced through bodysense.

phusanakicca
: function of experiencing tangible object.

pīti
: joy, rapture, enthusiasm.

Puggalapaññatti
: Designation of Human Types, the fourth book of the Abhidhamma.

puthujjana
: "worldling", a person who has not attained enlightenment.

Rāhula
: the Buddha's son.

rasārammaṇa
: object of flavour.

rūpārammaṇa
: visible object.

rūpa
: physical phenomena, realities which do not experience anything.

rūpa-brahma
: plane rūpa-bhūmi, fine material realm of existence attained as a result of rūpa-jhāna.

rūpa-jhāna
: fine material absorption, developed with a meditation subject which is still dependant on materiality.

rūpa-khandha
: aggregate or group of all physical phenomena (rūpas).

rūpāvacara cittas
: rūpa-jhānacittas, consciousness of the fine-material sphere.

saddārammaṇa
: sound.

saddhā
: confidence.

sahagata
: accompanied by.

sahetuka
: accompanied by roots.

sakadāgāmī
: once-returner, a noble person who has attained the second stage of enlightenment.

samādhi — concentration or one-pointedness, ekaggatā cetasika.

samatha — the development of calm.

sammā — right.

sampaṭicchana-citta — receiving-consciousness.

sampayutta — associated with.

Sangha — community of monks and nuns. As one of the triple Gems it means the community of those people who have attained enlightenment.

saṅkhāra dhammas — conditioned dhammas that arise together depending on each other.

saṅkhata dhamma — what has arisen because of conditions.

saṅkhāra-kkhandha — all cetasikas (mental factors) except feeling and memory.

saññā — memory, remembrance or “perception”.

saññā-kkhandha — memory classified as one of the five khandhas.

santīraṇa-citta — investigating-consciousness.

Sāriputta — chief disciple of Buddha.

sasaṅkhārika — prompted, induced, instigated, either by oneself or someone else.

sati — mindfulness or awareness: non-forgetfulness of what is wholesome, or non-forgetfulness of realities which appear.

satipaṭṭhāna sutta — Middle Length Sayings 1, number 10, also Dīgha Nikāya, Dialogues, no. 22.

satipaṭṭhāna — applications of mindfulness. It can mean the cetasika sati which is aware of realities or the objects of mindfulness which are classified as four applications of mindfulness: Body, Feeling Citta, Dhamma. Or it can mean the development of direct understanding of realities through awareness.

sa-upadi-sesa nibbāna — the attainment of nibbāna with the khandhas remaining by the arahat, thus not final nibbāna at death of an arahat.

`sāyana-kicca`
: function of tasting.

`savana-kicca`
: function of hearing.

`sīla`
: morality in action or speech, virtue.

`sīlabbatupādāna`
: wrong practice, which is clinging to certain rules ("rites and rituals") in one's practice.

`sobhana-hetus`
: beautiful roots.

`sobhana kiriya cittas`
: kiriyacittas accompanied by sobhana (beautiful) roots.

`sobhana(citta and cetasika)`
: beautiful, accompanied by beautiful roots.

`somanassa`
: happy feeling.

`sota-dhātu`
: element of earsense.

`sota-dvārāvajjana-citta`
: ear-door-adverting-consciousness.

`sota-dvāra-vīthi-cittas`
: ear-door process cittas.

`sotāpanna`
: person who has attained the first stage of enlightenment, and who has eradicated wrong view of realities.

`sota-viññāṇa`
: hearing-consciousness.

`sukha`
: happy, pleasant.

`sukha-vedanā`
: pleasant feeling.

`sukhuma`
: subtle.

`sutta`
: part of the scriptures containing dialogues at different places on different occasions.

`suttanta`
: a sutta text.

`tadālambana`
: retention or registering, last citta of a complete process of the sense-sphere.

`tadārammaṇa`
: as above.

Tathāgata literally "thus gone", epithet of the Buddha.

tatramajjhattatā equanimity or evenmindedness.

tejo-dhātu element of fire or heat.

Theravāda Buddhism 'Doctrine of the Elders', the oldest tradition of Buddhism.

thīna sloth.

Tipiṭaka the teachings of the Buddha contained in the Vinaya, the Suttanta and the Abhidhamma.

uddhacca restlessness.

Udāna Verses of Uplift from the Minor Anthologies.

upacāra access or proximity consciousness, the second javana-citta in the process in which absorption or enlightenment is attained.

upacāra-samādhi access-concentration.

upādā-rūpa "derived rūpas" the rūpas other than the four Great Elements.

upādāna clinging.

upādāna-kkhandhas khandhas of clinging.

upekkhā indifferent feeling. It can stand for evenmindedness or equanimity and then it is not feeling.

vacīviññatti the rūpa which is speech intimation.

vatthu base, physical base of citta.

vāyo-dhātu element of wind or motion.

vedanā feeling.

vedanā-kkhandha group of all feelings.

Vibhaṅga "Book of Analysis", second book of the Abhidhamma.

vicāra sustained thinking or discursive thinking.

vicikicchā doubt.

vinaya Book of Discipline for the monks.

viññāṇa consciousness, citta.

viññāṇa-dhātu
element of consciousness, comprising all cittas.

viññāṇa-kkhandha
group of all cittas (consciousness).

viññāṇañcāyatana
sphere of boundless consciousness, meditation subject for the second stage of immaterial jhāna.

vipākacitta
citta which is the result of a wholesome deed (kusala kamma) or an unwholesome deed (akusala kamma). It can arise as rebirth- consciousness, or during life as the experience of pleasant or unpleasant objects through the senses, such as seeing, hearing, etc.

vipassanā wisdom which sees realities as they are.

vippayutta
dissociated from.

viriya energy.

visaṇkāra dhamma
unconditioned dhamma, nibbāna.

Visuddhimagga
an Encyclopaedia of the Buddha's teachings, written by Buddhaghosa in the fifth century A.D.

vitakka applied thinking.

vīthi-cittas
cittas arising in a process.

vīthimutta-cittas
process freed cittas, cittas which do not arise within a process.

votthapana-citta
determining consciousness.

vyāpāda ill-will.

Yamaka the Book of Pairs, the sixth book of the Abhidhamma.

yoniso manasikāra
wise attention to the object.

Books

Books written by Nina van Gorkom

- *The Buddha's Path* An Introduction to the doctrine of Theravada Buddhism for those who have no previous knowledge. The four noble Truths - suffering - the origin of suffering - the cessation of suffering - and the way leading to the end of suffering - are explained as a philosophy and a practical guide which can be followed in today's world.
- *Buddhism in Daily Life* A general introduction to the main ideas of Theravada Buddhism.The purpose of this book is to help the reader gain insight into the Buddhist scriptures and the way in which the teachings can be used to benefit both ourselves and others in everyday life.
- *The World in the Buddhist Sense* The purpose of this book is to show that the Buddha's Path to true understanding has to be developed in daily life.
- *Cetasikas* Cetasika means 'belonging to the mind'. It is a mental factor which accompanies consciousness (citta) and experiences an object. There are 52 cetasikas. This book gives an outline of each of these 52 cetasikas and shows the relationship they have with each other.
- *The Buddhist Teaching on Physical Phenomena* A general introduction to physical phenomena and the way they are related to each other and to mental phenomena. The purpose of this book is to show that the study of both mental phenomena and physical phenomena is indispensable for the development of the eightfold Path.
- *The Conditionality of Life* By Nina van Gorkom

  This book is an introduction to the seventh book of the Abhidhamma, that deals with the conditionality of life. It explains the deep underlying motives for all actions through body, speech and mind and shows that these are dependent on conditions and cannot be controlled by a 'self'. This book is suitable for those who have already made a study of the Buddha's teachings.

Books translated by Nina van Gorkom

- *Mettā: Loving kindness in Buddhism* by Sujin Boriharnwanaket. An introduction to the basic Buddhist teachings of mettā, loving kindness, and its practical application in todays world.
- *Taking Refuge in Buddhism* by Sujin Boriharnwanaket. Taking Refuge in Buddhism is an introduction to the development of insight meditation.
- *A Survey of Paramattha Dhammas* by Sujin Boriharnwanaket. A Survey of Paramattha Dhammas is a guide to the development of the Buddha's path of wisdom, covering all aspects of human life and human behaviour, good and bad. This study explains that right understanding is indispensable for mental development, the development of calm as well as the development of insight.

- *The Perfections Leading to Enlightenment* by Sujin Boriharnwanaket. The Perfections is a study of the ten good qualities: generosity, morality, renunciation, wisdom, energy, patience, truthfulness, determination, loving-kindness, and equanimity.

These and other articles can be seen at www.zolag.co.uk or www.scribd.com (search for zolag).

CPSIA information can be obtained
at www.ICGtesting.com
Printed in the USA
LVOW11*1241050618
579601LV00004BA/24/P

9 781897 633274